"It wasn't until I read Quiara Alegría Hudes's book that I realized I've spent much of my life running away from who I was as a girl in a tiny apartment in Brooklyn and from the mother who was then just a young woman with curly bangs and a lot of secrets. I write about myself for a living but I seem to only remember the sorrow, because I can see the scars—but there was joy in those early New York summers, even when I felt like the loneliest girl in the world. Reading this book felt like those summers, the first ice cream cone from the first ice cream truck down Myrtle Avenue, the choking sob thrill of a memory lost on every single page, over and over again, and I cried from the relief of knowing that this was my city, this was my community, this was my legacy, this was my family, this was my story too."

—KARLA CORNEJO VILLAVICENCIO, author of
the National Book Award finalist *The Undocumented Americans*

"In her vibrant memoir, *My Broken Language*, Quiara Alegría Hudes takes us on an unforgettable tour of her neighborhoods. Negotiating between languages, cultures, religions, and the most important boundary, the haves and have-nots, Hudes takes us with her to visit her relatives, leading us up the front stoop into the living room, past the household shrines. But more than being a translator for these vivid families, Quiara Alegría Hudes teaches us the grammar and the rules of the languages spoken and unspoken. Through music, food, storytelling, and memorable depictions of these worlds apart, Hudes has created a must-read book that is difficult to put down. Her generous intimacy causes us all to examine—and honor—our families' broken languages that create a rich emotional legacy for the people we become."

—PAULA VOGEL, emeritus Eugene O'Neill Professor
and chair of playwriting at the Yale School of Drama

"Our histories, our spirits, our words, our racial diversity, our stories, our names will not be silenced thanks to Quiara Alegría Hudes. Her story helps us understand that our textured, rich cultural realities are to be valued, shared, and celebrated. The knowledge of Native and African elders grounded in nature's forces is alive and Hudes's journey urges us to understand and embrace the multiplicity of the spiritual energetic threads that guide our unique existence and contributions. It is in boldly standing in our truth that the misinformed histories that dominate the public narrative will be destroyed. Hudes is telling us: Say it loud, say it proud, we are the keepers of their stories, the spirit of our ancestors, and the storytellers that will pass forward their stories."

—DR. MARTA MORENO VEGA, founder of the Creative Justice Initiative and Lukumi Priestess Omo Obatala

"A wonderful and absorbing narrative . . . Hudes presents an exquisitely told and deeply personal narrative about notions of home, family, and belonging. It's a master class on how we might all find the courage to tell our own stories on our own terms."

—KIMBERLY DREW, author of *This is What I Know About Art* and co-editor of *Black Futures*

MY BROKEN LANGUAGE

MY
BROKEN
LANGUAGE

A Memoir

Quiara Alegría Hudes

ONE WORLD

NEW YORK

Published in the United States by One World,
an imprint of Random House, a division of
Penguin Random House LLC, New York.

ONE WORLD and colophon are registered trademarks
of Penguin Random House LLC.

LIBRARY OF CONGRESS CATALOGING-IN-PUBLICATION DATA
Names: Hudes, Quiara Alegría, author.
Title: My broken language: a memoir / Quiara Alegría Hudes.
Description: New York: One World, [2021]
Identifiers: LCCN 2020037277 (print) | LCCN 2020037278 (ebook) |
ISBN 9780399590047 (hardcover) | ISBN 9780399590054 (ebook)
Subjects: LCSH: Hudes, Quiara Alegría. | Hispanic American
women dramatists—Biography. | Racially mixed people—Pennsylvania—
Philadelphia—Biography. | Language and culture—America. |
Philadelphia (Pa.)—Biography.
Classification: LCC PS3608.U3234 Z46 2021 (print) |
LCC PS3608.U3234 (ebook) | DDC 862/.7 [B]—dc23
LC record available at https://lccn.loc.gov/2020037277
LC ebook record available at https://lccn.loc.gov/2020037278

Printed in Canada on acid-free paper

oneworldlit.com
randomhousebooks.com

2 4 6 8 9 7 5 3 1

First Edition

Book design by Jo Anne Metsch

FOR THE GRRRL DESCENDANTS
OF OBDULIA PEREZ,
PAST, PRESENT & FUTURE

Words carry power; they have their own aché.

—MARTA MORENO VEGA

CONTENTS

(Note to reader: I changed a bunch of names.)

PART I

_____

I Am the Gulf Between
English and Spanish

A MULTILINGUAL BLOCK
IN WEST PHILLY

Dad was hurrying mom in English. "Let's go, Virginia," as he leaned against the tailgate sucking an unfiltered so hard I heard it crackle all the way on the stoop. Mom propped the screen door with her foot, ordering me to carry out boxes in snaps, gestures, and screams. And Titi Ginny was telling mom to pay dad no mind in Spanish. "Siempre tiene prisa," she whispered with a tilted smile, turning dad's impatience into a sweet little nothing.

My brat pack came to wave me off and started in on the obscene gestures whenever mom turned her back. Chien was first-generation Vietnamese. Ben and Elizabeth, first-gen Cambodian. Rowetha lost her Amharic after leaving Ethiopia. We all spoke English, unlike our parents, who all spoke different languages from one another. This was my West Philly crew, my pampers–to–pre-K alphabet soup. I assumed all blocks everywhere were like it—as many languages as sidewalk cracks, one boarded-up home for every lived-in, more gum wads than dandelions. But mom told me no, nature would reign at our new rental house on a horse farm.

Titi Ginny unlatched the screen so it slammed, and handed me a pastelillo grease-wrapped in paper towel. A snack for the drive. I wanted her to re-create our current layout in the new spot, to move next door so I could sneak across the alley and watch cartoons in her lazy boy. There was a spot between two pleather cracks, duct-tape repaired, where my butt fit perfectly. My Sunday morning throne. But mom said there were no alleys where we were moving, and no such thing as next door either. That gave me something to think about.

Anyway, Titi Ginny's softball team was waiting in Fairmount Park and she had to be on second base in an hour. So she rolled down her driver's side and promised to visit the farm, my big cousins in tow. Mary Lou, Cuca, Flor, Big Vic, Vivi, and Nuchi. She'd cram all their stinky teen butts in her backseat, and they'd see the country for the first time. "Bring Abuela and Tía Toña, oh, and Tía Moncha, too," I said, marveling at the prospect of hanging with my fam outside of Philly. Titi Ginny turned the key and every version of dios-te-bendiga rolled off her tongue. There were a million ways to say god-bless in Spanish. Dios te cuide, dios te favoresca, dios te this and te that. There was only one way to say it in English, and you only said it after a sneeze. Then off she went before off we went.

Dad slammed the tailgate and mom teared up in the pleather passenger side. "Extrañaré a mi hermana." Dad stayed quiet, probably didn't understand. But I knew the Spanish word for missing someone sounded like the English word for strange. Sandwiched between them, I sensed mom's worried profile. She had talked the move up for months, but saying goodbye to a sister was a whole 'nother thing.

"Then why do we have to move today? Can't we finish out summer on the block?"

"Because, Quiara, I been stuck a city girl since I was eleven. But before that, before I came to Philly, I had a whole farm to myself. Mami gets to be with nature again, where she belongs, like in Puerto Rico." And her tired eyes made room for a little spark.

How she told it, mom had been changing scenes all her life, same as geese veeing over the art museum. There was always a next stop full of new promise. Even Abuela's memories about PR were made of a million places—towns, cities, and barrios. Too many to keep track. This time, I got to join mom's migration.

Pulling away from the narrow block, the rearview showed my crew double-dutching and playing shoot-out. No final waves, hollers, or stuck-out tongues. Whatever's the best language for saying bye, I'd flubbed it cuz the city already forgot me.

The horse farm was on a twisty road flanked by woods. Perky little hills worked a number on my bladder. Despite a strong midday sun, the road was all green shadow thanks to trees thick and tall as god's fingers. My old block's trees were like zoo elephants— one or two specimens stunted by a cement habitat. But this chaos of greenery had my heart calling dibs. Monster claws made of vine and bramble reached for our truck. Far as I had known, plants began in the soil and grew to the sky. But not here, where greenery grew sideways, diagonally, and downward. "We are your new brat pack," the woods whispered, seeming mischievous as my old crew, and also like they wouldn't tell on you.

When I got out of the pickup, I walked to the edge of the woods and stared. "Introduce yourself. Go talk to the trees," mom said. I ventured in, ferns feathering my shins, and didn't stop walking till I couldn't see the house and the house couldn't see me. Jack-in-the-pulpits were terrariums of rainwater and drowned flies. Mushrooms shriveled and swelled. A baby toad peed a puddle in my hand. In that moist wilderness, mine and mine alone, I recited a poem aloud. An original, from memory, about the Chuck Taylors that my dreams were made of. The trees listened close, gave a standing ovation. Their mossy velvet roots invited me to sit and felt so soft I almost forgot Titi Ginny's lazy boy.

2

SPANISH BECOMES A SECRET; LANGUAGE OF THE DEAD

"Please, mom? Can we go to Titi Ginny's this weekend?"

"Ay, how many times do I have to say no?" Mom rested, sweating, against the hoe's tall handle. Ribs heaving above spent lungs. All morning she had sliced the hoe's blade downward, troughing and trenching a patch of earth out back. Now they reversed roles and the hoe supported her momentary repose. "Go cut me an eight-foot piece, entiendes?" She handed me a knot of twine. I found a measuring tape in dad's workshop garage, and an exacto knife for cutting. Two important tools, I told myself, for an important task. When I returned with the measured and cut section, she told me to anchor one end in my fist. I held it firmly against the dirt, pink earthworms wriggling near my wrist. Mom lifted the twine's loose end and walked a steady circular path using the rope as a tether, marking her course with a walking stick. In just minutes, she had etched a circle into the freshly turned soil. Its symmetry was flawless. Next came the compass, which I got to hold, as mom located north, east, west, south, and center. She marked each of the five directions with a river stone, conch shell, or raw quartz. The garden would be a living medicine wheel, she told me.

For the remainder of the weekend, whether baking bread or sweeping cobwebs from the ceiling, mom paused on the hour, headed out back, and jotted numbers in her marble composition book. "This column is time of day. This column is the sun's position. This one, shadow length. So I know where to plant each herb. Back in Puerto Rico, Papi taught me. He couldn't read or write, so his brain was his notebook. My job was to bring coffee to him while he farmed, then bring back the empty cup. Little by little, I observed his methods. He would share a tidbit about the plants, seasons, moon cycles. For a man who never stepped foot in a schoolroom, your abuelo was a genius." A genius who died in Puerto Rico before I was born. The man and the island were mysteries to me, and the title Abuelo felt too familiar for, essentially, a stranger.

"How come he couldn't read?"

"He knew a little. Mami taught Papi the basics. But when he was younger than you, Papi lost all his elders to a hurricane. An entire community carried out to sea and, whoosh, swallowed by the ocean. He was one of two children who survived. Grew up like a slave in poverty, but with his indigenous science knowledge."

She compiled a notebook index of herbs and scooped me up for long drives to nurseries that might sell them. Angelica. Rosemary. Eucalyptus. Rue. Lemon balm. Yerba bruja. Basil (albahaca). Verdolaga (purslane). Peony. Artemisa (wormwood). Various types of mint. Parsley. Marjoram (mejorana). Hot peppers. Pazote.

And many, many sages. Because of its strong personality and curative properties, sage was to be planted at center. Mexican sage. Purple sage. Pineapple sage. Lemon sage. Rooting young herbs in loose soil made mom glow with a radiance I'd never seen in Philly. Depending on the humidity, her hair might be a tall springy afro, pyramid down in loose curls, or lie smooshed beneath a bandana save a strand at the ears. As summer progressed, she darkened from new-penny bright to old-penny rich. But some things never changed: her ski slope nose, the overbite that emphasized her tiredest smile, and slender shoulders with enough soft to lean your head on.

Monday through Friday mom still left home early and came home late, the bone-tired breadwinner. I had no clue what she did in the city, but the long train ride home was standing-room-only as briefcases pummeled her knees. She returned soggy-limbed, a marionette whose strings had come loose. Mom's curls and clothes that had been impeccable in the morning drooped off her brow, shoulders, and hips. She looked like a neglected laundry line. I was usually already in bed and only heard her entrance, the muffled footsteps in the hallways, the mattress's sigh as it accepted her troubles. Often, a fight would suddenly energize her and I'd stare at the ceiling to mom and dad's vitriolic screams.

On Saturdays the notion of retracing her daily commute made her wince and so despite my pleas, our weekend hangouts at Abuela's and Titi Ginny's became a memory. Titi Ginny never did come to visit, not alone or with the promised carful of cousins. Instead, mom and I spent weekend daylight gardening or strolling the farm's hills, while dad caught up with his carpentry in the garage.

The rituals began.

.   .   .

"Join me out back if you want," and the screen door closed behind her. By the time I leapt up realizing the Spanish thing—the
god thing—was about to go down, she was halfway up the hill. I
followed her past the circle garden and up through the wild grass,
breath thickening, windmilling my arms to show the grasshop-
pers how free I was. Way on top, overlooking the cows and
horses, was the warmest patch of grass in the history of warm.
That close to the sky, mom's skin wore the sun like a candy coat-
ing. Boy, did she shine.

Mom opened her marble notebook and let my fingertips
graze the pages. The grooves etched by her cursive were deep,
willful things. As usual, she had a little boom box and a few tapes.
Yoruba drumming, Andean pan flutes, music played low to accompany the recitations. What would she read today? A Lakota
prayer translated into Spanish? A psalm she'd adapted so god had
a feminine ending? A journal entry telling of auspicious dreams?
An original poem about nature?

"Mom, what's 'pecho' mean?"

"Chest."

"What's 'tierra' mean?"

"Earth."

"What's 'madre' mean?"

"Stop interrupting and listen."

Our hilltop rituals were the only Spanish I had now. Back in
Philly, at Abuela's or Titi Ginny's, Spanish was common as a can
opener in a kitchen. But on the Malvern horse farm, it was an
outdoor-only language, a mom-and-me secret. Whenever dad
was in earshot, mom kept to English.

I peeked in her cloth bundle. She had spent weeks drying sage and eucalyptus, then steeping the leaves in rubbing alcohol and oils. A bottle of the potion rested in her bag. Perhaps today would be a shiatsu massage. The human body, she had told me, has the same five directions as a medicine wheel. After slathering her palms in the stinky stuff, she would press her thumbs deep into my ribs to loosen my summer cough. My shoulder blades, typically made of bone, became pliant under her circling knuckles. Then, one breath later, I would wake up alone, long after she'd finished and left for the kitchen.

But today on the hill, mom did not reach into the bundle. The notebook stayed closed and the tape deck sat unloaded.

"When I was your age," she began, "something scary happened. It was frightening because I didn't understand. I want you to be prepared, Quiara, in case you have a similar experience."

She told five-year-old me about her own life at five, speaking in English so I'd understand every word.

Don Genaro perched on a stool beside mom's bed, his neck swollen as a ripe guayaba from diabetes. It was improper for a grown man to enter a girl's room, and so mom knew his visit must be urgent. While asleep, mom had witnessed his whole journey. How he rose from his bed a few blocks away and limped along the callejón past her window, dragging one chancleta as usual. Don Genaro's walk was unmistakable from the sound and everyone in Arecibo knew when he was coming. The entire moonlit journey, calling my mother's name in an agonized voice. "Virginia! Virginia!" In her sleep she saw him come up the porch and into the house. Opening her eyes, mom discovered the elder standing at her bedside. "Alert everybody, inform everyone," Don Genaro said. Mom knew it was her neighbor there, real as rain, but that it was not normal.

Ginny, mom's nine-year-old sister, shared the bed. She woke up to mom's screaming and ran straight for Mami and Papi, same as she had many nights before. They asked mom the usual question. "Who's here?" Previously, her answers were vague. "Strangers," she would say. "People I don't recognize." Tonight was different. "Don Genaro is here," mom told her parents.

Papi's usual scowl deepened. Juan Perez was not a religious man, though his connection to the earth ran deep. Church, for him, was his farm and the elements: sun, air, water, moon. But his daughter's nightmares were consistent, full of uncanny details, and where could they have come from if not some legitimate experience? This was agrarian Puerto Rico in the fifties. No one had TVs. There were few books and no movies. Outside influences were minimal.

Obdulia and Juan Perez rushed next door to wake the neighbors, who were Don Genaro's relatives and received him frequently. That's how my mom knew him. Don Genaro often brought a cookie for little Virginia and her sister Ginny when visiting his family next door. The tiendita on the corner sold penny treats and was perfectly situated on the way.

The two young sisters stayed in the house as instructed. Under veil of night, Mami, Papi, and the next-door neighbors headed for Don Genaro's home: up the callejón beneath mom's window, turning left at the tiendita, knocking on the elder's door. There would be no answer. Don Genaro had already passed.

.   .   .

A few times that year, mom lay in bed with her sister, inhaling the fragrance of magnolia. The tree stood at the porch's edge, right in front of the cupboard, and when its huge flowers blossomed they unleashed a nauseating perfume. Like most farm kitchens in Arecibo, theirs was an indoor-outdoor hybrid, with the cupboard mostly outside. Hand-carved in the 1930s, it was Papi's pride, a fine piece afforded by many harvests. Gandules and batatas earned him his one antique. Some china rested on its shelves, a few nice forks and knives. All the little fine things used for the holy days. As mom drifted into sleep one night and magnolia filled her lungs, the sound began in her dreams. Glasses and china shattering against walls, utensils crashing to the floor, a deafening clatter. Then explosive footsteps coming at the house and something dragging behind them. One other sound, too: a cáscabel, ringing, ringing. Who knew its source—there was no cáscabel in the china cabinet. Decades later, as a santera in Philadelphia, mom learned the cáscabel's ceremonial purpose: to call los Egun, to summon the ancestors. But at five she knew only the bell's ringing assault: tákata tákata tákata.

Though the nightmares only happened during the magnolia's bloom, the great tree flowered multiple times a year. Too frequent for comfort, the dreams grew overwhelming. "If you hear something, say a prayer," her mami instructed. "Shut it off."

At first it worked. Prayer lifted the burden, for a bit. The awful sound of the cáscabel diminished, until new dreams blossomed in the place of old ones. Now mom dreamed of people, strangers lined up along the family's sloping street, from the top of the hill to the small valley below where the sewer pipe drained. Hundreds of people waited to cross over to another land, as if the large cement tunnel were a sort of doorway.

Obdulia was devout, a churchgoing woman. Despite leaving school in the second grade, she read the Bible daily and with a scholar's devotion. Her brother, mom's uncle, was a Methodist minister and the entire extended family maintained Christian households. For a long time the family kept mom's proclivities quiet. What girl needs that stigma? But when Don Genaro was named, word got out. The next-door neighbors had witnessed it, after all. "Tiene facultad," folks whispered.

Opposite the family's wooden casita was Juan Perez's farm. The plot of land was cooperatively parceled and worked by three men. Set back from the main road's foot traffic, the farm was a good spot for make-believe and solitary exploration. There was a hog to avoid, rows of gandules to maze through. A bank of quicksand once swallowed a horse neck-deep and mom watched three men wrest the beast from the pit. There was a safety fence around a pond, its latticework overgrown with fruit. Picking sour parchas and pulpy guayabas was one of mom's regular pastimes.

One afternoon, she was surprised to discover a crowd cross-ing the farm toward the reflective water of the charca. In Are-cibo, a crowd meant an event. Perhaps a casket procession or a Día de los Inocentes parade. At the first sign of a group, kids would come running. This crowd was different, though. Con-cerned men, a search party. What could they be looking for? There was nothing on Papi's land but crops, a few animals, and the water reserve. After scouring the premises and turning up nothing, the men left the farm, crossed the road, and stepped onto Juan Perez's porch, where Obdulia stood waiting. When mom followed the crowd to eavesdrop, Obdulia ordered her into the house. "Go get your papi and stay in the bedroom, don't come out." She did as told and watched from the window as Obdulia and Juan Perez lowered their voices and the search party was quietly and swiftly sent away.

That was the end of it until a few weeks later, when a neighborhood man was found hanging in his apartment. In the suicide note, he described the cabinet where he'd hidden the girl, his victim. Despite some decay, the child's body revealed evidence of brutality and rape. Such monstrous acts were unheard of in Arecibo. Grief and shock gripped the town. Obdulia and Juan Perez could no longer keep the truth from little Virginia, my mom. The search party had come that day having heard of a child with gifts, a child whose abilities might help them locate the missing girl. Mom's parents had refused the request.

For mom it was bitter news, discovering that she might've prevented something awful but was never given the opportunity. Then again, if her ability was real, why did she need to be asked at all? Shouldn't the truth have come with no prompting, in her dreams? The murdered girl from the caserío had been a schoolmate. Was it mom's fault, in some small way, that her young neighbor was no longer sitting in class?

Mom grew sick. Light, no matter how dim, triggered headaches. Ginny, who had always spent evenings brushing her baby sister's long hair, watched as the bristles became a thicket of fallen strands. Bald spots revealed the dome of mom's head. Her trigueña skin turned sallow. Dr. Sandín was a kind tall man with light skin who made house calls. At his urging, Obdulia and Juan Perez closed mom in a room with no natural sunlight. Vitamin shots were prescribed, kidney problems discussed, reading glasses ordered. Mom lay in her parents' bed, afraid of what terrors sleep might bring, shivering and delirious all waking hours.

It was time for the tree to go. The curative properties of magnolia blossoms were widely recognized, and Obdulia suspected the tree's powers went beyond the medicinal. Its scent might be bringing in the spirits. Plus, cutting it down would allow Juan Perez to expand the porch. He was already converting their wooden casita into a cement home. The magnolia's removal promised real benefits.

Once the tree was uprooted, mom's visions faded. The visitations ended. Denying the gift became mom's gift. At a young age, mom mastered the art of being incomplete. With self-subjugation came relief, cool as charca water.

Mom's hair grew in again. Her girlhood resumed.

My mother finished the story and we sat in silence until, in the distance, gravel popped beneath tires. We heard the donkey across the road hee-haw, announcing dad's return from a weekend carpentry job.

"I better get started on dinner," mom said. Lying on my back, eyes squinted tight, I tried to imagine her as a scared bald-headed child, but all I saw was a strong-jawed twenty-something beauty with a bandana trapping her curls.

"It's a secret?" I asked.

"People use things they don't understand against you," she said.

"Does dad know?" But my gut sensed he didn't.

She thumbed my chin gently. "Have you ever had dreams like that? Or received visitations?" There was something beyond tenderness in her eyes. A wish. I thought not responding would be answer enough, but mom sat waiting. Eventually, I shook my head the least amount necessary to mean no. "If you ever do, come talk to Mami. There's nothing to be afraid of. And if you don't, that's okay, too. Just remember, the night I got pregnant with you, I saw the lights come into me." She kissed my forehead, then gathered her skirt to stand. Mom's tenderness couldn't veil her disappointment, nor could my silence camouflage mine. Motionless on the ground, I watched her like a downed boxer sees the feet of his victor. I wasn't sure whether the woman walking down and away was my ally or a newly met stranger.

But she had trusted me. That mattered. Same as the woods confided in me on occasion: a still-moist snakeskin, an unearthed arrowhead. Perhaps listening was my own inward dream state. Maybe guarding the vault's code was an honor, even if I didn't own the treasure inside. Having attended no church except this hilltop cathedral, having read no scripture except mom's marble notebook, I imagined god in her image—whispering Spanish, breasts and belly soft, hiding, cautious, from a misunderstanding world. Yes: my confidence offered refuge. By the time she hollered dinner from the back door, I was figuring my rung on the ladder was all right. Maybe other Sundays she'd have more secrets to tell.

3

ENGLISH IS FOR ATHEISM;
LANGUAGE OF WOODWORKING

Dad was sucking down a Camel unfiltered, his long hair cascading down the chairback, eyes hidden behind a sci-fi paperback. Asimov, Vonnegut, and Bradbury had overtaken his bookshelves and now created skylines all over his study's floor. Each cracked spine testified to multiple rereads, and half-missing covers were the norm. Sometimes I'd sneak into the study when dad was away and fan through yellowed pages, savoring the smell of woodchips and weed. These books were the only evidence of dad's past. If he had parents, they went unnamed, undescribed. If he hailed from a place, he never indicated so. It seemed to me he'd emerged from the woods a forever adolescent hoisting a hundred books over his shoulder and a bong in his back pocket.

"Is god real?" I asked.

"God is the opiate of the masses," dad said, reclining in his wooden swivel. His thoughts on any given matter were often too big for sitting upright. Dad could've said anything in that lazy repose and I'd have taken it as inarguable fact.

"Do you know what genocide is?" he asked.

"No."

"How about slavery? The Holocaust? You'll learn. Probably not in kindergarten. They're terrible things people have done to each other in the name of god. Religion is the root of all evil." He paused for a moment, double-checking that his point was complete, then returned the book to his face.

I closed the door behind me but could hardly move in the hallway. If religion was evil, then was mom evil, too?

All week when I saw him, I lost the courage to ask, until Friday, when I worked up the resolve. The school bus deposited me at the stop sign, a quarter mile uphill on the road that led home. Our house wasn't visible past curves and brambles, but as I got closer I heard dad's table saw shrieking. This would be the moment. I knew they argued hard and hateful, and always after my bedtime as if eyelids shut my ears, but if dad thought mom was actually evil, well then, case closed: he denied her special sauce, her main ingredient, her ABCs. And my toes got that tingle of stepping too close to the edge, and three woozy steps later it felt like I was crossing a bridge built of twigs.

Closer to the house, dad's smoking cough beckoned, a cavernous basso echoing his first cigarette at thirteen. I came into the garage, greeted by a milky way of sawdust. Specks of light hovered, suspended, slow danced. Dad glanced up and nodded hello. His focus was contagious and I fell silent as he worked. He tilted a hefty wooden slab back and forth, checking it out, a cigarette dangling from his lips. It looked like a dull, plain piece of wood, but after eyeing me to check if I was paying attention, dad cascaded rubbing alcohol over the plank. Suddenly loops and curls glistened on its surface. "Curly maple." He spoke the words like sacrament. "Curly maple," I repeated, a flock of one. Within minutes, the alcohol evaporated and the wood grain receded back into dullness. In the coming days, he explained, he would sand the plank, starting with rough coarseness, getting progressively finer. Then he would tung-oil it over and over, day after day, until the just-glimpsed glow reached permanently into the grain and held shine. For this project, he would use only mortise and tenon joints, enabling him to build without a single nail. "Joinery, if done right, is stronger than nails," he said.

"How can that be?"

"A nail creates a disturbance, a hole. It compromises the wood."

Dad's workshop was my after-school program. Sometimes I would venture a question as he worked, request an explanation. He spoke in the fewest words possible, each syllable decisive and considered. But today's question was a boulder at my locked lips. If religion is the root of all evil, then is mom evil, too?

The sky was striped blood-orange by the time dad checked his watch. We hurried to the pickup and chased the runaway sun around bends as green bramble darkened to silhouette. The hardware store closed soon, and dad needed sandpaper. His unfiltered Camel crackled like a miniature campfire. He didn't puff the cigarette so much as exorcise a demon from it. Five inhales and the thing was spent. Then he cracked open the window and in the rearview I saw it fly like a comet.

Mom had told me one of his secrets. How in boyhood he attended survival camp each summer. Twenty-one days with a compass, knife, and no companions. The goal being to survive. Just dropped him in the wilderness. Abandoned a young boy with no way to contact home. How fucked in the head is that, mom said. I imagined little-kid dad whittling sticks beneath the stars, preludes to the hand-sharpened pencils littering our home. Then one summer, when dad was thirteen and already a confident survivalist, his session came to an abrupt, premature end. Two weeks in, a camp official emerged, hurrying through the woods. Time to go. Not a moment to spare. It had already taken a few days to locate dad. The home news was this: another heart attack caused by diabetes. Her fourth and last. Dad was choppered off the mountain to attend his mom's funeral. Can you imagine, mom sighed. Learning about his mom's death from a stranger? But for me, something clicked. Dad's sadness always seemed a little bit holy. I had tried asking him about it, but he had quickly brushed past a "Yup, that was sad," to say he could start a fire in a damp forest without a match. Survival camp was the one part of childhood he enjoyed, he had said, which was more words than he'd ever spoken on his mom.

Now, with the sun completely fallen, dad pulled into the True Value lot and cranked the brake. Past the window posters, a cone of light beamed onto the register. Still open. Inside, we found various sandpapers and dad selected a progression of rough-to-smooth. Each one left different size scratches on my fingers. And even though the lady had unbolted the door for the day's final customers, dad took his time talking me through each level of coarseness. He'd have paused the world from spinning just to educate me in the True Value aisles.

The lady rebolted and we lingered beneath signage as dad lit another unfiltered. "Bailey's Irish Cream and hot fudge?" Baskin-Robbins was still open and one parking lot over. And with his offer, my simmering question dissipated. "Religion is the root of all evil," dad had decreed. Then does that make mom evil? I had reeled. But there in the empty unlit lot, I saw the crack in his foundation. Dad as an atheist—I couldn't quite buy it. His words didn't match his way. Dad the mystic, I thought, as if righting a crooked painting. Mom had taught me about mystics. It wasn't the typical father stuff that made dad one, though he had done it all. Keep your eye on the ball. Aim for the bull's-eye, hold the bow steady. When I let go of the bike, you stay pedaling. Sound out the word. No, his mysticism was an ability to be both a thousand miles away and right here with me, a creativity born of boyhood alone on a mountain. Despite his unrelenting intellectual certainty, dad spoke of a nail-less bookcase like psalm speaks of valley.

No longer would I trust the man's declarations, no matter how far his chair leaned. If his words didn't match his way, why bother seeking explanations? Why not simply observe the carpenter at work, trusting the unspoken—the felt and seen—which was more reliable anyway? So that's what I did every summer day, until kindergarten began.

4

A NAME THAT IS A MASK

Malvern was only an hour outside Philly, but it was a whole different universe. The woods, donkeys, and horses didn't account for the half of it. We had moved to a monolingual, pale world. Its language uniformity was so complete as to be creepy, zombie-esque. How the shopkeepers and mailmen spoke English confidently and pronounced all their vowels the same exact way. How within houses I visited, the kids, parents, and elders shared the same language and never paused for translation or to remember a word. Though Malvern folks didn't pray to ancestors like mom did, I could tell that if they did, even their ghosts would speak English. My Ingles was as good as the next Malvernite's but mom's wasn't, and I sensed trouble ahead.

At kindergarten roll call the teacher pronounced my Q the English way, so my name sounded like slime. After squinting at some error in the attendance book, she swapped the letters in my middle name. "Algeria?" All the kids screamed "Ewwwww!" because they'd heard of an African country like that. "Algeria? Algeria!" I told them it was Alegría and meant happiness in Spanish. "Then why's it sound ugly?" a boy snorted. By the time the Pledge of Allegiance arrived, I had stopped correcting them. "Alegría" was amputated from my book reports and homework like a gangrenous toe. I had to contain the damage to "Quiara" and "Hudes."

According to mom there had been a Ciara, a few Kiaras, and many Chiarras before me but never a Quiara. She invented a conjugation of "querer" to mean beloved. Whenever a classmate mocked my name, my guts coiled hot as a stovetop. Still, beneath the burn of mockery, I harbored a superhero's secret because I was a brand-new word.

Alegría was chosen not for its sunny meaning but to honor Ricardo Alegría, a Puerto Rican anthropologist. Mom described the Taíno ceremonial grounds he uncovered and documented. Never having been to the island, I couldn't really imagine petroglyphs or standing stones. Before El Profesor, mom explained, our island's indigenous roots had been silenced. But then Alegría wrote his books on the Taínos. "A library shelf holds tremendous power, Quiara. If it's not written down, it doesn't exist." Though she had never attained college, she talked with reverence about books and scholarship. "El Profesor brought us into the light. He was a revolutionary, so your middle name, Alegría, is revolution masked as happiness."

Hudes came from dad, of course. Dad rarely spoke about Jewish stuff, his surname being no exception. If it was rooted in some language or meant anything, it was news to me. All I knew was that the *u* was squishy, like in "beautiful" or "cute," but strangers said it the double-*o* way like "moo" or "boot." A silent *u* in Quiara and a spherical *u* in Hudes. A name that broke its own rules.

Three weeks into kindergarten mom brought a birthday cake to school, spongy yellow layers intercut with jam. She had jarred the stuff herself after picking wild raspberries on the farm. A shag carpet of icing covered the thing. Hundreds of florets had been piped individually, painstakingly, as she hummed boleros into the night.

The kids saw mom's copper skin and loose bouncing afro and turned to me. "Are you adopted?" a boy asked. My guts stove-coiled and I shook my head no. "Then what are you?" he said, genuinely curious. Truth was, I hadn't a clue. To me, Puerto Rico was a past-tense island. Jewish was murkier, no place at all, and dad shrugged any time the word was spoken. A group of class-mates circled around, anticipating my answer. Their eyes buzzed with excitement. I resented that in this English-only town, mom's skin tone and molasses vowels rendered her a headline. And that my difference from her now signified anything at all. "So? What are you?"

"I'm half English, half Spanish," I ventured, as if made not of flesh and blood but language. And it felt okay. The kids seemed satisfied by my declaration.

5

AN ENGLISH COUSIN COMES TO VISIT

Over a year in, and still no titis had pulled up in a caravan. Back in Philly, mis primas y tías had always passed through, rotating between our stoop and Ginny's, swapping babysits and gossip. But not once did they visit the farm, so what guests we had fell in line with Malvern's way: English only.

But Simon, my cousin from dad's side, came from Philly for the weekend. Considering how few playmates I had on the farm, and how few friends I'd met at school, the chance to show an older boy—a city kid—my personal wilderness was thrilling. I was back to my old brat pack self, showing off tree-climbs, plunging a thorn into my arm to elicit a pearl of blood, then savoring Simon's delicious "Ewwww!"

The beehive was hidden beneath a clump of wet leaves, in a distant patch of woods halfway past the cow pasture. I led the way along the path to the algae pond, mud squishing between my bare toes. I knew the second I stepped on it: the papery texture underfoot, the crinkle of a collapsed hive. Bees emerged from their home like a soul leaving a body. A buzzing cloud overtook me. "Run!" Simon screamed as electric pain rippled everywhere. We bolted out of the woods, hollering past unimpressed cows. I screamed from terror and pain and Simon screamed, sure he was watching me die. I couldn't outrun them. It was ten minutes to home if we ran at top speed. There were hundreds of them—a killing amount. They found my pinky finger, knee, and neck. They clouded my forehead, hovered at my crown, clasped in my hair. "Your shirt! Your shirt!" Simon hollered. Looking down, I saw my sweater covered in dead bees. They dangled from the yarn, sequins of death. I ripped off my sweater midstride, threw it behind me, and for one blessed breath the terror paused, the bees quieted, and there was only a strange, tangential thought: I am naked. This is my belly. These are my flat pink nipples and he is seeing them. Then the grass found my cheek and rest found my body.

I came to, limp in dad's arms. How much time had passed? Dad kicked the screen door so hard it unhinged, and was careful not to knock my head as he fed me through the frame. He strode to the nearest bed, placed me down atop the blankets, and gently pulled my clothes away to see how the bees had undone me. "Not my underwear," I whispered, too weak to hold them in place. As the two of them gazed down, I saw Simon's fear blossom into curiosity, then mischievous excitement. He made a scandalized O of his mouth, pointing at my hands, which made their best fig-leaf cover.

I wished mom would catch my soul's distress call, just as she'd caught messages from other spirits in distress. She needed to come quick, close the door against all glances, heal me with eucalyptus oil and feminine hands. A million times she had dressed, bathed, and healed me, and each time her eyes told me what my body was: no more or less remarkable than grass, plant, or pebble.

Either my distress call got lost in the transom or mom got stuck in traffic coming home.

Turns out I was not particularly allergic and the constellation of bumps never really swelled. We spent the afternoon in my room, headaches coming and going. Simon and I recounted the event over and over, no embellishment necessary. How many stings had I racked up? "Hundreds," he declared with widest eyes, spooked by the recounting. We marked each sting in blue pen as we tallied. Then it was time to check my torso, but I lifted my shirt only halfway. Simon looked at me, the hope in his eyes bright. He had seen my nipples plenty, as had every kid in Philly. In my hydrant days, I happily frolicked in the only bathing suit I owned: my Wonder Woman panties. But today, I told Simon two stings were hidden from view and he added them to the count, disappointed as he drew his hash marks. Then I climbed into bed and pulled the covers tight, the day's tumult making my head throb.

My body means something different to others than to me. That's what I lay there thinking. It's not that I resented what my body meant to Simon: a curiosity, a potential game of doctor maybe, the low-level scandal of a cousin's private parts. Whatever, back in Philly the brat pack was always doing grown-folks shit, oftentimes initiated by me. What bugged me was that his curiosity happened atop my wound, that in a moment of pain, I didn't set the score on what me meant.

I faked sleep for hours. When Simon waved goodbye, we were two helium balloons that had lost our lift. We never did finish tallying the bee stings.

6

LANGUAGE OF THE FOREST

Mom's bonfire live-in with a hippie on the run was, in the end, a spectacular failure. When I was in second grade they split, and mom and I returned to the old Philly block, two suburban discards.

Dad's every other week. Dad's on weekends. Dad's every other weekend. Dad's once a month, if that. The R5 tracks became my compass. Trains left on the 12s, 32s, and 52s. I was a migrant in my own life. I was told to find an aisle seat near the conductor, clip my nails if a man sat next to me, and if that didn't repel him, move immediately. But rules be damned, I rushed for the window each time, leaning my head against the smooth glass. Dust always dotted the panes' exterior from dirty rain that had dried, and I would stare past it as though my life lay beyond—a blur in the distance, going, going, gone. Mom had done this commute and grown exhausted. Now, the route being mine, I felt not tired but cold. The air-conditioning, the glass. I might have been scared on the hourlong ride or on the isolated platform waiting to be picked up. I might have been saddened by a family rent in two. But my ear and forehead propped against the cool windowpane? Anesthetic.

Conductors nodded hello, tipped their SEPTA caps, called me by name, even stopped the train if they saw me sprinting to the platform. But their smiles barely masked it. Damn-ass shame, their eyes told me as they punched my ticket. An unattended nine-year-old commuter.

Mom's Spanish was no longer reserved for backyard rituals, just out of dad's earshot. Now an hourlong gulf stretched between English me and Spanish me and in all those migrations I discovered the disparity. How the fifteen minutes from 30th Street Station to Overbrook was rubble, graffiti, broken factory windows, junk tires piled high. How three minutes later, by Merion, the Main Line was an oasis of gleaming brick, emerald lawns, restored wrought iron. The sudden change sickened me, for what it implied about mom, my titis, Abuela, and primas. My Perez women were messy derelict squalor. My English dad was manicured Americana.

Mostly my urban childhood, interrupted, resumed. Our tumbledown twin home had sat loyally waiting. Cobwebs had multiplied in unreachable corners. Floorboards creaked louder, with the same cracks so wide you could pass a note to the floor below. The second-floor landing was still haunted so you had to bolt upstairs before the spook snatched your ankles. The alley's padlock was rusted shut, no key in sight. Titi Ginny hadn't waited for

us. She had a new North Philly address now, nearer to Abuela.
Without two titis on one block, my Perez cousins didn't come
around as much. Same block, same rooms, everything different.

But I still spent weekends and after-schools at Abuela's, where
Spanish surfed on bus fumes—crashing on every corner and
through open windows. I relaxed in mom's return to anonymity.
She was neutral once again, and neutrality, Malvern had taught
me, was a luxury. Still, even in Philly, mom and I occasionally required explanation.

"Are you looking for extra hours? We just lost our nanny."

"I'm her mother. Have a blessed day."

It felt like my life's intact boat had crashed, boards splintering off
and drifting in disparate directions. It was baffling, watching
parts of myself get further and further from each other. I rifled
the back corners of mom's drawers, unlidded high-shelf shoe-
boxes. Anything for a clue as to what had happened, our family's
before or our after. A stack of old boxes in the basement beckoned. The juiciest secrets, I knew, were housed in the bottom
one. In it was an old upholstered photo album that I squirreled to
my bedside and gazed at nightly. Picture by picture, my parents'
love affair unfolded. I slid favorite snapshots from cellophane
sleeves, fingering their matte finish and round corners. Here
mom and dad were, barely twenty, hiking atop a waterfall or col-
lecting driftwood on a late-autumn beach. There they were at the
Rainbow Gathering, launching canoes into a pine-edged pond,
the braid down dad's bare back so long it grazed his woven belt.
Here were four openmouthed kisses in a photo booth. Or mom's
nine-month belly anchoring a naked body, her sumptuous breasts
backlit in a window. But the candid of them standing with dinner

plates at some party mesmerized me. I became convinced it was this shot that held the answer, so I studied it day after day. Dad was possibly still a teen and mom had just pushed into her twenties. Arms wrapped together, they'd become a single universe. Their bodies were lithe, draped in vaguely Indian fabrics, sexy. Mom, dark and luminous, smiled into the camera and imagined a grand tomorrow there; dad stared diagonally down and away, hoping the warm saturated aura of the woman beside him could patch up his terror. The weaving cling of their arms reminded me of parachuters plummeting in formation. They were as hypnotized by love as a midnight fawn is by headlights. .

The breakup went like this, or so mom blurted out in unsolicited tirades: while she was off earning rent money, dad invited a punk-rock sculptor into their bed. When that affair soured, the sculptor's best friend filled the vacancy.

"That's not true, mom. Susan and Sharon were dad's friends."

"I have the letters. They're in a stack of boxes in the basement. You want to read them?"

"No."

"He left them around everywhere, practically begging me to discover. But when a woman wants to be blind, it's amazing what she refuses to see."

"Susan taught me to use a glue gun and assemble found objects into art. Sharon lent me her rock-climbing shoes and I scaled a sixty-foot cliff. Those are things friends do, mom. I hung out with them and dad. Men and women can be friends."

"The fact that he had you buddying up to his playthings . . . Don't talk about shit you don't know, Quiara. I know. *I know!*"

"Well, they never yelled at dad like you always did!"

"Óyeme bien, Quiara. I never liked hanging with the hippie crowd. All that weed, tu me entiendes, I'm not into that. But I decided to surprise your father and show up at one of their gatherings unannounced. All heads turned my way like *uh-oh*. . . . Pues, this uppity chick, the squeaky-voice fake-smile type, introduces herself and will not leave my side. This lady is hell-bent on embarrassing me, all night picking fights, criticizing my advocacy work en el barrio. Because she had graduated college and traveled to Nepal, that made her some kind of expert on Hispanics? Fuck off, bitch. Another white feminist with all the answers. Everyone knew, Quiara. The whole party was hip to your dad's affairs. They had played matchmaker, puedes creer? While I was busting my ass putting groceries on the table . . ." Mom sighed a bunch of times in quick staccato, then lowered her voice to truth register: alto. "I'll always love your father, because he gave me you."

"So what did you do? At the party?" I asked.

"Gave that bitch a piece of my mind. Don't question my integrity, puñeta, when I been on the ground, busting my ass for a community you don't know shit about, because you volunteered at Habitat for fifteen minutes!" Then she sighed some more. A babalao had warned her, mom said. She'd gone for an unrelated consultation and he'd read the divination chain and asked inquisitively, "You're happily married?" "Very," she had responded. "When you return home tonight, you will have no marriage." Mom had laughed in the babalao's face. "Y mira lo que pasó, Quiara," she said. "Look what happened. Orula doesn't lie."

I zoned her out. It was too much. Her torrents too exhausting. And these words—"Orula" and "babalao"—that she lobbed my way, explosives on a battlefield, and I didn't even know what they meant. But in their plosives and round vowels, I sensed a new language emerging from mom. One that, apparently, she wasn't pausing to explain.

I determined to get dad's take straight up, like I'd done with god. He met me at the train for a weekend visit and with each curve of the country road I wrestled my nerves. *Did you have an affair with . . .* Too accusatory. *Did you cheat on . . .* Too blunt. *Did you have sex with . . .* No way. Finally, we pulled into the driveway and my time was up. "Did you take off your clothes and get under the covers with Susan?" Even I was embarrassed by the naïve wording. For a second, I worried he'd misinterpret my question as a birds-and-bees inquiry. But the way he slumped when switching off the ignition meant he knew.

"Why Susan specifically?"

"I know you've done that with Sharon. You're getting married soon. But you and Susan stopped being friends while you and mom were still together. So, did you? Take off your clothes and get into bed with Susan?" Dad's yes changed our relationship forever. That's how my carpenter god climbed down from his sawdusty pedestal and became the lonely stranger I saw on occasional weekends.

"I wish I knew how to lie to you, Quiara," he said. He had spent so many years as my hero and there in the bucket seat of his parked pickup we held a wordless ceremony, beholding the new canyon that glittered between us. Its span was panoramic, its beauty devastating. Then we got out of the truck and went inside.

In the immediate wake of their separation, a melancholy lumbered from dad like a bear from hibernation's cave. I saw it during weekend stays at the farm that had only recently been my home. He met me at the R5 platform and lit a cigarette as his truck pulled onto the country road. "I've been thinking," he said, one hand on the steering wheel, "about leaving Malvern. I'm not sure where to, but some place far, where nobody knows me. Maybe California, by the redwoods. Start over from scratch. What do you think, sweetie? Would you want to come?" His voice cracked a bit as he laid out dreams and goals. "Money would be very tight until I could get some jobs. I probably couldn't buy you new school clothes. It would mean leaving your mother and friends and family, possibly not seeing them for a very long time." I was moved to be cast in dad's escape fantasy, but the timing seemed off.

"Aren't you and Sharon getting married, like, in a month?"

"Yup," he said.

The next time he met me at the station, he had cut off all his hair.

Picking me up from the train, dropping me back at the train. Pulling into Wawa for gas, unfiltered Camels, and black coffee. This became our ritual of coming and going. There were more bucket seat confessions as though I was his one and only confidante. His relationship was loveless, he said between drags. No carpentry work was coming in. Their lack of nice clothes and Florida vacations fell on his shoulders. Listening was now daughterhood. Talk less, cry never, and demonstrate devotion with eye contact and head nods.

As to how a girl should behave at her dad's wedding, no instructions had been provided. I knew very little about what the day would bring and didn't realize till the morning of that it would happen on the horse farm, a twenty-minute walk from mom's now-withered circle garden. The first time I visited dad after leaving, I had run out back to pick some sage, to roll it in my palms and smell its strong medicine. What had greeted me was a circle of wilted stems. Plants shriveled and bent, untended broken things. By the day of the wedding it was a bald spot.

Far beyond the hills where mom and I once prayed was a blue-stone mansion owned by old-money Main Liners. An elderly matriarch oversaw the farm estate, including the house that we rented. The wedding ceremony would happen by her manicured hedges, the reception overlooking her lily pond. But first, strangers gathered for portraits. Feeling socially adventurous, and unaware of any protocol, I squeezed into a large group photo. Unfamiliar folks were calling out across the patio, waving arms, shouting, "Get in! Hurry!" So it seemed the social thing to do. But after the first flash, Sharon tapped my shoulder and curled her finger, beckoning me aside. She lifted her veil and bent to my eye level, smiling. "This is a portrait of my family members. I'll let you know if you're needed. Today is my day." Her smile seemed reasonable, even kind, but it was no kumbaya when that word left her lips. *My.* I had never heard it used as a weapon before. *Today is my day.* She adjusted her veil and returned to the photograph.

I left. My ballet flats became handhelds as I ran past cows and horses, past the algae pond where bees had pocked me, past the high spot on the hill and the bald spot below, into the woods. The twenty-minute jog wrecked my stockings, and now I walked too close to the forest's interior bramble, letting thorns catch my dress and snag its fabric. I kicked a few old mushrooms into oblivion, exploding them loose from fallen tree trunks. *Today is my day.* Why hadn't she just let me in the photo or at least explained who the strangers were? *Today is my day.* Why had I presumed affinity, thinking the wedding might, in fact, be our day? I shouldn't make that mistake again, I thought. I shouldn't assume any our, ever, and it was best to relinquish all desire to belong. Solitude was reliably safe and enjoyable. The woods understood that, they had taught me well. I spent a long time visiting my old friends: the ferns, the toads, the moss. Finally, relief found me, now that I had decided who to be. The girl alone. The girl who despises the English word "my."

Buoyed by this new self-awareness, and lightened by all I had let go, I was prepared to return to the wedding. Sharon was a college grad whose aspirations didn't include a depressed stepdaughter with an angry Boricua mother. And dad had never intended to kidnap me into a great tomorrow, he had only mumbled a nice wish in his truck. But it would not upset me now, with my new armor of solitude. If the breastplate and helmet were heavy, such was the cost of warrior protection. Even the dirt stripes beneath my fingernails whispered: You have a quiet forest within, retreat there and none can hurt you.

After the long walk back across the farm, I discovered the folding chairs had been moved. No longer a ceremonial grid on the grass, they now circled luncheon tables. Buffet trays were picked over. Crumpled napkins littered tabletops and people milled here and there, wineglasses and car keys in hand. "How was it?" I asked a stranger. "Lovely," the old woman said, "didn't you think?"

I cruised the crowd's perimeter hoping dad would extract himself. I didn't expect much. Maybe thirty seconds or a minute.

He'd clap my back, muster a "Where ya been, kid?" with a fatherly blend of reprimand and forgiveness. And I'd offer him the simple truth. "Sorry, dad, I lost track of time." But for the remainder of the evening he did not approach me, and now, knowing who I was, I could live with his silence.

PART II

*All the Languages of
My Perez Women, and Yet
All This Silence . . .*

7

LATINA HEALTH VOCAB
FROM THE LATE '80S

Mom hadn't always been into community activism. Before my birth, she started her professional life as a carpenter, doing nontraditional work in restoration. But soon after my entrance, during our original stint on the West Philly block, the common-law feminists across the street would steer mom's path wide of woodwork. Ms. Penny was frumpy and friendly with an unbrushed pouf of curls. Ms. Nancy, a professor, was tall, husky-voiced, and no less warm, always handsomely put together in ascots, suspenders, and wool trousers: trans before I'd heard the word. They were the original white folks on our block, before dad moved in. Coming and going, they made a point of brief hellos with us kids, otherwise leading a quiet life behind closed doors and drawn curtains. Mom called them brave and told me to address them with the courtesy reserved for sanctified elders.

It was the Good Old Days. Before the Horse Farm. Before the

R5 Train. Back then, I'd be running the alleyways with my brat pack and come home thirsty, knees all scraped up, to find Ms. Penny and Ms. Nancy in the living room with mom. Far as I could tell, the topic was professional womanhood—words like "union" and "rights" and "labor" flung with animation as I gulped water and snacked. Even though mom grew to resent white feminism, she never had an ill word about those two: rebels who built bridges right to mom's doorstep. Through connections from her professorship at Temple, Ms. Nancy connected mom with training for women entering the trades, to get union jobs with equity salaries. Soon mom was organizing the other participants, cofounding Tradeswomen in Nontraditional Jobs in our living room. The women shared relevant info gleaned from union pals, swapped tidbits overheard at day jobs. The stories about union women getting harassed by their male counterparts horrified mom, so she tried for a nonunion gig building sets for Channel 17. The boss man seemed supportive and promised freedom to work as she pleased. Mom pounced.

Still, she wasn't living to her heart's content. The organizing, not the carpentry, had made her come alive.

It was through her relationship with Lilian Chance, the old-money matriarch who owned the horse farm, that mom's life path veered toward real advocacy. Mrs. Chance came from a long line of suffragettes, and while we lived on the farm, mom took the initiative to knock on her door. Back in Arecibo, elderly folks were to be checked on regularly, and mom carried the tradition with her to Malvern. They both loved gardening. They both had unhappy partnerships. And even if Mrs. Chance's marriage to a renowned engineer left her isolated, she was tremendously wealthy, could afford top-shelf spirits any time of day, and found renewed joy in mentorship.

"You need to go do your work," Mrs. Chance told mom. "I'm going to make a phone call for you." She reached out to Women's Way, a grant-making and advocacy umbrella in Philly run by upper-class white feminists from the Main Line. It was an inner sanctum of highly educated tough old-money cookies who had met through Daughters of the American Revolution. One phone call later, mom went to work for CHOICE, a reproductive health and childcare hotline housed in downtown Philadelphia.

But mom's deepest spark of activism had been lit years before my birth, during one of the scoliosis massages she used to give Abuela. Applying firm touch to Abuela's hip relieved the back pressure, and one day mom saw a small scratch on Abuela's belly she had never noticed before.

"Que es esto?"

"La operación." The operation.

That's how mom learned of sterilization abuse in her hometown, Arecibo. Abuela insisted it didn't matter, water under the bridge, which made mom all the more insistent that the scar be explained. The details Abuela reticently spoke, downplaying each bit, were alarming. In the mid-fifties in Arecibo and neighboring municipalities, poor women of reproductive age were given vouchers for cash and services in exchange for receiving cutting-edge birth control. "They always throw in a candy to catch you," Abuela said, then described the long line of women who rode the carro público into town. In the hospital, Abuela went to sleep, woke up, and was sent home. Pin-pan-pun. A revolving door. Laparoscopic tubal ligation was not yet legal on the mainland, but it became so prevalent in Arecibo that schools shuttered after birth rates plummeted. Never mind that hospitals didn't test women beforehand, so that Abuela was unknowingly sterilized while pregnant with mom. Never mind that the doctors emphasized the ease and reliability of this birth control, conveniently neglecting to mention its permanence. The medical establishment correctly wagered on Puerto Rican women's silence because what Boricua would publicly declare her barrenness? Or let the town know she'd been bamboozled out of motherhood? Keep it quiet and move on with your life. Don't make a scene. Abuela was luckier than many, with a full roster of young'uns. It had been happening forever, anyway. Indeed, mom would learn that in the decades leading up to Abuela's operación, the island's sterilization rate reached one-third—the highest in the world.

But that day, massaging her mother, mom quietly freaked out. After completing the laying on of hands, she immediately logged the details in her diary.

"I had never heard of that shit before." Mom told me Abuela's tale while organizing a conference on sterilization abuse. Fourth grade had come and I was acclimating to the after. After the Horse Farm. After the Split. Mom and I now had more time together and I spent it, in part, proving myself a respectful listener. She rewarded my attention with battle tales of her life as a dissident, in the trenches fighting for health justice. For the conference, mom had flown in the physician who risked her career to bring the sterilization abuse into light. "Dr. Helen Rodríguez Trías is a true American hero," mom said. "We were the guinea pigs, Quiara. It was population control. She uncovered all the government documentation to prove it."

Beneath my engaged front, though, la operación was difficult for me to wrap my head around. A voice inside me whispered,

That can't be real, that doesn't happen. My own body had never faced such danger. Not when the bees attacked, not standing alone on a late-night train platform. That's urban legend stuff, a *Twilight Zone* plot, I thought. But even as the doubts swirled, I knew they only doubled the importance of mom's advocacy and added to a silence whose cost had been too high.

Mom had to be on time for the conference, and first stop was greeting the keynote speaker at Terminal A. With one foot stuttering on the gas and the other stammering on the brake, mom's driving was not for the faint of heart. The herky-jerky ride made me yank a plastic bag from the glove compartment. It was chockfull of the "sick bags" collected from Acme and ShopRite, and they were used regularly. Luckily, she turned into a lot and my head began its slow unscrambling. She covered the car windows, slid out of jeans, and squeezed into the magenta suit that had been hanging by the rear window. She applied lipstick in the rearview and handed me the conference brochure, asking me to check for typos. She could apologize to the participants if times or titles had been misspelled.

For the event, I was placed in a room with typewriters and given the code to the Xerox: a young poet's playground. I planned the next issue of my self-published teen idol mag, listing possible titles and potential cover stories. I typed Beatles lyrics, imagining Paul inking them on stained cocktail napkins. A one-pager came out in a burst of energy, about a man who lived in a box before hitting the numbers. Occasionally I peeked into the conference room, impressed by all the well-dressed and distinguished-looking Latinas. Mom stood at a podium addressing this powerful crowd, her reverbed voice a blend of ferocity and feeling. The words were still new to me. The stories she told, like the story of my grandmother's sterilization, came from what felt like another

world. But that world was now mine. I knew none of it, till I
knew all of it.

I had never gone to work with mom—I had hardly known
what her job was—but now, out of necessity, her office and car
became second homes. Dad's garage workshop had been a rhap-
sodic after-school program, the floating sawdust a daylit cosmos,
my silent reveries interrupted only by power tools. But there was
no room for daydreaming when mom took the wheel, flinging
state-of-the-union sermons about Latina health crises. It was a
loud-ass, mile-a-minute crash course and I better keep up, and I
better listen hard, and I better believe because most of the world
sure as hell didn't. As she sped down the Parkway schooling me
in what SIDA stood for, I mourned the soulful gardener's shiatsu
massages. This outspoken firebrand, awash in urgent matters of
the flesh, rarely had time for tendernesses now. What happened
to the soil-palmed gardener, hoeing in the sun, confiding in me
of her ghost dreams?

Mom broke down the catastrophic infant mortality rate in the
Hispanic community—of which, make no mistake, I was suddenly a part. Our babies died at twice the rate of white ones, so
take note. She shared mounting evidence of an AIDS crisis deci-
mating Hispanic women. There was, she insisted, a two-block
North Philly pocket where mothers were dropping like flies. It
came through their needle-sharing partners, mom hypothesized.
Cervical cancer was through the roof, she moaned, because Latin
American women thought a speculum betrayed their wedding
vows. No Pap smears, no cancer detection. The undocumented
mushroom farmers who lived outside the city were having basement babies, afraid a hospital delivery would get them kicked out
of the country. Even police brutality threatened our pregnancies.
Mom brandished forensic photos of a bruised pregnant dome. I

was to note the wounds formed the shape of a cop's boot. The woman had been assaulted by uniformed officers in broad daylight for lingering near a fight rather than clearing the crime scene. The baby came out with a lump on his head.

How to get the word out to the women most affected? How to urge Latinas to visit the bilingual OB-GYNs mom had vetted? How to assist in filing civil suits against the police? How to explain stovetop methods for needle sterilization? How to convince that prenatal care would help rather than lead to another barrio tale of fatal hospital neglect? As long as Latinas didn't phone the hotline where mom worked, all the resources she mustered were as good as useless.

She had responded powerfully to each case encountered: conferences with councilmen, marches with top-notch Hispanic leadership, multiple petitions, contentious Fraternal Order of Police negotiations, press releases of bruised bellies and urgent statistics. The incremental changes that resulted, however, affected those nearest the levers of change: politicians, healthcare providers, police commissioners, community leadership. Mom was not yet reaching la gente with the depth or breadth that marked a bootstraps trailblazer.

"They don't have phones!" mom shouted to the dashboard one night. "They don't have fucking telephones!" And though that struck me as sad, indicative of a poverty I'd once wished Malvern could glimpse for a second, mom said it like she'd struck gold. "Bingo! Maferefún! Cabiosile pa' Changó! Thank you, Creator, for always pointing my compass toward the path!" We sped through North Philly with the windows rolled wide as mom shouted multilingual praise to busted streetlights. She thanked gods I had heard of and plenty I hadn't. At Abuela's, we had late-night rice and beans in tin bowls. Abuela fed a daily stream of

blood and zip-code family, accepting payment in the form of stories, which, en el barrio, were never in short supply. The only
things more bottomless than Abuela's old pots were her listening
ears. I related, preferring to absorb the cacophonous oral histories quietly, but savoring them nonetheless.

That night, as we spooned pegao into our mouths, mom laid
out The Vision. Abuela listened, nodding as if the gentle gesture
might lull an ailing barrio into good dreams. By the time we
made it back to West Philly, mom's adrenaline was spent, if not
the pilot light glowing inside her. Our cheek kisses and good-
nights were formalities, and we traipsed off to separate dead
zones, bone-tired.

That's how Casa Comadre was born, mom's bricks-and-
mortar community center for a phone-less demographic. It was
an old row home smack-dab on North 7th, tidied up on the
cheap, whose warmth outshone its spartan décor. Almost immediately, curious women poked their heads in. Then hung around
for a cafecito on the sofa. Then attended the workshops where
mom presented female anatomy charts so body-chat could proceed with shameless specificity. The comadres opened up about
their lives. Their needs—nutritious food, dental work, safe harbor from violent partners—were urgent and painful to behold,
and yet their laughter, educational history, working-class and
dirt-poor concerns, and even their eye contact felt like home.
Mom designated and trained Block Ambassadors to go speak
with women who were reticent to be seen entering the building.
Now mom could reach forty-somethings who'd never had a Pap
smear, explaining gynecological procedures while chauffeuring
them and holding their hands during checkups. One such visit
caught the cervical cancer early, and when word spread, more
women came. Now mom could sit face-to-face with undocu-

mented women and convince them a hospital delivery would be legally sound. Mom assembled a bilingual team of legal and medical professionals who swore to answer her call any hour, ready to head to the hospital and advocate like hell.

I was inching toward preadolescence, murky still on the nuances of booty, but comically well versed on AIDS and STDs. The herpes pamphlets littering our backseat made for better reading than English class. And as I became schooled in the Latina body, I grappled with the notion that I might have one. If mine was, as mom insisted, Boricua through and through, did I not carry sterilization abuse in my cellular memory? Yes, mom said. Health and sickness were shared by the collective, not siphoned individually.

But my skin tone more closely resembled those of mom's white supervisors at the hotline. She frequently took potshots at her managers' la-dee-dah pedigree, branding them elitist and out of touch. She had been hired through an exclusive network after all, Daughters of the American Revolution, the kind of feminist club sure to deny her entry. For the entire seven years mom worked at CHOICE, she could never reconcile herself with management's whiteness. Gloria Steinem's visit was the cherry on top. When the famous feminist chose CHOICE and its affiliate programs as a stop on her Philly tour, the office was over the moon. "This is big, man!" mom hollered in thick morning traffic, drumming the steering wheel. "I'm going to put the Latina health movement on Gloria's radar! Today, Boricuas are going to get a national audience!" But that evening's drive home was stifling, and we bypassed Abuela's for drive-thru and straight-to-bed. "Same old tired shit." It turned out that Gloria's reception was management-only. Mom watched the all-white crowd through a window whose reflection revealed she was not alone.

Behind mom stood her lone African American coworker and single Latina colleague. All three witnessed the superstar feminist through a sheet of glass.

Which part of that divide did I fall on? Would I have been invited to the courtyard or forced to view it soundlessly from a distance?

That was the management dynamic when Casa Comadre came up for budget renewal. It was criticized as a divergence from CHOICE's central mission, an unfocused and even rogue programmatic sidestep, the work of a cultural zealot whose passion superseded protocol. With an outsize focus on the need-filled Hispanic community, mom's flagship program was a major resource sap for the cash-strapped organization. Eighteen months after its founding, Casa Comadre was defunded. Mom had shed pounds in the wake of her separation, then dropped another pants size during a below-the-belt custody battle. After Casa Comadre was denied, her cheekbones hollowed inward, as though readying to grow tusks. Drive after drive, I saw her soft shoulders yield to bone. Her knuckles gripping the steering wheel became spindly. She was hollowing out, wasting away because there were Latinas in crisis and those who would see them suffer. In this way, mom and I shared something new. She could smell it on me and I could smell it on her: the loss, the bafflement, our common perfume. When I boarded the R5 train, I was a Latina in crisis, too. The ride out to dad's was simply a variation on her theme. That damn stretch of train tracks from 30th Street to Overbrook: rubble, graffiti, dereliction. And boom, the Main Line arrives as the American oasis: lawns, gilt wood shop signs, mailboxes etched in historic detail. If I had once questioned mom's tales of coerced sterilization, I now believed and was pained by her suffering.

Latino leaders citywide formed a committee dedicated to Casa Comadre's survival, and the *Inquirer* printed a feature lauding the center's successes in an under-resourced neighborhood. In the article's accompanying photo, mom looked focused and ferocious. It was an action shot taken during a conversation, and her mouth is open delivering unheard words that seem equal parts authority and love.

In the end, no committee or article could save it, and the center shuttered. Mom left the job where she'd spent seven of her best years, her twenties now complete. Our house's sadness became saturated and we could barely stand being home. In those days we avoided West Philly. It became a site of sleeping and laundry only, every corner a reminder of loves once felt, fathers once favored, advocacy once activated. So instead of hanging out there, mom, a born workaholic, threw herself into maniac hours in a new social justice position (with a new white boss who would become a second mother to her). And me, I became a North Philly expat, with Abuela's house as the capital of my new dual citizenship.

8

SPANGLISH COUSINS ON
THE JERSEY TURNPIKE

f you won a shopping spree and loaded your cart full of cousins, that was Abuela's house. They streamed in and out, staying for five minutes or two months or eighteen years. They were from Lehigh Ave, South Jersey, Florida, and PR. There was always a new one I'd never met plus the daily rotation of usual suspects. Cousinhood in my big-ass family was a swim-with-the-sharks wonderland.

I was the hump cousin. Younger by years than my own generation. Older, by more, than their emerging crop of babies. Wedged awkwardly in a no-man's-land where I had to make friends with 'em all or be alone. Always hovering, always listening, ears perked up like Abuela, though I held the perimeter while she was central as the sun. Sometimes a burst of cousin laughter would crack my shell and I'd emerge, poking my beak into their sunlight, waddling up to their joy, wings wet and yearning to fly.

At two years my elder, Tiny was the closest in age. Already in her early teens by the time we moved back to Philly, she was just four feet tall and compensated with bangs teased to heaven, aqua-netted to diamond firmness. With underwire bras and C-cups, her boobs accounted for half her body. Despite her frequent stays in North Philly, she couldn't fully conceal her suburban South Jersey airs. Her parents had fled the 215 dysfunction, Ricans with their noses in the air, like an aboveground pool was some ethical distinction. But they still relied on barrio childcare at Abuela's.

Tiny was perpetually ill, a Victorian recluse in the wrong time and place, and spent sick days at Tía Moncha's right next door to Abuela's. Her menstrual flow required Hoover Dam intervention. Girl had her period three out of four weeks, plus cramps, nausea, and migraines, making her swallow pink horse pills at twice the prescribed dose. When Tiny wasn't fetal or hunched over the toilet, the two of us would play War with an incomplete deck or watch shirtless boys bike up and down American Street from Tía Moncha's porch. "He's mine," she'd point out. "I call him," I'd say. We'd sit in some sexy manner as the boys rode up to us and asked what bands we liked. "Menudo," Tiny called out. "Guns N' Roses," I shouted. "Corny bitches!" they yelled back, popping wheelies in their wake. To band-aid the disappointment, we bought penny chicle from the bodega and Tiny taught me to snap it like a firecracker.

Cousins JJ and Danito were old enough I could play with them, young enough I could babysit them. They were originally Flor's sons but Titi Ginny had adopted them in grade school. When I swung by Ginny's house, they thundered down the uneven stairs and pulled me to the G.I. Joe bin. If we excavated Ginny's yard today, we'd find the remains of a hundred action figures. They loved whupping me at Nintendo—Ginny had a knack for finding "new" cartridges at church sales. JJ and Danito named the sticker price on Madden Football or NBA Jam, then bragged how Mami Ginny had paid cents on the dollar. Balling on a budget. JJ inserted the cartridge and after a moment of silence or static withdrew it, jiggled it like spun gold, breathed holy in the slot. Occasionally, the game loaded. "Press A," they shouted. "I am!" I shouted back. After mopping the floor with me for an hour, they grew bored and fled to Norris Square. Real football was happening at the corner of Hancock and Susquehanna. I'd stay in Ginny's kitchen listening to my walkman until her husband, Tío George, called the boys home for dinner, showing off the loudest whistle in North Philly. I knew mom would be swinging by soon to scoop me up and take me home, but I hoped it might be one of those after-work hangs when, insisting she had only five minutes to spare, mom pulled up a chair and we crashed the family meal.

Candi, JJ and Danito's biological sister, was also adopted away from Flor, but by Abuela. She was shy and studious, with a smile that tended to pout. Mostly I recall her in Abuela's living room, wearing Catholic school plaids and leaning over her homework. She would show me how to dot the i in her name with a heart, then run out for hopscotch or house with the block's young'uns. Out the window, she joined the circular foot traffic of freeze tag. I, in turn, crowned headphones over my ears and pressed play on my walkman, watching the kids from the kitchen. A few piano notes later Whitney Houston assured me the children were our future, as Candi tabbed open a grape soda and traded sips with a knob-kneed block kid. By the song's symphonic swell, Whitney crunching those high notes—*if I fail, if I succeed*—the kids were throwing soda at each other, staining T-shirts, then communally crushing the can with Payless Mary Janes. Mere inches from the gorgeous idiocy of childhood, I waxed poetical, just outside the action.

When Cuca invited me to Six Flags with the big cousins, I was Cinderella being invited to the ball. These weren't the rug rats of the family, my usual crew. Five to ten years my elder, my big cousins were gods on Mount Olympus, meriting study, mythology, even fear. Cuca, redheaded Joe, Mary Lou, Flor, and Nuchi. Saying their names filled me with awe. They had babies and tats. I had blackheads and wedgies. They had curves and moves. I had puberty boobs called nipple-itis. They moved in unison, a complex organism, dancing, laughing, cursing, and gossiping. They were electrons and protons, some positive, some negative, circling and orbiting in a dynamic flow. They spoke Spanglish like Greg Louganis dove—twisting, flipping, explosive—and laughed with the magnitude of a mushroom cloud.

That my cousins moved as a universe unto themselves made them a microcosm of their North Philly home, but exceptionally homogenous when compared with the larger city. Elsewhere in Philadelphia, I noticed that opposites found each other. Litter stagnated alongside new skyscrapers. Homeless folks made cardboard cities a block away from the Liberty Bell. Every path crossed the Italian Market, reeking of fish, crates of squid stacked curbside, storefronts ripe with the stench of pig slaughter and peach rot. Hard hats lined up at Pat's next to suits from downtown. Chinatown flip-flops and Rittenhouse Square loafers tramped atop flower petals and fruit rinds. The Italian Market sidewalks were slick with mess, though an occasional bucket of water washed the grime downhill. Middlemen gesticulated and bluffed by open-air produce vendors; taxis collected mink-clad blue-hairs. The cheesemonger would cut a free slice if you braved the stench. Tourists and the homeless braved it.

In the Italian Market's old cookware store my aunt Alice, from dad's side, manned the coffee counter. She had eloped and fled suburban Long Island for the anarchic hubbub of Philly's white working class. It suited her well. She wasn't the only émigré. Seemed to me if you threw a stone in any direction at the Italian Market, you might hit a down-and-out expat who'd left the trust fund, running.

By sixth grade I was taking the trolley and bus alone, exploring any pocket of Brotherly Love I pleased. Rittenhouse Square, Old City, Chinatown, University City . . . so many Philadelphias in my restless foot traffic. Bakery cases and heat lamps boasted regional specialties; old men played international games on park tables; the tuning of AM/FM dials revealed nostalgias rooted in different hemispheres. The one commonality was porousness, how insiders and outsiders traversed blocks together, riding upstream for a bit in shared waters. Within all the mismatch and chaos, I could be both interloper and core constituent—a tug and pull I knew well, being of two cultures.

North Philly was different. What scarlet letter el barrio wore on its corners I couldn't tell, but its motions and commerce were strictly internal. A colony on Mars couldn't be more sealed off. My big cousins moved by some internal logic to a music all their own, impervious to and unseen by the rest of Philly. Being with them was a VIP pass to the most delicious, if segregated, social club. It was a separate world, like my mother's circle garden had once been, and I recognized in this separation not just safe harbor but something resembling a scream.

·　　　·　　　·

Our trip was courtesy of Coca-Cola. That summer they were running a promotion. Collect a bunch of cans, get a half-price ticket to Six Flags in New Jersey. We piled in a double-wide hooptie with four different-size tires and zero operational seatbelts, soda cans clattering in the trunk. Though it cost more, we gassed up in Philly cuz there was duct tape where a fuel cap oughta go and full-service Jersey didn't mess with that crap. Every time we hit a bump, I could hear half-melted ice swish in the cooler, as bodega ham and Wonder Bread took a swim.

I got the hump in the back. My thighs stuck to the pleather seat and pressed up against Flor's warm bare legs. Cuca's shoulder pushed sweatily into mine. Zooming north on the turnpike, my cousins blasted La Mega and yelled Spanish lyrics at passing cars. There was a thick parade of trucks thundering along the highway. "Yank your fist like this, Qui Qui," Flor said, cranking her arm. An eighteen-wheeler pulled up alongside us, rattling the hooptie with its gravity. Flor pinched my thigh and cooed warmly, "Go 'head, Qui Qui, don't be afraid!" She had coined the nickname, coronating me Qui Qui when I was still in pampers. The childish title always sounded best in her mouth. But now all my big cousins chanted, "Qui Qui! Qui Qui! Qui Qui!" Finally the cab was level with the back window. The driver's eyes flicked in our direction and I seized the moment, leaning into the cushion of Cuca's shoulder so I was visible to the outside world, balling my right fist and cranking an invisible airhorn. The typhoon of sound that came at us when the trucker honked back was trumped only by the wild cheering of my cousins. "Okay, Qui Qui!" Flor hollered, and we all fell back laughing.

Now Redheaded Joe, whose eyelashes were freakishly blond for el barrio, told scatological jokes that were Egyptian to me. The X-rated ones he told in Spanish, but even the English punchlines flew over my head. I was certain they entailed sex and poop, but neither word was used, nor any synonyms I knew. Still, I laughed when they did. Nuchi giggled through her missing teeth and Cuca—proper Catholic, wait-until-marriage Cuca—cracked up, then slapped Joe's shoulder hard, cuz he was corrupting her. And Flor had news about the new roller coaster. Six Flags had been running ads all summer long, but Flor knew some folks who'd actually braved it. They returned not just with apocryphal tales of steep drops and breakneck turns, but with actual-factual shitted shorts. "I hope y'all brought clean draws!" she laughed.

Carsickness was common for me but today was different. My thigh started to sweat where it touched Flor's and my guts felt like stew. AC was not one of the car's few features. By the time we pulled into the Six Flags lot, I couldn't un-hunch. "Look, Qui Qui, it's a long walk to the ticket booth. By the time you get there, the fresh air will make you feel better," Flor offered. But extracting myself from the backseat seemed herculean. "Should we take you home?" Nuchi asked kindly, the group's responsible elder.

"No, I just want to take a nap. Please go without me."

Redheaded Joe tried to lift me out of the backseat. "Let me give you a piggyback," he said, but at ten years old, I was too heavy for that, plus my body was limp with nausea.

Nuchi and Cuca consulted with each other. "Should we call Titi Virginia? Quiara, you want to talk to your mom?"

"It's just carsickness. It wears off eventually." I would've been embarrassed if I hadn't felt so sick. Despite initial reticence, they eventually agreed to start the fun without me. I'd join when they returned for a sandwich break. I curled fetal in the back, eyes throbbing shut, my hair wet spaghetti against the hot pleather, the car now my own personal hell as all four doors slammed.

Later, half-lulled from a knockout slumber, I was vaguely aware of my cousins' voices coming through open windows. They were eating sandwiches on the trunk, spreading mayo on slices. Who needs mustard? Flor, pass me an orange soda. Ey yo, these pork rinds be poppin'. Apparently, hours had passed. They compared notes on which roller coasters had the shortest lines, which carnival games gave the most tickets. Wake up, Qui Qui, you feeling better? Want to join us? I muttered "no" from the depths of hell and they headed off. Again, I fell into the blackness of sleep.

As we drove home I whimpered between stomach pangs. A pathetic, woozy chorus. "Sorry I ruined the day." I was sure it was the last invitation they'd extend. "No, bendito, Qui Qui, we felt so bad leaving you like that." Flor ordered everyone to roll down the windows, fresh air being good for carsickness, and she tapped my head, gently guiding it to her warm shoulder.

During the ride south, they were subdued. Wiped out and whiplashed after all those rides, but also shielding me from the fun I'd missed. They'd recount the adventures another time. Intimidated as I had been by their earlier adult humor, their compassion came at me in surprising unison. They put on La Mega and listened in silence. By exit 5, Redheaded Joe was snoring, and Flor used my resting head as a pillow for hers.

I missed the goodbyes as Flor and Nuchi and Redheaded Joe were deposited onto various North Philly corners. When we rolled up to American Street, it was just me and Cuca. I crawled straight for Abuela's bathroom—I hadn't gone all day. My guts were throbbing, my back hunched and radiating heat. Though I could uncurl myself enough to unbutton my shorts, pulling them to my ankles felt like Armageddon. At which point I saw my panties. Red, brown, and moist. "Cuca?" Her footsteps hopped upstairs and she tapped on the door. "¿Estás enferma, Qui Qui?" I waddled to the doorknob, cracked the door, and asked if this was what a period looks like. Suspended at my ankles, my panties made a horrible hammock. Then Cuca snorted, a tear shot out her eye like a BB pellet, and she unleashed a magnificent laugh made of rejoice. She disappeared down the hall and I heard Abuela's bureau drawers open and shut. Cuca returned with clean fresh parachute panties, improvising a tune. "Oh my gah! Qui Qui's a woman now!"

She knew the precise shower temperature to ease the abdominal pressure. Clean and refreshed after, I pulled on Abuela's bargain-bin panties, which were fit for a queen. Cuca brought me two Bayers and a cup of room-temperature water. Then skipped across traffic to buy a box of pads. "Don't tell the bodega man!" I pleaded. The Always were thick as a Bible and rough as a brown bag, two features that struck me as the height of sophistication. Every fifteen minutes I changed them with vigor and industry. One drop of blood, time for a new one. "You only need to change them every couple hours," Cuca said, smiling. "But won't the blood, like . . . dirty me?" I asked. "Relax! A little dirt never hurt anybody!" She laughed, smacking her teeth, enjoying the mentorship.

For the balance of the evening, North Philly was an oasis. The *Wheel of Fortune* marathon. My tranquil stomach. A strong night breeze making the screen door slam over and over. It was all right as rain. Flitting around, prepping for the work week, Cuca periodically swung by the sofa and kissed my forehead. Eventually I dozed off as Vanna White paced with a calm regal smile.

9

BODY LANGUAGE

One of the two birthday girls had gone missing. No matter. Brooklyn babies, South Jersey cousins, and North Philly aunts crammed the kitchen like sardines. Singing along to Juan Luis Guerra's latest, gossip laced with vulgarities, cheek-kissing the incoming tide of arrivals. Abuela was the default host of all parties, funerals, rosaries, fights, bingo nights, late nights, overnights, emergency adoptions, breakfasts, after-schools and lazy Sundays. If Abuela could've hosted her own funeral, she would've.

The Fourth of July, an auspicious birthday. None of us knew Abuela's age. Far back as I recall, she was ancient—Moses with the tablets, except she's holding una cuchara de cocina. The wrinkles, I suspected, had been present at birth. The increasing hunch of her osteoporosis was the only evidence of time's march forward. "Are you eighty, Abuela?" "Pienso que sí, no se." Surely, there was a baptismal record back on the island, but that was a galaxy far, far away.

Abuela's wrinkle of a sister, Tía Moncha, lived in the adjacent row home. They had a tidy way of passing ingredients through the back fence. You need some rice? You're out of corn meal? Toma, coje el teléfono, it's the cousins from Puerto Rico! But today Tía Moncha had actually walked down her stoop, traversed fifteen feet of sidewalk, and grunted her way up Abuela's steps to join the festivities. They shuffled toward each other in a giggling embrace, eyes pooling with cataract tears, their frizzy buns in left-right stereo. How far they had migrated from tropical farms, rows of fibrous yuca and ñame left unharvested, to be side by side in this urban mayhem.

Flor, the second birthday girl, wasn't around. I'd last seen her in November and the incident still burned like sunlight through closed eyelids. It had been another afternoon at Abuela's. I was lounging on the plastic-covered sofa as *Looney Tunes* played— one of two VHS tapes Abuela owned. Flor was upstairs giving Danito, her youngest of three, a bath. Suddenly Danito started wailing deep and fierce, a baritone cry no toddler should know. Flor shouted IF YOU DON'T SHET THE FUCK UP! Then, a series of thuds. I knew it without seeing it, just from the sound. Danito's skull had met the bathtub. Cuca flew up the steps to intervene, four at a time, superhero-like, the way they say a granny can lift a car off a kid. *Looney Tunes* played on. I dared not move from my spot on the sofa. I homed in on Bugs Bunny and bit my lip. I became a statue facing the TV, shut my eyes when the ensuing mayhem bled into my peripheral vision. But I had no way to stop the sounds. The rotary phone clicked in a frenzy of spins. Abuela wept and whispered psalms. Cuca told Flor to get the fuck out. Don't let the door hit you. I heard the screen door's

spring expanding and contracting, arriving footsteps on linoleum, decisive voices. Doctors were called. Titi Ginny, a pediatric
nurse, discussed the steps that must be taken immediately. Mom
would do the driving. Someone cradled Danito like a freshly
fallen chick, draped in a white towel, davening, ice held at his
crown. But I looked away before I saw who. And thankfully,
thank god above, I heard Danito cry. It seemed impossible: Flor,
my cuz with a laugh warm as September sun, had been plucked
from sanity and blown to chaos, a dandelion seed on the devil's
breeze. "Drugs," mom said on the car ride home. "Before that
shit came into el barrio," she sighed, "we were just another poor
neighborhood trying to make do. But then came the overnight
sensation." Her straight-ahead stare put an end to further questions.

Now, on her birthday, Flor was who-knows-where. Her boys,
Danito and JJ, came to Abuela's party sweaty and soiled from
Hunting Park, where they played ball with Tío George. Candi,
Flor's middle child, and Cuca now licked a limber on the stoop,
coconut melting a river down their forearms. Flor's sisters, Mary
Lou and Nuchi, were in the kitchen, shining with sweat. Tía
Toña, Flor's mom, called the bingo game. And Juan Luis Guerra
sang us into ecstasy. Asses bouncing to claim one slice of North
Philly. Heck, even dinner danced. Tap tap tap as arroz compelled
the lid into movement. I walk-danced to the kitchen, my moves
noncommittal, removing the top so my face got a rice-fragrant
steam bath.

Change had come for me, too. High school was a few months
off, a fresh start beckoned. As years passed after leaving the horse
farm, the malaise had soaked marrow-deep. By now, I could

hardly inhale without grief's noose yanking. If I forgot the depression for a moment, it came slicing back unprompted, catching me off guard. I was haunted by dad's marriage and new kids—their suburban tableau hovered always in the back of my mind. Every time I took the train out and dined amongst their sunniness, a beast started tramping my insides. And yet, in that season of change there were shifting consolations. I was old enough now to take the Greyhound alone to New York, where my aunt Linda from dad's side, a composer, taught me to read music. My new Russian piano teacher let me play Chopin's Nocturne in B-flat Minor. There were boys and girls to kiss. Mixtapes to make for summer hangouts. Bottles of wine to sip when mom was working. *One Hundred Years of Solitude* to finish so I could return again to page one.

Juan Luis Guerra's latest, *Bachata Rosa,* came that summer and had us an inch off the ground. That tape lifted us. Clarion trumpets, power-synth hits, Afropop vocals—the old world, new world, and middle passage braided like cornrows—just $7.99 at the local Sam Goody or free if your busted antenna caught La Mega. Cuca played the tape till it melted in the deck, then quick-dropped $7.99 for its replacement. In his lyrics, romance in tough times was our way. His caribeños loved bigger than farmhouses and factory jobs. This throbbing, thriving music hit our tape decks midway through the zombie apocalypse. Latinidad in a nutshell: die loving. Its virtuosity transcended era, yes, but the joy mattered double in a decade of hijas lost to alleyways.

That Fourth of July we could all feel the dawning precarity. Every few minutes I peeled the shirt from my torso, but it slurped right back on me like cling wrap. That there was no AC in a rude July, that both doors hung open begging for some breeze, still did not account for the sweat blanketing us. The constant commerce of our touch made it triple-hot. Arms around shoulders, salsa spins, cheek kisses, butt pinches, pile-ons and huddles before a Kodak disposable. Tía Toña, presiding over tabletop bingo, demanded kisses and bendiciones from all entering children, who had to push through other butt pinches, cheek kisses, and lift-ups to arrive at her side. I watched the procession from the nosebleeds (aka the backyard slab of concrete) until Toña summoned me to her. "What piano piece are you playing now?" she asked, and clung to my hand the entire response. "Pregúntala en español," mom said, so that all the bingo elders looked up, eager to see me bumble. "Ay, Virginia, déjala quieta," Titi Ginny cooed. "Coño, I can ask my niece however I want!" said Tía Toña. In Spanish, I described my recent piano recital until the elders, mom included, nodded approval. The meatiness of Tía Toña's palms sandwiching mine was equal parts grotesque and baptismal. The harder she pressed, the stronger my urge to flee and yet the longer I spoke. There in her grip she touched me—daydreamer me, thinker me—into the material world. For a family whose migration was four generations deep and counting, a laying on of hands meant lineage, location, resting place. After I extricated myself and headed for the kitchen, the warmth of her palms lingered on mine.

I served myself some rice and beans, went to the staircase, and rested the tin plate on my knees. Seated just inches outside the swirl, I had the perfect vantage on cousins and aunts, a flock breaking right and left in rhythm. Even their proximity and touch did not fully account for why my Perez women glistened, swampy. I knew shit was goin' down by how hard Nuchi, Cuca, and Mary Lou danced that day. Like if their hips slowed a bit, Flor's absence would be all we had left.

Nuchi's booty tested the limit of spandex. Prima's curves had curves. Because she was tall enough to cast a shadow across the room, her imposing frame seemed to be in the living room, dining room, and kitchen all at once. Nuchi didn't so much walk as thrust, and menacingly so. On her figure, the subtlest dance moves became acts of aggression. If Nuchi danced in your direction, best thing was to get out the way. That's why I spied her from the steps. Watching agog, timid, trying not to get ensnared in the dance and gossip that formed a sticky web. She felt my eyes and shot me a smile. "Hi, Qui Qui!" She waved and I blew kisses back, recalling her Six Flags tenderness. Her eyes looked tireder than that distant day, but her towering majesty and righteous thighs were a dare. Try not to stare. Try not to gulp. Try not to feel a wee bit violated. Two years later, addiction would render her skeletal. She would become a walking dagger. But for now, the spandex was tight and right. White bike shorts, white sports bra, white hoop earrings. Everything white except her trigueña skin and rainbow elekes. Las siete potencías—the seven Lukumí Orishas—orbited her neck in a protective oval. She had brought her four babies to the party and they were fixed to hips like tool belts. Teens held babies, kids held babies, bowlegged babies, pamper-butt babies, grumpy toddlers frowning on the porch.

Mary Lou was slender, boasting fewer curves. With an exposed midriff her dance moves looked slinky times ten. A wooden rosary hovered at her cleavage—Jesus pointing down at the sin. But it was Mary Lou's joy that was outrageous, that made her so fun to watch from the steps. A happy that needed no café, that woke up that way and let loose on the world. Rejoice was her daily rhythm. With a pronounced overbite, mid salsa-step, she proclaimed she was moving to Florida "porque aquí no vale!" If she hated the neighborhood, she had a cheerful way of showing it. Mary Lou chased Nuchi's babies around, planting an embar-

rassment of kisses on their foreheads, tutoring them how to do
the butt. "Do the diaper," she goaded as they obliged or ran away.
"Right, Qui Qui? Tell them!" "Do the diaper! Do the diaper!" I
rapped on cue, chewing my rice, swaying my fork in time. I ate
slowly on the steps, counting out grains, prolonging my excuse
not to dance. Then through Mary Lou's joy, though, came a hissing sound, directed at her only child. Ashley was five and from
the steps I watched Mary Lou cutting her down with razor eyes
and a ferocious yell. Punishing love-strictness. *I will not let these
blocks make a mess of my daughter.* Her meanness had originated in
protective ambition but had grown into "I'm tired as shit" and
"Life ain't working out" and "These blocks be getting me down."
A year later, Mary Lou's equine body would topple, an aneurysm
knocking her to the floor at age twenty-seven. Ashley would
grow up motherless, in girlhood's ocean with no compass, her
mami's strictness a phantom voice.

Tía Toña climbed the stairs, squeezing by me and using my
shoulder as a resting spot, before disappearing into the bathroom. She was already large by this Fourth of July, but would
soon be too massive to get up from the sofa. Having your husband die in his forties and a kid die in his twenties will do that to
you. Gotta do something with all that sorrow. Might as well eat
it. But for now, before the final death—Mary Lou's—Toña was
almost spry on those steps. Perhaps after using the bathroom, I
thought, she snuck into Abuela's room to cop a look at the
X-rated playing cards. Each card boasted a different naked man,
Black and Brown beauties captured in nature: leaning on rocks,
splashing in waterfalls, their flaccid cocks arranged in scenic repose. My gin rummy skills peaked that summer.

Flor had been the lone Perez who could pull me onto the
dance floor. "Come on, Qui Qui, baila conmigo!" and she'd yank

my hand till I succumbed. To Flor, dancing was stand-up comedy writ on the flesh, and ass-shakes were the punchlines. My awkwardness became an asset when she took the lead. That day, in her absence, I remained on the steps. Mine was a dance of the eyes and ears, watching, wondering what a life that corporeal must feel like. Motionless on the staircase, I had the privilege of spying on life, if not the courage to step onto the dance floor. I had never read a book like Abuela's living room but still I savored it my preferred way—like the private, treasured pages of a novel.

10

SOPHOMORE YEAR ENGLISH

Freshman year the reading was lively enough—*Romeo and Juliet, Animal Farm,* "The Cask of Amontillado"—but I was the only kid who raised my hand or, for that matter, whose eyes stayed open the entire period. Our textbooks were generations old and had run out of spaces to write your name. Held together by duct tape or not at all. It was an arts school and my sleepy classmates weren't lazy, they just stayed up late charcoal-sketching or hammering bass riffs or sculpting soda bottle bongs instead of reading English's assigned pages. We were given three weeks to read *Animal Farm,* indulgent even for a slow reader like myself. At the end of which it was clear no one knew what "four legs good, two legs bad" referred to. Even as my zine thrived, I grew restless.

Sophomore year I jumped ship for Central, an academic magnet that drew kids from all zip codes. It was a competitive school with four-digit enrollment whose milieu was decidedly African

American and white. Us few Latinos and a smattering of Asians contributed to the "other" portion of the pie chart. Now I had trouble keeping up with the pages. *Gulliver's Travels, Their Eyes Were Watching God, Narrative of the Life of Frederick Douglass.* Page after page of direct hit. They jangled me, incited me, and none more than *Death of a Salesman.* My jaw clenched at Arthur Miller's picket-fence tableaus: sunny suburbia masking nightmare magma. Loman was sure some throne was his birthright; when it eluded him he grew disconnected, disconsolate.

"What do you think, Quiara? You wrote this in your reading response: 'The roots of the grass lawn are rotting.' Say more."

"It just annoys me how Loman thinks he's tragic. Two sons healthy enough to throw the pigskin. A marriage intact. Like, what's so awful?"

"You tell me. What's his problem?" The teacher trained his eyes on me.

"Well . . . Loman's a *Brady Bunch* guy, the kind of patriarch smiling in an insurance ad. The billboards and TV shows make him out to be some kingly provider archetype. And I guess he drank the Kool-Aid and then, like, eventually had to face the fact that he's average. So that's his tragedy. Being average. Which I don't find tragic."

"Write that down, everyone," the teacher said. Shit, I wrote it down, too. The class took it from there, launching into discussion, as Arthur Miller yanked my shoulder hard and hoisted me out of the room, a child snatched in the night. I came untethered from my desk, tossed through a chasm, to be deposited on dad's lawn in the burbs. There stood his house, witnessed during my now-occasional visits. Their impeccable manners and happy pantomime couldn't hide dad's malaise. I knew him too well. The more my suburban siblings thrived—gymnastics trophies and marching-band portraits—the deeper his unvoiced depression seeped until I could no longer tell tree trunk from invasive vine. Was he dad any longer or only a latticework of what-ifs and minor failures? I was his biggest failure, but his unhappy marriage and inability to find carpentry work didn't help. Dad and Willy Loman. Willy Loman and dad. American archetypes. A crisis of inconsequence. Might dad's misery lead him, one day, to an end like Willy's? Alone in the garage, hosing exhaust fumes through the window, leaving us all to sort through the mire? I walked into a distant hallway of memory and conjured dad's thick ponytail, how majestically it had grazed his lower back, how once when I was tiny I asked if I could Tarzan-swing from it. He had smiled and said yes. And I swung with abandon from his hippie hair until, worried I was hurting him, I let go and dropped back to earth.

All these literary patriarchs paraded their woe like it was some main event. Hamlet brooded, Romeo beat his chest, Willy went mad. Why didn't they dance like the Perez women? Were they so above the fray? No billboards or sitcoms had declared my Perez cousins queen, and I now saw freedom in this. No false thrones, just the shitstorm of life. Grab a shovel and sing a work song. Build a throne that's real.

The classroom phone rang, a TNT detonation. I was to report to the principal's office. "Bring your backpack, too." I closed *Salesman* and stuffed it in my bag. My cowboy boots echoed in the cinderblock corridor. How strange, these empty hallways. Most kids were in class. I passed charcoal portraits of Langston Hughes and bulletin boards showing who'd made JV. The main office was filled with smoke, which haloed around the principal and obscured his bearded face. A rack of pipes stood on the desk, small wooden saxophones hung out to dry. He suggested I call home.

"Do you have a quarter?" he asked.

"No." He handed me a coin and sent me on my way. Outside the main office were antique wooden phone booths. The folding door clattered, sliding shut. My first quarter was returned: no answer at home. On the second try, the coin was swallowed and the call went through: it was Abuela's house. Screams rang out in the background. Mary Lou was dead.

After school, the SEPTA platform was an adolescent carnival. But midmorning, with me alone by the subway tunnel, it was a limbo world, cavernous and moist as a grotto. Water traced mineral outlines on walls, pooling by the tracks. Though SEPTA rides were prime reading time, *Death of a Salesman* remained in my backpack. Instead my jaw clenched, biting on a question. Central High was a magnet school. It enrolled kids from all over the city. Why did classmates from other zip codes have a lower funeral count than me? How come the Birkenstock set from Mount Airy and the South Philly headbangers shook their heads when I asked if they'd seen open caskets? Moments before, I had wondered at our Perez resilience compared to the Willys and Romeos. Now I catalogued our disappearances. What was wrong with the Perezes? What were we dying of?

Tía Toña's losses were now complete: Husband and son dead. Flor still off on an extended drug jag. Nuchi spiraling to a skeleton. And Mary Lou gone. Tía Toña had graduated to accomplished mourner. She could school Pavarotti on vocal projection. It's all I remembered from the first funeral I'd attended, that of her husband, Guillo. Upon arriving at the church and passing through its marble foyer, Tía Toña collapsed in a fit of wailing and chest-pounding. The awful scene made me wonder if I'd felt a real feeling ever and made me doubt whether I wanted to. I took her cries as an essential form of womanhood: powerful, dangerous, grotesque, steeped in the tragedy called love. Nothing repulsed me more than the possibility of myself laid so bare. Please never let me be that way, I had prayed, as men surrounded her and attempted to peel her from the cold church floor. She violently kicked them, took their concern as a provocation. God deserved to hear her scream.

Now, stations passed as I neared Toña's fresh batch of wailing, alongside others' whispered prayers, and an inevitable barrage of guests bearing flowers and cigarettes. This loud-soft whiplash would continue till midnight, then start up at the next day's rosary session. A routine we knew well.

At Abuela's house I sat in the stairwell, beholding the mourner's parade. Ritz crackers went untouched, Gouda cheese grew waxy. A pot of café had been brewed hours earlier and sat half-full, cold on the stovetop. The Brooklyn cousins arrived, mascara smeared, passing tissues. The tabletop was crowded with bouquets. Enrobed in cellophane, a field of carnations. The screen door slammed in constant announcement: neighbors and family cycling through, having a smoke on the porch. December air kept pouring inside but no one cared. Toña wailed and hollered upstairs. When Ginny arrived with the boys, little Danito took my hand and looked me in the eye. "I'm sorry for your loss, Qui Qui." Only in elementary school, he was already an experienced griever. Kid had fucking grace.

Through it all Ashley slumped on the sofa, eyes glazed and cast toward the linoleum. Eight years old. No doubt she was replaying the scene from earlier that day: she heard a weird scream, ran downstairs, and discovered Mary Lou on the kitchen tiles. A cereal box in her hand. Some Cheerios littering the floor. Everyone patted Ashley's head or scooped her into embraces until her dad showed up and carried her away unceremoniously. "Let's go." She slumped over his shoulder, a rag doll of loss.

Years earlier, Mary Lou had selected me as miniature bride. Hers would be the real thing, a church ceremony with handwritten invitations. Mom sewed me a white gown to replicate Mary Lou's. Beneath a thick white ribbon at the waist, the skirt flared out, an explosion of tulle. Beadwork covered the bodice. Opal sequins were hand-sewn onto gloves. For months mom hunched at the sewing machine, peering through a monocle. She was a portrait of devotion in the soft lamplight, her palms guiding the fabric through the machine's steady current. The dress was complicated and ambitious, requiring weeknight work, too, despite mom's standing-room commutes. She was the image of constancy, sewing the wedding dress, in miniature, she'd never gotten to wear with dad.

The day before the wedding mom trimmed my bangs. She took an iron to my hair and curled the bottoms inward, just above my shoulder. Then she pooled the gown in a circle on the floor and said, "Step in," before tunneling it up over my body. Slowly I fed each arm through a delicate sleeve. It took her many minutes to button each pearl up the back, and she hummed to pass the time. Then we went outside. We still lived on the horse farm and she eyed our expansive surroundings. "By the circle garden, so I can get the trees behind you and the hills to the left." The woods next to the pasture burst with reds and yellows. "Tilt your head like this," she instructed, then took my picture. Beneath a huge autumnal sky, I posed resplendent and pensive.

We repeated the process the following morning before driving into the city. I stood in the corridor of St. Ambrose Church, hiding in a foyer beside Mary Lou. Our dresses matched perfectly. The only difference was her high heels to my flats. My older cousin was smiling and nervous, bouncing at the knee. She marked my cheek with a red lipstick kiss, then smiled a crescent of mischief and snapped open her clutch. In that quiet moment, as she dug through her purse for makeup, I felt wildly alive. I loved how the lid clicked open, how the pink stick emerged like spiral steps. I loved the waxy wetness as Mary Lou patted a bit of color onto my lips. Her touch was Creator, turning me human. I had always disliked the itchiness of gowns, the clownishness of makeup. But the ceremony of dressing up meant touching older women, and that made it worthwhile. Mary Lou's fingers trembled as she held my face still. "There! Your mom's gonna kill me!" Then I walked the aisle. At the altar stood her sweetheart, a tall Boricua with indio skin. He was handsome and confident like Mary Lou, and only slightly less goofy. Afterwards, one big sloppy kiss later, they ran outside to the North Philly curb, church bells a-ruckus, and dove giddily into an honest-to-god limousine. It had the whiff of importance, which I mistook for permanence.

Soon I would return to St. Ambrose Church, dressed in black head to toe. Soon we'd drive the streets of North Philly, a motorcade of orange funeral stickers. Slow-going, a wending path, horns honking toward the cemetery. But tonight, the rosary must be started.

Mary Lou had come to babysit one summer evening. I was twelve and had been a latchkey for years, but I think it was mom's excuse to give Mary Lou spending money in tight times. And to me, it was a welcome way to hang with her and Ashley. Ashley walked in with a Big Gulp the size of her torso. Her long hair was tangled and cute and she was acting like that soda was Dom Péri-gnon so I helped myself and made a real show of it.

"That's mine! Don't finish it!" Ashley blurted. Mary Lou went postal. They'd barely arrived and she was already screaming at her daughter.

"Your soda? Abuela ain't teach us about no yours and mine! Sih' down!" Mary Lou pulled her hard to the floor. "You, too, Qui Qui. Sit. Don't worry, you're not in trouble, but she is and I'm gonna teach her a lesson." I sat. "Now we're gonna share this soda and if you complain, Ashley, if you so much as think about complaining, you ain't coming back to Qui Qui's house EH-VER. Me entiendes?" Now Ashley pushed away the Big Gulp, wiping tears with a fist. "Drink. It." Finally Ashley did. My turn was next, and I didn't even like Mountain Dew. Shit, even Cola Champagne or Black Cherry Wishniak—real bodega gold—wouldn't be worth all that. But we kept going in a circle, drinking the stuff. It was a bummer and took forever, sip after sip. We got full but the Big Gulp was only half-drunk. Our bellies bloated. Ashley kept puff-ing hers out extra big till we couldn't stifle the giggles. Finally, Mary Lou removed the lid and chugged half the Big Gulp without stopping to breathe. My and Ashley's eyes grew wide until Mary Lou slammed the cup upside down on the floor. Empty. She paused for a moment. And then from her mouth came what started as a burp but grew to an injurious audio event. It was a Jurassic, cavernous belch and as it continued she began reciting the alphabet. In pitch. She made it to M before running out of burp. We were rolling, all three of us, crying and kicking. "I peed my panties," Mary Lou said. "Me too," Ashley chimed in. I hadn't peed. "Then you weren't having enough fun," Mary Lou said.

The first night's rosary ended before midnight. Mom had an aura of calm, driving through empty streets. Philly had gone to bed. She took the long way home, forgoing the expressway, weaving through residential blocks, lingering after traffic lights changed. "Mom, it's green, you can go now." Fifth and Girard, even under veil of night, was an event horizon: wealth and want converged right at this intersection. Just north of Girard, blight. Just south, brownstones and burglar alarms.

Mom's vaguely westbound route deposited us on Mt. Vernon Street, a purposeful detour. Mt. Vernon was her old stomping ground, where she lived after arriving in Philly as a preteen. Back then the area had been a Puerto Rican enclave, but no more. The block had always been nice—I remembered when Abuela had a floor-through—but it was full-on dignified now. American flags hung above doorways, with the stripes sewn on rather than printed. Spotless brickwork, polished brass. Bankers and judges had moved in, restoring the homes to their original single-family design. The Perezes had joined a Puerto Rican migration deeper north into smaller row homes made of less sturdy goods.

Mom slowed the car and looked around, before continuing onto the diagonal Parkway. Behind us, City Hall's clock was a midnight moon. William Penn balanced atop the tower, the night's bronze sentinel.

"Mom, what's an aneurysm?" I hadn't dared ask at Abuela's.

"A blood clot in the brain."

"What causes it?"

"Genetics."

"Was it preventable?"

"Mary Lou's brain was a ticking clock, and none of us had a clue." The answer brought some small relief. An accident of fate, a genetic marker, seemed a death that might happen in any city or suburb, to any family, rich or poor, white or Brown, Spanish or English. It was a tragic way to go, but not sociologically complicated. Mary Lou: age at death, twenty-seven.

Maybe in mom's fatigue, she would let a little truth slip. Maybe midnight was the hour of answers. I risked a second question, this time about a different cousin.

"Mom, what did Big Vic die of?"

"Kidney failure."

"Why did his kidneys fail?"

"Dialysis doesn't last forever, sweetheart."

"What put him on dialysis in the first place?"

"He took too many ibuprofens."

"Like, Advil? Why?"

"He was a big guy, he took more pills than he needed."

"But he wasn't big at the end, he was skin and bones."

Mom paused. "Big Vic might've had AIDS."

"Might've?"

"Your Tía Toña gives me a different answer every time."

"How did he contract AIDS?"

"The dialysis, probably," she said.

"Mom! Mom." Unsure if she would answer or if the truth was forever dammed up in her, I realized: there are words that have willpower, that compel you not to speak them aloud. "Was Big Vic shooting up? Was he using dirty needles?" She didn't respond. Big Vic: age at death, twenty-four.

"What about Guillo? Did he OD on Advil, too?" I asked. She was unmoved by my sarcasm.

Mom sighed. "If you ask Toña, she'll say liver failure."

"Liver failure due to what?" I said.

No response came. Guillo: age at death, forties. Whatever it was, this plague that hit us hard, it would remain unnamed for another night. My evidence for a universal conspiracy against the Perezes was anecdotal at best. Nonetheless, I vastly preferred how Mary Lou had passed—in a manner no one was ashamed to speak aloud. I rolled down the window, letting the breeze hammer my palm. The river beside us reflected a black sky and the twinkling lights of Boathouse Row. The radio remained switched off. So this was the soundtrack to our soundtrack. This was what DJ Circumstance spun in the background, behind all that Juan Luis Guerra: silence.

"Should we drive to the art museum?" mom asked, flicking the turn signal. She U-turned and drove the curving roadway up toward the monumental sand-colored pillars. At the top of the parking lot she rolled to a stop. I knew what to do—get out and unhook the chain. Mom lurched forward, I rehooked the chain in the car's wake and got back in. We pulled slowly onto the museum's grand upper plaza. The fountains were off for the night. Floodlights uplit the Grecian friezes. No pedestrians, no tourists. Just mom and me.

"Guillo probably died of AIDS," she said, switching off the ignition.

A few times a year we'd end up here, after the security guards had gone home, atop the famous steps. It was a favorite late-night rebellion of mom's. Sometimes in celebration, others to kill time. There beyond us twinkled the City of Brotherly Love. Somewhere in that cluster of lights, a founding father had written about self-evident truths, but I had no faith in self-evidence of any kind. Linda Loman's warning swirled in the darkness. "Attention must be paid." I missed my cousin.

11

THINGS GO UNSAID LONG ENOUGH . . .

Because they were not my mother or father, because mom drove me out of North Philly at the end of each funeral, the deaths felt only half mine. I imagined siblings and parents cleaning dishes after the rosary, trashing wilted carnations a week later, pouring murky flower water down the toilet. Meanwhile, my mom would still be there in the morning, brewing coffee. I would still hear the steam-hiss of the iron as she prepped for work. Our daily routine would proceed undisturbed. The gaps left by these deaths were two neighborhoods over, a car ride away. The truth was I had never wept for a cousin's death. Not one tear. I cursed myself for that—what casket-side teen doesn't need a Kleenex?—and I feared that not crying meant I hadn't loved them enough. Perhaps weeping and dancing live in the same place within us, and I had shuttered that part of me away. The part that touches grief, euphoria, and god. Without tears, I could never legitimately call them *my* losses, only *ours*.

Ours meant the Perez family. The Hudeses had mourned, to be sure, amongst the mightiest griefs in history. A generation before dad's mom died too young, the death camps, the six million. When the name Hudes got a typewriter's close-up in *Schindler's List,* I ran home and called dad. "Tell me, tell me." And he did. As a seven-year-old, he'd seen the tattoos on a few relatives' arms. My bewilderment and sorrow in that moment found solace in context. English teachers had already assigned me Elie Wiesel's *Night,* Anne Frank's *Diary of a Young Girl.* Those books had title pages and final paragraphs. Spielberg's film had an opening sequence and final shot. The horror of history, made slightly less unbearable through the telling, the forensic understanding, the bearing of witness.

But whatever beast stalked the Perezes was present-tense and its appetite was peaking. No title pages or final paragraphs to name it, no opening sequences or final shots to help me see. This reaper nipping at our heels, pulling up a chair at our Thanksgiving table. In Compagnola Funeral Parlor on North 5th. At Riehs Florist on Girard Avenue. We had accounts there, we bought funerals on credit, first-name basis with the staff. I had no sociological study diagramming the crack and AIDS epidemics, nor an evidentiary grasp of the human cost of residential segregation. I had no sense that we were living and dying through a discrete dot on the American timeline—the eighties and nineties. I had only a handful of funeral cards featuring blond angels with Latino names looped beneath them.

Sadness was not quite the feeling. A bitter pebble tossed in my stomach. Churning, polishing its bitterness with every toss. The unfairness of it. Because for every birthday dad didn't call, for every pair of socks not bought, there was a bendición from Titi Ginny, a packet of bodega chicle from Cuca. The Perezes did so much heavy lifting and yet racked up funerals like baseball cards.

I look back and think maybe mom explained Big Vic's and Guillo's deaths quite clearly that night at the art museum steps. Maybe I filtered out the truth and retained only the confusion. I'm forty now and thought if I asked how Big Vic died today, mom would at least spit out one fact, maybe two. It seized my mind on Thanksgiving. Stuffing the turkey is when you inquire about AIDS in the family, right? Or is dusting off the gravy boat the more respectful moment? As the question left my mouth I was certain of my fraudulence. Vic had probably died of MS or stomach cancer, and dramatic me had blown things out of proportion. Things go unsaid long enough, the silence becomes all you got.

Mom pulled yams from the oven. Burned. She jabbed the hardened molasses with a knife. "Well? There's two versions of how Big Vic died," she said. Here we go again. Exactly as I remembered. Ask a question, get a labyrinth.

"The first is that Guillo, Tía Toña's husband, had a kept woman back in PR. Guillo thought he was slick, giving her Toña's empty house like he had property to spare. But that was my papi's home, not Guillo's, and everyone in Arecibo knew. My papi had been a respected man. Tía Toña was all set up in Philly so Guillo thought she'd never find out. Pero tu sabes, Boricua news travels fast. A neighbor tracked down Toña's Philly number, called her and asked, 'Who's the lady going in and out your house? Just curious, wanted to make sure it's not a squatter.' The neighbor was putting on a polite front, to not embarrass Toña. Bueno, Toña flew back, put the bitch out, threw her stuff in the street, sold the house immediately, and pocketed the take. Not a penny to Guillo. But the HIV was already in his bloodstream."

I tried to untangle exactly what mom was saying. Female-to-male HIV transmission is difficult to pull off. When I mentioned this, mom raised an eyebrow: "This woman was a well-known prostitute, a total hussy. She'd probably been infected by multiple partners." That dubious assertion did not increase the slim occurrences of female-to-male transmission. Mom sniffed my doubt. "I'm telling you what I was told, Quiara. Anyway, Guillo got sick fast. Big Vic, being Guillo and Toña's only son, moved in with his father and became his caretaker." The image struck me, it was almost biblical. Big Vic the hustler, the macho, his neck ringed with 24-karat rope, as live-in nurse. Son dressing father's mosaic wounds. Son bathing father with a damp cloth. Son emptying father's bedpans. Son repositioning father so bedsores wouldn't worsen. Guillo's body becoming the locus of father-son interdependency. "It was early days, no one had heard of AIDS. To most people, it was a gay disease. And Guillo wasn't gay so it wasn't AIDS, right?" She shot me a glance. "And even if it was AIDS, which they refused to admit, no one knew about preventative measures. Rubber gloves? Please. That's opposite of how we learned. We were taught there has to be a laying on of hands. Entonces, many fluids were exchanged. Dressing the sarcoma, emptying urine and feces in the bedpan. Many, many fluids. Big Vic took such good care of his father, Quiara. He never left his side."

"I was sure I had made it up somehow. But I was right. Big Vic had AIDS," I said.

Mom shrugged and mumbled, "Maybe." As if her entire explanation had suddenly dissolved. "I'm telling you what I was told, Quiara," she said. Guillo had died in '89, Big Vic in '90. Hardly early days. HIV prevention ads wallpapered the city in those years—mom had done some of the wallpapering herself. Silence Equals Death was the mantra back then. But why prevent transmission of something you don't have? It's amazing, how strong our secrets held. Had Guillo even known or had he kept the secret from himself, refusing testing?

Mom launched into the next version of Big Vic's death, but I was fatigued by the first. No doubt she had saved the more salacious tale for second. I no longer wanted to hear it. I felt ill, depressed; that rumbling adolescent helplessness came rushing back at forty. "You know Big Vic was a dealer, right? He was associated with a vicious network, the most violent and feared drug ring in Philly, but he was low-level, he didn't participate in any of that." Her characterization of Big Vic as some bit player made me nearly laugh the burnt yams out my mouth. Decades later, were we that committed to our fairy tales? As if I hadn't seen how Vic used to walk el barrio like a goddamned emperor, gold chains stacked, hairline crisp as a hundred-dollar bill, with his girl Monica in fly shades and rhinestone manicures. It didn't make me love him any less. I could hold the reality of his income and heart in a single glance. Christmas Eves, Big Vic parked outside Abuela's in a Santa hat, popped the trunk, and let the kids go at it. He could fit half a toy store in his car. "Choose what you want!" and he'd smile as we went to town.

Mom continued. "So. Big Vic got locked up for some minor offense. One eight ball, they had nothing. It was all a setup. Use the pawn to get the queen. He traded down jail time for info." She didn't use the word *snitch*. "The police knew the ringleader's name and address. They had been trying to nail this woman for a long time, but their raids came up empty. But Big Vic knew where the stash was." Mom's voice grew animated, she started laughing through the tale. "So, in bust the cops, storming the woman's house, and they head straight for her altar. She's like, 'No, por favor! Anywhere but there! You can't touch the Orisha!' They lift the lid of her Obatalá sopera, which you can never do, you must never open an Orisha like that! And what do they see? A mountain of eight balls. Just like Big Vic told them! The woman made a whole scene about it. 'Ay, that's cascarilla! Ay, that's ceremonial chalk!'" Mom was cracking up now. "Coño, you gotta admire the creativity, meng! Only en el barrio, tontería como así! Entonces, once she was locked up, Big Vic knew. His days were numbered, they were prepping for war. He went into hiding, got more elekes for protection. But her associates were into the dark arts." She said "the dark arts" like a gat dang movie trailer. "They found the kind of Palero who, for the right price, would kill a guy. The curse they chose has a very high success rate. You drain a person's blood, spiritually speaking, and give him a certain amount of days to live." She muttered what the number of days was, but I was pissed and had shut down. Was she really telling me Big Vic was jinxed to death? "I know you don't believe in that stuff," mom said. "But there's a lot you don't understand, Quiara."

"Whichever version you believe, he went quick. It took him fast." That much I remembered. On Memorial Day he was strutting through el barrio, a blinged-out T-rex. By Christmas it looked like a hatchet was stuck in his neck, that's how far his Adam's apple protruded. Knees so knobby the cane hardly kept him upright.

We placed the gravy and cranberry sauce on the table. Called the kids in from the TV room. Time was approaching to say our thanks.

12

POSSESSION'S VOICE

There was a turtle in my bathtub.

"Can we get a terrarium?" I asked. When mom didn't answer, I followed up. "Is he a pet?"

"Don't get too attached," she said. "Don't name him."

For a week the turtle and I exchanged glances. He was suspicious of my power, I of his fate. Out of our mutual distrust, a strange camaraderie emerged. A shared perplexity at our divergent lives in unexpected juncture. A week into his stay I lifted him from the tub. He hissed and retracted, a sharp claw grazing my wrist. It startled more than hurt, but I dropped him and he hit the tub with a bang. I cursed mom and tried again, this time holding his shell at the midsection, my grip more assured. I set him on the floor gently. Soon his head poked out, he cautioned a step. Then he was off. Darting beneath my bed, lumbering into the closet and out again, looping around the brass legs of my nightstand. He could've beat the hare by a length—a turtle in a rush is a marvel to behold. His relief was mine, too. His knobby legs and cumbersome torso made the sprint admirably ridiculous. The poor creature was hardly capable of walking on the tub's slick linoleum. Now he reveled in the friction and grip of my bedroom floor.

The turtle kept being in the tub. The length of his stay kept surprising me.

When high school friends came over and used my bathroom, they emerged quickly, spooked. "Were you gonna mention the turtle?"

"Oops, sorry. Our terrarium tipped over and shattered."

"Where do you shower?"

"In the downstairs tub."

"What's his name?"

Mom's directive loomed, gave me pause. "Turtle."

"Your turtle's name is Turtle?" I tried to play it off as ironic, a cheeky meta-name.

At night he tried scaling the tub's porcelain walls to his freedom. Instead his claws merely fluttered, scratched, tapped, and rested. Over and over, driving me mad and then numb. After months of the turtle's nocturnal clawing, the sleep deprivation had me desk-drooling through dreams all first period. I damned the creature, cursed my mom. I jammed toilet paper into my ears, covered my head with the pillow till I choked on my own exhales.

Then one afternoon I strode into the kitchen to discover mom hunched over a cutting board and bowl, tugging hard. One hand gripped a half-hollow turtle shell, the other pulled at maroon flesh inside. The bowl was filled with wet raw meat. Mom's knives were no match for the turtle's sinuous, belligerent musculature.

Why was I the kid who knew death like an old knock-knock joke? Why hadn't the reaper chosen my white friends to toy with? First Guillo then Big Vic then Mary Lou and now the turtle—minus an open casket and undertaker's stitches. Just reptilian flesh clumped in a mixing bowl.

That night no sound came from the bathroom. There was no flutter of claws requiring me to blast a tape. The quiet hooked my neck, lassoed my lungs till they breathed shallow. I got up in the dark and walked toward the bathroom. The floorboards creaked beneath me, filling the room with a little bit of sound. I walked in, cold tile beneath my feet, enshrouded in silence once again. The tub loomed, empty and shadowed. A slick sepulcher without its entombed. I sat on the floor, back against the porcelain, and cupped my head in my palms. I owed the creature that much. A few hours of night watch, a few hours too late.

I forced myself to stay there all night, trying to pinpoint the start of mom's Philly awakening. When had the altars appeared in our living room? When had she allowed god to flood her days once again, or been initiated into what laypeople and horror flicks called Santería? Why hadn't she invited me to reprise my role as witness, an honor I had savored out on the horse farm? It was not forbidden that I watch the toques and bembes, but direct invitations had never been extended. Instead I was told something would be happening downstairs and if I didn't want to see, best to stay in my room. Here in the city a network of venerable Afro-Caribbean theologists thrived. In a community that looked more like mom, I was no longer needed as ballast.

When I discovered mom in the kitchen—pure dumb luck—curiosity flooded me. *Mom, why a turtle? What's the significance?*

Tell me what blessing this is meant to bring. Questions piled up in my closed mouth. But explaining herself, I knew, often required self-diminishment. A concession to a world that kept pointing fingers.

There was a goat in the basement. I hopped down the steps, twirling my bike's U-lock key. My thrift-store Schwinn was a forty-pounder, equal parts red paint and rust. Two speeds only and trash-truck sturdy. I pumped a few squirts of air into the old tires and suddenly felt eyes on me. There stood a goat, plain as day, its head angled inquisitively. A chewed-up strip of *Inquirer* dangled from its beard. He seemed pleased by my company, as if he'd been expecting me. "A spot of tea?" his keyhole eyes seemed to ask. I backed up the stairs, closed the door gently, and decided the 34 trolley was faster than my Schwinn. "You should have a sleepover tonight," mom said that afternoon, casually sorting through mail, not glancing my way. Then she added for clarity, "At a friend's house, not here." So, I left with a sleeping bag. Returning home the following day, I called out and discovered an empty house. I beelined for the basement door but, gripping the knob, lost my nerve. I wobbled to the sofa and threw myself down, listing my grievances, craving the decency of a god-damned explanation. Eventually I traversed the living room again, turned the knob, tiptoed down. Every bit of hesitance, I thought, might reverse time. But the goat was gone. The newspaper, too. The piss was mopped up and the floor, usually dusty and dull, gleamed.

There was a chicken in the backyard, inside a cage. Its wattle was flaccid as a crushed worm, its beak a sickly pink. I cursed its orange tripod feet, how the toes were coarse and speckled brown. Every detail was one whose demise I must anticipate, unless, of course, I freed the creature. So I would. White feathers thrashed at the cage, whipping up a cloud. Our cement backyard became a snow globe with every flap. I crept toward the cage, studying how to unlatch it without getting pecked. We established a groove, the chicken joining my silence. He fell still. At last I reached out, unhooking the door with a click. Wings now exploded in a whup and a whirl. Feathers burst like backyard fireworks and beak pounded palm with the force of nails. I dashed into the house and darted up the steps all the way to my bathroom, where I slammed the door and cursed on the toilet. The chicken had not broken my skin, nor had I freed it.

That night I was determined to watch. Was I not complicit? Did I not owe the bird the decency of witness? When its guttural plea pierced the house, I raced down the stairs in time to see the bird suspended by its legs, jerking wildly, then falling limp. Its blood ribboned out, a molasses stream, into a dish. Death's hush came quick and a metallic whiff of blood flew at me. I crouched at the first bend in the stairwell, out of view. Limbs afire, tears cutting. Strong hand over mouth, I remained undetected as spit gurgled through my fingers and fell in pendulums. So now the tears came. For a bird. When I hadn't needed a Kleenex for my cousins' funerals. Nice, Quiara.

Eventually the tears grew bored with themselves. Still, I watched. Even as I disavowed this Lukumí offering, thick was my compulsion to see what scared me the most. Was it god I feared? Or my implicit connection to mom's spirits, my single degree of separation? This numinous impulse was rooted in her at birth. She had entrusted me with tales of her five-year-old visions. Was

I an heir, too? Were mom's ceremonies lurking, dormant, in my marrow?

Mom did entrust me with some menial tasks, which I executed dutifully. Monday mornings, I was to place espresso at the feet of Eleguá, who lived near the front door. I returned last week's demitasse to the kitchen for washing. When mom cooked, the first plate was piled high until beans pooled at the edge. "The Orisha eat first," she said, handing me the feast. I carried it to the sunroom, where the soperas lived. There I stood in awe of the majestic altar mom had built. Halved oranges covered with honey and cinnamon for Oshun, an indigo urn housing Olokun's secrets, for Changó a red crown and mahogany axe. Babalú Aye leaned on a crutch—his woeful, pathetic eyes offering me kindness. La Caridad del Cobre was a Brown virgen atop ocean foam, waves cresting at her ankles, multihued cherubs hovering at her crown. Hills of fruit were arranged on the floor, while rattles, brass bells, and coconut shells mingled on various perches. In English the word was altar but in Spanish the word was throne. At the foot of el trono, I placed the dinner plate.

On occasion, I was the recipient of blessings and protections. When my depression raged until mom feared I'd hurt myself, baños y limpiezas were prepared. She mixed flower petals, oils, powders, and perfumes into water, praying over the swirling bowlful. Or she brought me to revered elders, where I'd step into unfamiliar bathtubs to receive cleansings. They would tip the large mixing bowl over my head, and the downward cascade would wash away bad energy. The baños reminded me of mom's old shiatsu massages with eucalyptus oil. Afterwards, stinking and messy, I savored a dual sense of groundedness and expansiveness. I squeamishly picked flower petals and herbs from my hair, but the patient touch of female elders lingered. Other times mom enlisted me to participate in fruit ebós. Her energy was soft and luminous on these excursions. After driving to Wissahickon Creek and hiking into the woods, we left a sealed brown bag with specially prepared fruit near water's edge, tucked into a tree's roots. Another day, during a crowded Odunde procession, we stood on the South Street Bridge and dropped melons into the Schuylkill River, alongside neighbors throwing money, flowers, y miel. That Philly afternoon, aché rained down.

When mom and I visited elders in Philly's Lukumí community, I was welcomed into living rooms with grace and warmth. Hands-down the most diverse spaces of my youth, Benetton would've paid top dollar to snap pics. Of mom's two closest padrinos—both Cuban—one was dark-skinned Black, the other ruddy-cheeked and fair. Ceremonies and celebrations were primarily Black Latino gatherings, with shades of Brown and White present, too. In an African-rooted philosophy and practice, I knew a gringa couldn't just saunter in, cavalier. Invitations, mom always said, were never to be presumed. But time and again, greeting me at the door of tenements, apartments, and row homes, elders saw my skin and my spirit and told me, *entra*. With wise eyes, in one soft sustained glance, they seemed to ascertain and warm to my core. I often wondered *what did they see* and hoped I'd see it one day, too.

"What's Ainalode, mom?" I asked her the afternoon I received protective spiritual beads. My clothes and hair were still a bit damp from the limpieza and I slowly pulled slender pompom petals from behind my ears. "Is Ainalode like, *god bless you?* Is it the same as *bendición?*" Since all the priests and priestesses there addressed mom with the word, I figured they were bestowing aché or something. "I *am* Ainalode." She laughed gently. "Ainalode is me. That's the name I was given when I was crowned with Changó. Everyone who does santo receives a name." Aha! So much for my self-diagnosed name amnesia. Previously, she would introduce me to an elder and I'd develop instant anxiety about addressing them, certain I had already forgotten or initially misunderstood their name. I'd hear others calling them something different and shrink into paralysis, cursing my bona fide name-retention disorder. I'd go to all lengths to avoid addressing elders directly and in the rare instance where I had to, I'd use formal awkward Spanish—Don this and Doña that. Now I understood. "So . . . Tía Toña and Titi Margie. Do they have Ocha names?" I asked. Those were two of mom's older sisters who were also advanced in the religion. "Yes," mom said, carefully peeling a tiny flower petal from my clavicle. "Tía Toña is Obanyoko. Titi Margie is Ochalerí." And she asked me to repeat, checking my pronunciation, as she lifted the shoulder strap of my training bra and pulled a flower bit from beneath it. Her smooth acrylic tips gave me chills as she fished away the petals.

By the next ceremony, no longer fearing the names, I could revel in their cadence. I observed how mom greeted her godfather, Padrino Julio, at the front door, but the second he put on that white ceremonial cap, he became Baba Funque. *Baba Funque.* Now, that's a name made of music. Testing the waters, I approached her other godfather. "Padrino Tony, what is your Ocha name?" "Oluchande," he told me. "Oluchande," I repeated. It felt marvelous to say. And as he smiled, I realized I had dropped my middle name years ago, fatigued by its difference. Meanwhile, this circle welcomed the complexity of new names in new languages. Time to pay attention, Qui Qui. Time to ask if you can accompany mom to the next tumbao or bembe.

Problem was, many ceremonies—big ones, in my home—were off-limits. The fact of my occasional inclusion made these exclusions personal. As if some devotion was too full-on, some mysteries too powerful for fragile Qui Qui. This was not about age, I was pretty certain, but about mom's tally of my intellectual and spiritual limitations.

Later that night, by the flow of the downstairs conversation, I knew real shit was under way. Batá drums thickened the atmosphere like humidity. I couldn't make out words, only general urgency. Some voices, I recognized. Sedo, my not-quite stepfather, a Boricua contractor mom had been seeing for years, got in a word or two. Padrino Julio's familiar cadence was lilting, with his signature trace of giggle. He was mom's mentor in the religion, an elderly Santero Obá whose kindness softened my reticence. He aimed affection my way without asking permission or demanding reciprocation; for that, I favored him. I knew mom was downstairs, too, as she had called me to greet Padrino Julio y le pidiera la bendición. I could not hear her at present, though. An unfamiliar male voice held forth, his authority galloping in on quick words and melodic inflection. No one interrupted or spoke over this powerful man. In their silence, I inferred deference and profound respect. I stood at the upstairs landing for a very long time, leaning over, hand to ear. Who was this houseguest? What did his presence signal?

One step at a time, that's how I descended. Telling myself *turn back* with every inch of progress. Toward the bottom I cursed my own curiosity. I sat in protest, hoping to stall my forward motion. But my desire to advance was strong and I descended the steps in a seated position. At last the living room unfolded before me. Three people sat at the table—mom, Sedo, and Padrino Julio. There was no strange visitor in sight. Mom was the stranger. She was a man. From her mouth flowed the voice I had heard upstairs. A plosive, nasal Spanish with some dialect spliced in. What creole tongue, what pidgin words these were, I hadn't a clue. A twang of the ancient rode the cadence. By the sound, this was a frisky spirit, and wise. Even the bones in mom's face were changed. Her slender nose widened, her overbite reversed so that her bottom jaw thrust forward as if rolling a marble between her front teeth. She was squatter now, her usually soft shoulders broad and firm. Se montó el espíritu.

The men sat with her, alert and listening. Padrino Julio fed her rum and asked questions, the answers to which Sedo transcribed in a marble notebook. He filled the pages quickly, his pen resting only when he needed a new page. Occasionally Padrino Julio sought clarity before the next question. The spelling of some unfamiliar town, perhaps, that he'd check on later. "Can you repeat that person's name, please?" She-not-she answered, then lifted Bacardi to her lips, tipped the jug, and swigged down a third of the nearly full rum. Surely she would vomit or seize. Aside from a beer during spring cleaning, mom never drank. But she slammed down the bottle and the interview continued apace.

My body railed, hating the scene. Knees trembling madly, teeth chattering, fingers squeezing my jaw into silence. I was a crab in the undertow, flailing as the current churned. I wanted to scream, "Stop! You're gonna hurt my mom!" To run and wipe sweat from this face that was not hers, to reach down her throat and yank out the spirit. First Guillo then Big Vic then Mary Lou, now mom? Everyone I loved, lost. Mom wasn't mine, I now understood. Never had been. She belonged to herself and the province of spirits, but never me. My thoughts turned to that distant Fourth of July. How hard my cousins danced, how propulsive and insistent their hips had been, as if conducted by some magnificent force. That gathering had been secular, this one was spiritual. And yet, a pulse is a pulse is a pulse. A drum is a drum is a drum. Yes, it was true, and here lay the evidence: dance and possession were dialects off the same mother tongue. I spoke neither. English, my best language, had no vocabulary for the possession nor the dance. And English was what I was made of. My words and my world did not align. That, perhaps, made me a lost soul.

Over an hour in, mom's stamina raged on. Eventually her breath grew labored. She stopped speaking, started again. She was disoriented, a bull in a ring going down slowly. Suddenly she stood with such thrust and violence that her chair flew back and crashed into the wall. Upright for the first time in more than an hour, mom lost her balance and collapsed in Sedo's arms. Shallow breaths, hair matted on her forehead. She looked around at our living room with vague familiarity: that wallpaper, this table, the stereo. Sedo chuckled, "Welcome back, negra. You can relax now." "Cuidao," Padrino Julio said when she stood, "all that Bacardi will go to your head." He chuckled as mom saw the half-empty bottle, dazed. Then she walked out back without so much as a stumble. "What happened?" she asked as night air swallowed them. Padrino Julio and Sedo began to answer as I stared at the still life, searching for clues.

So carefully had mom explained her activism. She had invited

me into her grassroots advocacy, tutoring me on the hidden
crimes against Puerto Rican women. There was a *know your roots,
guard your truth, never forget* vibe in those lectures—a motherhood strategy full of warrior specificity. The intentionality of
those explanations only made the mysteries smack of abandonment. What of our family's hidden deaths, my cousins' disappearances, her blossoming faith? No motherly sermons provided
those answers. Every time a riddle beckoned me closer, a fog descended, obscuring my view. My life required explication, and I
didn't have the language to make it make sense.

*God, give me a space where this fits—all of this loss and life. Give
me a language to voice the scream so others can hear and understand,
and in the understanding I can be made whole. Make me whole. God,
help me find the right words for begin and end because right now the
death and the dance overlap in ways that make a mess.* And even as I
prayed I had to laugh, because what god, precisely, was I praying to?

I yearned for a home that required no explanation, for a Western frame so I might see *that stuff* like my white friends saw it.
Yeah, Vietnamese and non-Latino Black friends shrugged at
mom's altars, unfamiliar. But too often, white friends paled when
greeted at my door by Eleguá, holder of all pathways, center of
the crossroads. He was a cement-filled conch shell with cowry
eyes, placed in a clay dish in the foyer. A few pennies and a shot
of espresso lay before him, tokens of gratitude. Worse than the
disgust on my friends' faces, though, was the embarrassment
that flooded me in response. Shame's hot furnace lapped at my
throat as I wished mom would worship a little bit whiter. Faced
with my guests' disgust, I remained silent rather than apologize
for mom, but I also remained silent rather than defend her. More
than once, I had the painful realization that friends who insisted

sleepovers be at their place were doing so by parental mandate. After hosting an initial hangout, their parents had picked them up and seen Eleguá, deciding this home was no place for their child. My friends confessed difficult conversations with their parents, torn because they had known and loved my mom's vibrant and warm hospitality. These parents weren't so cruel as to disallow the friendship, but I couldn't shake an anger that my Brown mother had been seen as threatening. Nor could I deny, though, that I often feared her gifts and her proximity to gods I'd never met.

I so wanted to take my dad's side, join his disavowal of any god, his assertion that religion was the root of all evil. It would have brought a perverse relief to write off mom's gift as gremlins of brain chemistry, to name some psychological diagnosis. But such a dismissal would have denied my gut. Belief, I knew, was beside the point. You don't stroll through a city going, "Do I believe in the skyscraper, the clouds reflected in its windows, the shadow it casts?" That's a question for lunatics and self-important pedants. The question was not did I believe in god, los Egun, the Orisha, Ifá. I had seen enough to know that shit went down whether or not I believed. The question was if my curiosity would lead me toward the altars and voices of the spirits, or whether I'd shut the door. Would I look *at* or look *away*?

Sometimes I stood in our living room staring at a wood and brass National Organization for Women plaque hanging on the wall. The word HERO was engraved above mom's name. It was accompanied by other framed letters and taped proclamations. State representative Ralph Acosta commended mom's invaluable work "meeting the health needs of our community." The "our" had an assertive, celebratory tone—one Philly Rican leader tipping his hat to another. There was mom's letter of appointment to the state chiropractic board under Governor Casey. An older Memo of Appreciation from Governor Thornburgh beside it. A citation from the Pennsylvania House of Representatives full of calligraphed *whereas*es and *therefore*s. Things she did not file away. Things she didn't keep secret. I was proud of them. Mom curated this self in the living room. Meanwhile the Orisha, aside from the ones who by mandate perched at a home's entrance, lived in the sunroom, away from foot traffic. Mom was a warrior out in the world but self-protection mattered in her home. So she hid her altars from the ignorant gaze of friends, neighbors, family. Even, perhaps, from me.

Heat danced on the South Dakota tarmac. Mom had left CHOICE Hotline and now thrived as a youth ambassador for the American Friends Service Committee, the activism arm of the Philadelphia Quakers. A bootstraps Boricua within a white service organization, mom was a natural choice for outreach to teens of color. This was national work for a national organization, and while each new assignment took her farther from her community, I sometimes got to join as mom's horizons expanded. We would spend a week on the Rosebud reservation, where she would meet with Lakota Sioux teens and discuss everything from alcohol addiction to safe sex.

Mom welcomed the shamanistic opportunity. The Lakota Sioux greeted her as a recognized indigenous Taína, spirit medium, and natural healer. Our trip would culminate in an invitation-only Sun Dance. Mom repeatedly impressed upon me the honor of this invitation. "This is not something taken lightly. You are to behave with utmost respect and deference." Our rental car cut a scenic route west. I followed the map's unruly folds, reconciling its printed landmarks with the barren landmasses around me. Through dust and haze, the Black Hills beckoned. Dark, low mounds. "Sacred ground," mom said. I knew the Jersey Shore, New York City, and Six Flags, but I'd never laid eyes on the belly of our nation. Which is what this landscape resembled— a flat ochre belly.

Crossing onto the reservation, the road became a red stripe dusting into the distance. Sparseness was the only decipherable city planning. Mom drove slower than usual, and we both paid attention. A corrugated steel structure sat back from the road. Topped with slanting tar paper. There were no windows, just a doorway and freshly hung laundry. Whatever held card castles together, the same principle seemed to be at play here.

"Is that a house?" I asked.

"What else would it be, Quiara? Coño, please do not be rude or ignorant around the elders."

No power lines ran by the road. "Do they have running water?"

"Some do." Flor's and Nuchi's and Tía Toña's blocks came to mind: burnt buildings, empty vials scattered, derelict lots full of weeds and old tires. Their homes tugged at my memory: plastic sheets for windows, duct tape holding up the ceiling. In North Philly, poverty was the cupboard's last slice of bread, offered to Qui Qui who had come for a visit. Our nation, it seemed, offered up a panoply of invisibilities. I stared out the window, quiet and observant.

Mom spent much of her time with a Sioux elder named Hildegard, a stout woman with thick braids worn a variety of ways. Hours passed as they whispered about women's work, spirit stuff. Though she was sturdy and physically capable, age had softened the woman, and mom seemed angular, almost juvenile at her side. Seeing mom in the position of student relaxed me. At last she was not the wisest in the room. Meanwhile, local teens took me to the creek and schooled me on dip. "Tuck it behind your bottom lip," as if that made the wad any less like coffee grounds. We perched on river rocks, holding menthol magic wands, flipping through well-worn teen idol mags. These kids lived in decent if cobbled homes, with windows and running water and disheveled bedrooms just like mine. But I kept thinking of the shacks and lean-tos and then in turn scolding my memory: *stop staring*. Mom had frequently told me, "You have no clue, Quiara." Though I hated that phrase, offered with more weariness than judgment in the face of things I didn't understand, I now conceded its accuracy.

Mom and I had attended powwows in Fairmount Park at Philly's perimeter. We liked the dance competitions, how the drums met our guts. Mom always knew which vendors sold good crystals and hand-grew their smudge sticks. And sometimes they'd say, "I knew you were coming! I have something special for you!" But the Sun Dance was no raucous celebration, no shopping fix. A field of blankets stretched beneath the sky. Families filled the expanse, whispering and sharing meals. Meat in clear broth arrived at my blanket, delivered on the hands of a quiet stranger. At the field's center, young men danced, their pectorals pierced by bone ornaments. The piercings were attached to long ribbons, which in turn were tied to a tree. Through their left and right breasts, the dancers were attached to the pole and therefore to each other. Their footsteps transformed earth into drum. The soil beneath me vibrated as though the men were attached to me. The drum's voice came at me on the breeze, quilting me and mom to strangers on nearby blankets, sonic stitchery. The ribbons, each one a radius, reminded me of drawing mom's circle garden in the dirt.

The ceremony had been going on for days. We joined for a long afternoon in the home stretch, the culminating hours. The drumming seemed to bolster the dancers' fatigue, and they undulated between energy and lethargy. At the ceremony's climax the men danced backward, outward and thrusting, until the bones ripped and broke from their skin. They were free. I watched, stunned, as they bled. Crimson trickled from the wounds and drew root-shaped paths down their chests. Mom saw how quiet I'd become.

"Women bleed during childbirth, but men don't get to make that blood sacrifice. In this ceremony, though, they do." I wasn't sure if it was her interpretation or something learned. But it resonated, felt personalized even. Blood sacrifice, it seemed, transcended my West Philly living room. Blood sacrifice was impervious to my voyeuristic perch and provincial qualms. It was not just mom's method of alienating me. Here was sacrifice of the self, of the sanctity of one's own skin, as a quest for completeness. Maybe in this life begging for explanation, I was the answer I was looking for—my own body, made of blood, bone, and language.

Soon after I landed back from South Dakota, my search began. For god, perhaps, or for my true mother tongue. Or for the fulcrum where those two balanced. I had often struggled to squeeze my reality into words that didn't fit me. Now I would go searching for better languages.

13

SEDO BUYS ME AN UPRIGHT;
LANGUAGE OF BACH

n Perez homes throughout Philly, womanhood was rampant. Girls, cousins, tías, abuelas, primas, hermanas, madrinas. To keep up with a Perez female, a male needed stamina and resilience. Facing the gale of our hungry bellies and heartbreaks, a man's sail would require sturdy stitches. Mercedes "Sedo" Sanchez was such a man. His chest was so thick it could bust open a barrel. His wide smile showed off big teeth, with gaps broad as harmonica holes. The main gap—smack-dab in the middle—was probably the first thing in his mouth and his teeth just grew around it. On his expansive forehead, atop thickest eyebrow, sat a penny-size mole. A mole like a setting sun. On another man the mark would've been a blemish but on Sanchez it was regal. He cut a striking figure at six foot two.

People stood straighter when Sanchez walked into the room. Curse words were folded and tucked in back pockets. Hands were presented for shaking. Out on the street, folks hollered as he passed. "Sanchez!" The name, said aloud, put some polish on the day. His joint, the Sanchez Bar and Lounge, was an after-dark oasis at the run-down corner of 5th and Dauphin. Pool tables, disco balls, a neon jukebox with bubble tubes, rum bottles aglow above blue-lit shelves. Tuxedoed waiters traversed the crowd, silver platters perched on their fingertips. A dollar Heineken got you entry to this barrio paradise, and if the bouncer was a no-show, Sanchez manned the door.

He was a well-known builder north of Girard, who wore polished loafers to his construction sites and got drywall dust under his nails. Then he returned the next day, loafers shiny and polished, handing out payday envelopes to his crew. He didn't have employees, he had guys. Sanchez even smelled good when walking his work zones, with a gait that was calmer and less showy than swagger. His presence quieted people like an ocean vista. The sea doesn't have to act strong and neither did he.

Mom was no withering flower. A formidable presence, the spirits came to her direct. They slipped in quick, a no-splash dive in the deep end. When that happened, she didn't have time to give warnings. She grabbed the reins and rode it. Mom weighed more during possession, too, like her veins had been filled by an iron spigot. She needed a man who could catch her when the spirit left. It never left lightly. It was a seismic exit.

Sanchez caught her. Every last pound. Without warning or hesitation. He had been raised a Catholic of the most pious order, so this wasn't a learned skill. It was his character, the weft and weave of his heart's cloth.

In the Perez family, there weren't a ton of dudes modeling dudeness. Most men—Boricua, white, or African American—fathered a kid or three, then took off, leaving the Perez women to their insular bubble. Big Vic and Guillo had died. Mary Lou's widower had moved back to Puerto Rico. Danito and JJ and Nuchi's four boys were boogie-nosed tots. And Tío George, Ginny's husband, was a milder genus, burrowed into his prized lazy boy, calm as the Eagles or Phillies allowed. But everything about Sedo was a culture shock.

In a constant campaign to culture me, he cranked up the Fania and stomped my toes, spinning rag doll me too close to walls and furniture. No morning was too early, no evening too late, for him to curse local politics at volume eleven. Every election, the Democrats spat promises like sunflower shells: they would fix the schools, the potholes, the blight. Every election, Puerto Ricans delivered the vote, Sanchez yelled, and the Democrats dropped them like yesterday's lotto tickets. "The Democratic Party never did shit for our people!" he cursed. He had, in fact, run for local office and a few of his campaign posters gathered dust in the basement.

According to mom, his folks named him Mercedes after the luxury car, to assure an abundant future. Mom pursed her lips, kissing her own condescension. She loved calling out haughty Puerto Ricans who nosed the clouds like their shit didn't stink. He couldn't remember when he'd changed it to Sedo, but it stuck. Two syllables blunt as a butter knife in steak. I called him Sedo, same as mom, which felt slightly disrespectful. But I saw no better option.

His biological children were punctual, I give 'em that. Every night during *The Simpsons* our phone rang. "Your mother's a whore," they whispered before hanging up. Sometimes they'd abbreviate it simply to "Whore." Click. He had left them, my dad had left me. So we were tied in the dad department, but they didn't know or care. It's not like I wanted their cologne-scented, crisp-hairlined macho in my kitchen every morning. No one had consulted me on the great daddy swap-out that was now my life.

One night they were really on a roll. Crank-calling a gazillion times in quick succession. Mom stormed up the steps, hands sticky from chopping sofrito. "Tell your friends that our phone line is not a fucking toy!" It rang again. She grabbed the receiver, double-palming it fingerlessly to not garlic-up the plastic. "Hello?" The word sounded through the earpiece: *Whore.* Click. She looked at me with surprise.

"Wait . . . Was that?"

"Yeah."

"That's why this thing's been ringing off the hook?" I had tried to shield her from the calls. Some nights she had been cooking and blasting Celia Cruz louder than the ringer, others she was out working late. Now it rang again. "Don't answer," mom said, running to rinse off the garlic. She returned clean-handed and grabbed the receiver with steady poise. "Hello?" Again, the word was hissed more than spoken. *Whore.* "That's just sad. Do you even know what you're saying?" mom sighed. The line went dead, the ring repeated, as did the slander. *Whooore.* "You know something . . . you may have a point. Call it to me again." They obliged. *Whoooooore.* "I bet you didn't think you'd be my teacher tonight. What am I?" *WHOOOOOOOORE!* When the line went dead, mom craned her neck to god. "I caught your transmission! Maferefún!" Her giggles gathered until the next ring, when she answered by simply blurting: "Give it to me." *WHOOOOOOOOOOORE!*

Mom lost it. Woman cracked up. Laughter flying like Sunday hallelujahs. Hitting soprano notes I didn't know she had.

"Stop, mom. It's not funny."

"They have no idea what they're calling me! How do we say 'whore' en el barrio?" mom asked.

"Puta?"

"How else?"

"Ho?"

"Exacto: ho! Now tell me, Quiara, what is a ho?"

"A woman who's shamed for her sexuality?"

"It's the shame men have given us from the get-go. The shame that is written into the Bible! But think, Quiara, what else is a ho? I want you to make this connection yourself." Racking my brain, I came up short. "HO!" she yelled, as if volume was a code-cracker. "AZADA! AZADA! AZADA! What is a ho, Quiara?"

"A gardening tool."

"And what does a hoe do?" she asked.

"Digs."

"It's an ancient tool with a sharp blade for clearing and turning the soil. When the earth gets tired, you break the earth, you wound the earth, digging narrow troughs and trenches so you can do what?"

"Plant seeds."

"Plant seeds!" she rejoiced, all affirmation. "They think they're shaming me, but they have no clue that they're praising me. We are not whores, we are hoes! We plow the land, we plow our reality! We plant seeds of potential! I am hoeing on Sedo's potential. I am hoeing on the potential of my community. I have been hoeing your potential since day one, hija!"

Resplendent and alive, she answered each call. The word "whore," when missiled her way, was met with the laugh of a honey-sated bear. Mom's laughter caught me, until both our feet hoofed the floorboards, both our fists pounded sofa and our faces contorted and torqued with pain. But still we laughed.

.   .   .

I was eight when Sanchez first appeared. The second mom brought him home, I was on alert. Man brought an earthquake. The blackout drunk rages at three A.M. Mom stripped his pants, tugging at the ankles, and washclothed the shit away as he hollered and cursed. I would spy these struggles from the upstairs landing. My jaw would clench with animal instinct and I'd despise the devil in his voice. I tried transmitting instructions telepathically. *Forget him, mom! Let him clean his own shit!* No matter how loudly I thought, mom never seemed to hear.

One rainy night I found trash bags out front, filled with his nice clothes.

"Where's Sedo, mom?"

"Straightening up or getting out." The following morning the bags were gone. The house quieted that week, as if listening for clues. Mom was tense for days, vague with the answers. She gripped my arm whenever near, as if to steady herself from stumbling. She offered unsolicited assurances. "We will be fine no matter what happens. You gotta believe in your mami, me entiendes?" She was shoulder-length from heartbreak, hollowed-out, teetering. She had lost love once, and it had nearly annihilated her. Would I watch her plummet again?

Finally, she was pulling onto the Schuylkill. The on-ramp from West Philly was a treacherous blind merge with cars zooming by on her left and an impatient line accumulating behind her. If a gap slipped by unclaimed, angry honks pounced like wolves. "What do you want me to do, fly?" she screamed in the rearview. She swooped into a lane and in that moment out came her decision. "What I have to figure out is if I'm ready to put in the time. I'm not young, Quiara, and this is a major project, an investment of my best years. Cleaning up a man is no one-two-three quickie. Pero, with all his imperfections . . ." And now her voice cracked. ". . . when all I had around me was death . . ." She trailed off, leaving me to infer what death she referred to. I knew. It was the shroud that fell on her in those skinniest days. I had watched my mother erode. Being a Brown woman battling a white man in family court. Dad's threats to kidnap me to California. Casa Comadre being destroyed when—and because—it flourished. "When all I had around me was death"—mom steadied her voice—"Sedo said get on your knees and give that to the universe. I tell you that was a powerful moment in my life. I will die thinking of it. He returned me to faith."

When Sedo resurfaced the next day, a chastened hush arrived with him. What mom anticipated as a years-long process—cleaning him up—he had begun to accomplish, it seemed, in those few days away. As time wore on, the temperance proved lasting. It's not that he had shrunk, but he came back home with a sense of permission and humility. I wondered if by drawing a firm line, mom had made good on her spiritual debt. If in his darkest hour, she had restored him to himself.

Sedo was a light-skinned Puerto Rican whose coloring might've matched my dad's, but otherwise they were a different breed. He was, above all, a fantastically groomed man, and mornings in our home became a symphony of macho preening. The hiss of the Niagara spray as mom creased his slacks. The hum of the clipper as she edged his hairline. Spanish radio pummeled my ears too early, Mom and Sedo's chatter bursting above it. She apparently knew every Héctor Lavoe lyric there was—news to me till I heard her sing them while spritzing cologne on his neck. He had never heard of the Beatles nor I of Johnny Pacheco, and we looked at each other like alien beings. Now it was all Eddie Palmieri and Ray Barretto as mom rolled lint off his dry-clean-only sweaters. They planned their day in Spanish. Argued in Spanish. Budgeted money in Spanish. Ridiculed Dan Quayle's IQ in Spanish. For the first time in my life, there was Spanish in my home. Not at Abuela's house or Titi Ginny's or in the bodega on American Street. Spanish was no longer a way station I passed through. It was in my kitchen as I poured my Cheerios and scuttled away.

Mom had done none of these things with dad. Not the ironing, not the hairline. Spanish—on the radio or in her mouth—was an infrequent visitor in my early years. Mom certainly never cooked rice and beans for dad. Back on the horse farm she had been an accomplished baker. I can still smell the yeast, feel my palm flouring the counter, hear the slurp and suck of the dough. Our tactile kneading. She was skinny in her bread-baking days. Her copper skin framed by Charlie's Angel curls, shirts buttoned low so her cleavage could say hi. A beauty with a rolling pin. But mom's last loaf of bread was baked on the horse farm. When they split, she became a stovetop cook, a rice and beans lady.

Still, above all these new behaviors stood the biggest change of all. Mom had never worshipped around dad.

So, which was the real mom? English-speaking never-prays Virginia? Or this new creature, stopping en route to the babalao's, browsing the cologne counter at Macy*s so her man could walk North Philly smelling fine?

The animal sacrifices had started in middle school. He was still Sedo in those days. But the night I witnessed mom possessed, I saw something else, too: a partner at her side. A man who earned her complexity. Soon after that I tried on "Pop" for size. He never dictated what I should call him and "Pop" seemed all right. Not too awkward or eager. An appropriate title for the man who caught my mother, probably the only person on earth up for that ancestral-level trust fall. His catch wasn't just taking her weight. It was a total yielding, an acceptance of a woman's full, impolite truth.

There was that Sunday early on (he was still Sedo then) when his voice boomed from the porch. "Quiara, prop the door!" His crew was out front, clumped around an old upright. They stooped over, breathing hard. "Well? Final stretch?" he said. Sedo was not one to bark orders from the sidelines. He took rear position—the most weight-bearing—as they hauled the piano up five front steps, sweat pouring from noses, tears of exertion raining down. Their muscles quaked beneath the terrible weight, and if that thing toppled over, they were goners. Once the steps were conquered, they discovered that the piano's old casters had rusted stiff, so even on a flat surface, the lifting must continue.

The piano was placed by the dining table. Someone had given it a slapdash coat of dookie-brown paint. Chips here and there revealed older colors beneath. Two keys, missing the ivory, resembled gaps in grade-school smiles.

"A church in Downingtown was about to be demolished." Sedo beamed, wiping hand sweat on his slacks. "They auctioned off the contents first, and I bought almost everything! So, what do you think, Quiara? Was this worth twenty-two bucks?" Sedo lived to find gems in a garbage heap and throw a few hours' work at a few willing guys. That's how our West Philly twin went from tumbledown to handsome: because Sedo and mom scoured auctions and estate sales and, knowing how to build, they patched our house's wounds room by room.

I sat and played. Bach's Minuet in G Major, the one classical piece I knew. I had learned it by ear on the school piano during recess. Tinny notes like chimes in a music box rang out. The keys required only the gentlest press to make music. The workers crowded around. They could hear it, too. She was sweeter than a lollipop, this worn-out piano. Sang like a parakeet. My fingers lifted from the final chord and I turned to face my audience. Their cheeks were still red from exertion but with brighter eyes.

"¿Quien la escribió? ¿Tú?" one asked.

"Bach."

"Bach," he repeated. The guys chuckled at the name.

Mimicking German pronunciation, I proclaimed: "Johann Sebastian Bach."

"Sabes otra?" Not knowing another, I replayed the minuet, life's aperture widening with every note. Indeed, later that night, when the crew had gone and mom and Sedo were out working, I would carry my radio downstairs, pop in a Phil Collins tape, and rewind it over and over, plunking around for notes that matched the song. "Against All Odds." An eighties power ballad of heartbreak. Though I did not know the word "triad," my fingers intuited their structure. Each chord was an easel balanced on three points: the major fifth, anchored by a major or minor third in the middle. First came A minor. Then B minor. A progression would emerge, unspooling a thread of sound. Within minutes I would play the first verse, a fawn fumbling on new legs. Soon I would sing-play the melodrama of the chorus through tears. Miraculous: to be saturated in feeling. The fact of my sadness, no longer sad. The notes did that. They soared where English and Spanish failed. All testimony and evocation, no mistranslation.

Soon my aunt Linda in New York would teach me to read

music so that at a moment's notice I'd hop a Greyhound north, hungry to advance. Soon she would sponsor weekly piano lessons and Chopin would knit an opalescent cocoon around my melancholy. Soon I would xerox "Maple Leaf Rag" at the school library, buy Gershwin's "Three Preludes" at the piano store on Chestnut. And since, in pursuit of my melancholy music, I would learn to brave New York's Port Authority alone and late-night West Philly on my way home from lessons, soon journeying solo to the library and Borders became second nature, so that Langston Hughes and Allen Ginsberg would become paperback mentors, all thanks to that upright.

For now, my fingers rested as Bach's final G-chord rang out. The workers nodded, smiling, easy converts to Bach's orderly music. It was dainty in a way life rarely mimicked, an ephemeral koan. From a thick roll of cash, Sedo thumbed twenties and fifties to each guy. Then made a declaration. "My daughter's a natural!"

That's how I got my first piano. And a few notes of a new language.

14

TAÍNO PETROGLYPHS

To escape and therefore understand my living room. To cram warring selves into one elegant space. To quell the grumbling in my gut and yet deeply mourn. To fathom the blood of it all: my own, my cousins', the Sun Dance's, the turtle's. Maybe sitting in quiet for an hour would light the way. No one at Quaker meeting pulled me to a dance floor. It was as if the whole space were Abuela's staircase. And the little girl within, who'd fled to the woods, again mistook refuge for safety.

When I'd first attended, fall of sophomore year, I'd sat alone in the empty room before service began. A few months into this trial run, it was still my habit. Other worshippers clumped by the simple wooden doors, chitchatting. *How are your tomatoes this year? Did you bring your bulgur salad for the potluck?* They wore ungelled hair, unironed skirts, and Mondale/Ferraro pins rusty with age. There were no stretch jeans or bleached hair or exposed midriffs, no Latinos far as I could tell. The few Black folks in the group seemed at ease with the frump. Mine was the gait of apologetic tourist. Pay me no mind, just looking. They demanded nothing of me—not a name, affiliation, or reason for attendance. They offered just enough eye contact to communicate that I could come or go with ease. But my shyness remained no matter how many meetings attended, and I rushed in and out, avoiding the commitment a hello might imply. Still, Meeting for Worship became habit. To a Joplin-playing poetry-writing child of volume elevens, silent worship might imply rebellion. Quite the opposite. Unvoiced contemplation was a skill learned at five, when mom led me out back and whispered god's name in Spanish, far from dad's ears. The quiet made me come alive. Zipping my lips meant swallowing my contradictions and confusions, guarding the flavor for only myself.

The brick building was an aged structure in a city of old things. Its wood shutters and plain footprint spoke of modesty. Shallow tides of light dappled the walls. The window frames held bumpy glass of a century prior, so that even the sun felt old in that room. It was a calm place, simply appointed, with unadorned benches in semicircle formation. The dull mahogany shimmered only at the armrests, shined by all those repeated grips to stand up or sit down. Soundproofing was of little concern when the structure was built, so our silence was accompanied by the dull music of 15th and Cherry Streets. A hissing bus, a cooing dove.

For an hour I sat amongst unassuming strangers. There was no leader or moderator, no Bible or hymnal. There were only these benches and this quiet now, an open space into which the spirit might enter. Occasionally someone stood to decry the Gulf War or sing "Amazing Grace" or offer ecumenical analysis of *Thelma & Louise*. Some meetings were talky, others proceeded without testimony. Some folks were less animated than Charlie

Brown's faceless teacher. Some wept quietly, or screamed. Others stood in rapture.

When it came to prayer, I was a novice. Should I ask god for a dance, like the prom-going teens in John Hughes flicks? The room's silence seemed profound from without but in the clatter of my brain felt mundane. *Think of nothing for ten minutes,* I told myself, and soon my watch's progress infuriated me, the second hand a slow-motion laugh. I remembered a few nonadjacent Ginsberg lines. *I saw the best minds of my generation / America I'm putting my queer shoulder to the wheel.* They played on loop, a mantra of misquotes. Next thing I knew, the carpet's diamond pattern grabbed my attention. *Focus, Quiara.* I needed a directive, a compass, a map. I tried remembering mom's Spanish prayers from the horse farm. Words surfaced—*tierra, pecho, creator, great spirit*—but no whole prayers. Mom's Orishas and ancestral guides, her full house of spirits, eluded me on that old wood bench. With each failure to tap into her cool divine current, my frustration coiled and glowed. The more I pondered life, the more bewildered I grew, a stranger to all I had seen, a fraud who went god shopping in Center City though the divine sat in my sunroom and by my front door. Why had mom shut me out since the horse farm? Why had she abandoned me, tradition-less, in pursuit of her gift? Was there not space for two on her path? Was my Spanish too shaky for any practical conversation with babalaos? Was I too white for the Afro-Caribbean river to roar in me? Was I too constant a reminder of my dad, who had disavowed spirits and scorned religion? *God is the opiate of the masses.* His old declaration thrummed at my organs. *No no no!* my original response roared. And I remembered that time on the hilltop, overlooking the cows, when mom asked if spirits had ever visited me. How tenderly she had masked her disappointment when I answered no. Was I a disappointment? Not the kind that stems from misdeed, for she sang to me daily of her pride. My grades, my Chopin, my latest in the lit mag. Those earned me kisses and songs of admiration. Instead, did something at my core disappoint mom? Some ingrained selfhood guaranteeing her displeasure would stick forever? And I finally let loose the thought I hated thinking, tired and obvious as it was, and unresolved as it would remain. Was I not Puerto Rican enough? The next thought was new. Was mom not Puerto Rican enough? Had years in Philly resulted in her own selfhood slipping away, rendering my halfness an abrasion in her migrant wound?

Puerto Rico. Its vistas stretched before me. I could finally imagine them because I had visited at last, thanks to Pop. Plunged headfirst into Luquillo Beach's turquoise waves. Tasted calabaza ice cream from los chinos. Seen the cement house her papi built and the farm across the road, which had become a nunnery. The images soothed me, pulled me toward a focused silence. And within that softer place, my knee began to tremble. No sooner had I stilled it than the shaking moved to my shoulders, stronger. Then my knees and shoulders quaked together, joined by my jaw, and I heard the rush of blood through my heart's chambers. I stood. *My mom and stepfather took me to Puerto Rico.* I was now both speaker and listener. *My mom and stepfather took me to Puerto Rico, and we were driving in the mountains. . . .*

We had been in Puerto Rico a week—me, mom, and Pop. We had double-parked by the highway for roadside bacalaitos. We had braved Viejo San Juan's weekend traffic so mom and Pop could play blackjack. We had hooked around to Piñones, chewing ensalada de pulpo as sandflies bit our ankles. And spent a day down south in the bone-dry Ponce heat. The mountain roads were different, an adventure unto themselves. Blind turns fed you, head-on, into school buses or wild horses ridden bareback. Last-second swerving was crucial, horn honks a matter of survival. Cars, trucks, stray dogs, and roosters formed two-way traffic on one-lane switchbacks. No barrier marked the edge or kept you on the road. "Suave, Papi! Suave!" mom cried, which he found hilarious. "Negra ya! Is this my turnoff?" Looking out the window, I saw no off-ramp at all, only a plunging drop over a cliff. It was barely afternoon and they had visited two open-air bars. Pop was tipsy, lurching cliffward. After the third bar mom took the wheel. To mitigate her own tipsiness (she kept up with Pop one beer to his three), mom dedicated one foot to the brake and one to the gas. The ride grew more sickening, what with stopping short and hiccupping on. My head all but came loose and bounced away. My eyes were rolling like Mega Millions ping-pongs. "Where are we going?" I muttered, semiconscious and miserable. "Here!" Pop laughed, stretching his arms wide. "Be here now!" Opening the window brought some relief. Gulp down that mountain air, taste its crisp citrus dew. All that greenery, a verdant drape, as if the island were a king who wore these mountains for robes. "Mira, Sedo, hay cocos frescos!" and I nearly fucking died—another stop—as she pulled into a roadside ditch. A folding table's sparse inventory included a few green coconuts and unlabeled bottles of hot sauce and honey. Mom bought everything. A machete swooshed through the air and voilà, the huge seed arrived in my palms with a straw. Abuela had told me of her old machete, how she'd used it to scare off burglars and bad guys. But I'd never seen one in use. Certain a revelation awaited me, instead cloying lukewarm liquid filled my mouth. I hated the flavor. Back in the car I cranked the window down, waiting for the coconut water to reappear any moment, all over the backseat.

When we reached a flat wide stretch of road, mom's driving slowed. She stopped, scanning the road, did a three-point turn. Finally, we pulled over. There was nothing around. Just an uncovered drain hole in the derelict road and a mud puddle that threatened to overtake the drain. Knee-high wild grass stretched to the horizon. A white cement structure was either a kiosk or modest home, before which sat an old man in a sun-faded beach chair. A loud wind blew as mom and Pop questioned him. "No hay boletos, no hay que pagar." The wind further muffled his naturally gentle voice. "Camina por allá," he said. Mom glanced at Pop, wary. It had been different last time, but that was in her childhood. The man insisted. When mom pressed a ten into his palm, he cried a little and clasped her hands, saying he only took it out of sheer necessity.

Wild grass sliced my shins. The dense mountain greenery had given way to stony, airy terrain. The breeze whipped, slapping our faces with its strong flat palm. As the wild grass shortened to crabgrass, the rocky ground became so eroded and sharp it poked through my rubber soles. Mom grew nervous. "They're coming up soon! Sedo, hold Quiara's hand! Cuidao!" She proceeded no further, boycotting our progress. "Turn around, Papi! Nos vamos! It's too powerful! The wind is too strong!" Pop waved her off. "Ya Negra, quieta!" And then the ocean appeared, way down below. We were atop a seaside cliff. Pop grabbed my elbow. I'd almost fallen into the thing. A hole in the rock, wide as an elevator shaft, shot straight down, no end in sight. The darkness swallowed Pop's flashlight beam. "Do you see it yet?" he asked. My eyes scanned the algae and lichen blanketing the cave walls. Slowly, a shape came into view. Tall as I was, carved in thick outlines. A sun. Its rounded beams hummed with energy. A second petroglyph whispered into sight and now a tapestry of carvings revealed themselves. The glyphs were large, their manifold forms bursting with testimony, all bearing witness to the natural world. There were animals and babies. Spiral shapes evoked hurricanes and waves. The carvings huddled together, their proximity purposeful. This was a book. Or an altar. Perhaps both.

Many old texts had found their way to my hands. *Hamlet, Romeo and Juliet, Death of a Salesman, Animal Farm.* But those were all reprints. Here was a first edition. A cliff-size ledger, immortalized in stone. A Taíno assertion that the sun ought to be recorded. Giver of life, opener of paths, the trickster sun that can also burn—the shapes were survival and resilience, paradox and reverence, knowledge and explanation. Here was Boriken before empire, before crucifix, gunpowder, or smallpox and maybe before English or Spanish. Here was the way Taínos spent their time: carving the numinous world in stone. They were writers.

Then Pop pulled me to another. Caves and carvings were everywhere. Mom screamed from a distance. "Step back from the edge! It'll suck you like a vacuum! Sedo, hold her hand!" She knew by how I teetered. Each cavern was a geological esophagus. *Swallow me,* I thought, eyelids closing, wind wailing at my shoulder blades.

I reached out to strangers on nearby benches. "Thank you for sharing," they said, shaking my hand. Meeting for Worship was over but I was still jangled by the quaking. Embarrassment lingered. While testifying, I had fallen silent here and there, unable to still my clattering jaw, or to annunciate clearly past the tumult in my throat. As folks meandered across the hall for potluck, I escaped into the Sunday morning sun. The brick courtyard and autumn sky, the yellow chestnut leaves, were welcome anchors back to the material world.

It had been, perhaps, too much god—being overcome by spirit, my pulse surrendering the reins. The sensation still rippled with some aftershocks and tremors. As I walked south on 15th, footsteps wobbly, adrenaline forced my progress until I remembered mom-not-mom at the table—speaking in tongues, transformed by possession. I nearly laughed aloud. Had I been like her for one deviant inexplicable moment? The city's colors and sounds throbbed around me, and I felt startlingly present.

I now craved something atheist, even vulgar. It was 11:35 A.M. If I hustled, I'd make it to the museum in time. I walked past the Logan Circle fountains, whose spray cooled my skin. The wide promenade of the Benjamin Franklin Parkway cut diagonally beneath a corridor of flags. The Rocky Balboa steps welcomed me up and the guard waved me through. Free. No sooner had I begun attending Quaker meeting than I had also become a weekly visitor to the Philadelphia Museum of Art. Admission was free before noon.

I sped through the Early American galleries, in austere shades of red and gray. Gold-leaf frames, hand-turned Chippendales, pasty old patriarchs immortalized in oil. Just beyond, at the building's outer reaches, the contemporary wing was a white-walled affair. The ceilings were vaulted like Catholic churches but undecorated, in contemporary minimalist style. Sunlight reflected on concrete floors. Familiar works formed a receiving line. The

Warhols, ironic and cheeky. I poked my head into the grotto of Cy Twombly's *Iliam* series to see if I had started liking it since last time. Nope. The lithe Brancusis curved hello. The blue Frank Stella was a geometric splat. Two or three breaths before the Chuck Close thumbprints—a few moments in short range, a few squinting from a distance. A moment of reverie before Richard Long's *Limestone Circle.*

My destination was the Duchamps. They beckoned like a bare shoulder at the edge of a dream. There was the wooden stool with the bike wheel—rebellious. There was the cubist nude descending a staircase—kinetic. The *Boîte-en-valise* was a sinister curio box. There was repurposed junk—a bottle rack, an infamous urinal. The *Female Fig Leaf* was a bronze square of innuendo. Duchamp even deigned to create representational art— a chocolate grinder with three drums in rotation, a portrait of Adam and Eve as blotchy humanoids with huge craniums. Duchamp was a swiss army knife, an attic of ideas, a flea market of art jokes. Ribald as a bathroom stall punchline, with the abandon of a master who'd earned every rebellion. Though I disliked Duchamp's sarcasm, I sensed freedom in how he treated virtuosity as a stepping-stone to something less rigid.

Tucked within the Duchamps, Room 182 was hidden in the back, the farthest gallery from the museum's front entrance. Last stop, folks. Nothing left to see. It had the footprint of a coat closet and, without windows or lightbulbs, was unlit. Empty as a shoebox. No art on the walls or placard. You might miss the thing altogether. But if you stepped inside long enough, your eyes would adjust to see a wooden door at the end. Primitive, hewn of wide-planked hardwood. A barn door, perhaps. Or a portal to a torture chamber. Hard to tell. Two peepholes glowed, beckoning. I pressed my nose to the wood. A sliver of life-size diorama came into view. A pastoral scene, lifelike, of a nude white woman on the ground, legs akimbo. Her hairless labia were asymmetrical, possibly deformed. One visible breast sagged like a small pouch of rice. The other breast, along with her face, was out of view. I angled and contorted, tiptoeing, pressing one eye then the other, trying to glimpse her face. No luck. This nude woman—whether resting after sex, or death-pale after murder—lay atop a bed of twigs like some X-rated Jesus in the manger. The oil lamp she clutched had a still-lit flame, so whatever had befallen her was recent. If she was dead, how was she still holding the lamp? If she was alive, why did she splay like that, so prone?

Étant donnés was nostalgic tableau, crime scene, rape fantasy, dime-store kitsch, and postcoital ciggy, all in one half-glimpse. Denying her face was the work's grotesque thesis. Her warped vagina, front and center, was the only identity the artist imbued on her. I stared and raged and fumed and fantasized. I glanced behind me to see if anyone was waiting. Then I looked some more. It wasn't just the vagina that drew me. The Perez women strolled around butt naked all the time. Cellulite, saggy tits, bushes—old hat to me. What really shocked about *Étant donnés* was that the cunt was all she got. Not a face, name, or story. It was a complete and effective violence, this omission of person-hood. I knew Duchamp had staged, with precision, my warring impulse to see and turn away. It was the same game I now played with my own life: peeking further for clues, thrilling at some an-swers, cowering before others. I looked some more.

15

LUKUMÍ THRONES

After repeated visits, Duchamp was another language I could decode. The autumnal palette that made the landscape serene, the pastoral motifs that normalized a predatory gaze, the total control over the viewer's experience, including the illusion of having discovered the unmarked room. Also, how Duchamp harnessed innuendo, injecting perversion into the viewer's brain. Duchamp made the gross thoughts your fault, not his. My burgeoning multilingualism felt pretty satisfying. I knew English, halting Spanish, and advanced conversational Duchamp. Plus more. On that sweet upright from Pop, I gained facility with Bach inventions, Chopin nocturnes, Mozart sonatas. Wrong notes, train-wreck fingerings, and botched dynamics were de rigueur at first but diminished with each practice, until mistakes grew infrequent. With enough repetition, I wasn't playing single notes at all, but phrases, then movements, and finally forms. At Central, I memorized sixteen lines of *The Canterbury Tales* five minutes before the oral exam. Nailed it. My emergent superpower, an increasing fluency in Western Canon, brought exhilaration and comfort because if you're fluent in a language, there's a place you belong.

But I hungered to decode my own home, to make it my center of belonging. To understand mom's many tongues and therefore close the distance between myself and the people I loved and the people I was losing—most of all my mother. I wanted to arm myself against Western Art's easy idiom, to master a more complex language, one that richly described my world. There was installation art in my living room but the Western Canon didn't provide vocab for all that. And while mom had many gifts, explaining stuff was not one. In fact, she seemed generally suspicious of explanations—like intuiting life's shit on your own was the only path to understanding. Her silent industry implied that, to her, explanations were surface whereas observation promised revelation.

During latchkey evenings, if homework was complete and Mozart was practiced and mom and Pop were out rallying with Philly's Latino leadership, I would stand before mom's altars. Study them. Memorize the items. Notice the air pressure in the room. Even touch the stuff. Once I ate a piece of the Ibeyi's candy (it was stale). Once I lifted the lid from Olokun's blue jar (inside was something dark and moist). Once I reached into Ogun's tiny cauldron and touched a bone. Once I dragged chair to cabinet and reached for Osun's silver chalice, tapping a pendulum bell. The altars changed frequently. Different Orisha were fed throughout the year, and on mom's Ocha birthday— her anniversary of consecration—they all came out at once. Repeat visits were rewarded, new discoveries awaited. Some altars were small—a few doodads tucked in a corner. Like Eleguá in the entrance foyer. Our front door never fully opened because he nestled just inside the hinges. His was a diminutive, primitive altar. A cement-filled conch shell for a head. His cowry eyes squinted, his cowry lips pursed. Eleguá sat on a clay dish, the kind meant for a houseplant. There were some pennies and pinwheel mints. A shot of espresso. Perhaps a candle. Eleguá tended the pathways, guarded the crossroads, gave permission for the ceremony to begin. Small yet mighty, Eleguá was the trickster. I was certain his cowry eyes penetrated my soul, and I observed him sideways or from behind to avoid his gaze. A few steps beyond, by the living room sideboard, lived los Egun, the ancestors. Mama Francisca was a hand-sewn doll with jet-black skin. She was mom's spirit guide, and fresh pompom flowers filled her vase.

Farther back, unseen from the main living space, the sunroom altar stretched floor to ceiling. A portal to a universe. Sheaths of fabric created backdrops, canopy valances draped from the ceiling, and its sheer scale was a marvel to behold. Clear valises of water refracted the light, candles rested on the floor. Rattles, bells, and cascarilla chalk sat alongside one another. Abundant fruit piled on straw mats. Pomegranates, plantains, cantaloupes. There were coconuts caked in thick powdered eggshell and oranges oozing with honey and cinnamon. El trono. The throne. It was an apt and accurate name for the place the Orisha sat. Each deity had impressive beaded mazos and embroidered paños in their specific color. Changó's warrior lightning was assertive red. Yemayá's ocean was motherly blue. Oshun's sensual river radiated gold and amber. Each had a dedicated urn housing its secrets, fed and nourished in hush-hush ceremonies. Together, the Orisha appeared totemic and diverse.

Atop a shelf were portraits of deceased family members. That's how I knew of Juan Perez's strong brow and arrowhead nose pointing downward, because of the small watercolor of mom's papi on her altar. It was the sole surviving image of my ancestor. A wealth of statuary stood on pedestals. Plaster Indian busts, Catholic figurines with black and white faces, and African carvings, each radiating a distinct vibe. Babalú Aye was an aria of trauma, the biggest statue, but hardly the fanciest, and less prominently placed than Changó and Obatalá. His tattered rags showed a meadow of open sores. Dogs gathered at his crutches, licking the cuts. You could count his ribs. It reminded me of Big Vic after he grew skeletal and got what looked like skinned knees all over his face. How had Babalú Aye predicted, centuries prior, that SIDA would take down my older cuz?

Over months and then years, the altars taught me how to pay attention and see them. On one occasion, I'd gotten so proficient at Chopin's Nocturne in B-flat Minor that I could play it eyes closed, without minding the fingering or keys. This allowed me to plunge into the song's eerie melancholy, and playing it left me emotionally raw, missing dad so hard it hurt. With arm hairs raised and tears falling, I fled to the sunroom. The estera, the straw prostration mat, was rolled up in a corner. Just as I had seen mom do, I unrolled it, lay belly-down before the Orisha, and shook the rattle. Just as I had heard mom do, I called out in a loud intentional voice, like an arrow shot toward the sky. "Eleguá!" I called out. "Olodumare! Babalú Aye! Changó! Oshun! Obatalá! Ogun! Oyá! Thank you!" I returned the mat to its proper place, then continued practicing Chopin. The Orisha now lingered on my fingers, dancing with the nocturne, and I sensed the dawn of a real bilingualism, appropriate and specific to me.

Mom was a decadent warrior seamstress. She knew every fabric store on South 4th Street (Italian-owned) and the Main Line (WASP-run). The proprietors saw in her a kindred soul, won over by her textile acumen. They squirreled away fabrics till her next visit. Together mom and I scoured hundreds of bauble drawers to find the perfect silver fringe for Yemayá or the best gingham button for Obatalá. We searched cubbies of trim, boxes of tassels. We unspooled ribbon to make Oshun glow. The day mom found Changó's red satin, the cashier measured four gleaming yards and sliced it with professional scissors—a scrumptious, clean cut. Then he folded the satin loosely, so as not to crease it, and carefully slid it in a paper bag. Mom could get lost in those fabric shops, same as me at the Free Library. Shelves stacked floor to ceiling beckoned to ardent believers. En route to finding whatever she had come for, a different treasure might tap her shoulder: "Take me home." That's how she found Obatalá's opal sequins. That's how I found Allen Ginsberg. He had been shelved, on accident, beside Eugene O'Neill and joined the altar of my backpack.

Mom sewed her paños late into the night. Thread spools clicked as she loaded new colors and her Singer's kick-drum pedal stirred me awake. "Mom's home, she's back from work," the sewing machine said. Lulled by the clatter, I returned to dreaming. Hours later she'd still be sewing, such was her devotion. The gift that stirred when mom was five had been advanced through rigor, discipline, and study. I had visited the homes of other babalaos and santeros, seen their living room altars—some simple, some fancy. But mom's were of the most magnificent order. Each detail chosen with reverence and surrender. Animal sacrifice was traumatic, spirit possession was disturbing, but the splendor in our sunroom merited contemplation. Only a fool would scoff, and a system that credited Duchamp's visual acumen above mom's was no ally, I knew. Mom had mastered a symbolic language. I was not yet there with Chopin. But I was trying.

16

SILENCE=DEATH

Once upon a time Vivi was like Cuca, Nuchi, and Flor—another big cousin in the cosmology, almost-woman to my tater tot awe. Huddled together on Abuela's steps, Vivi and co were a Mount Rushmore of cool. They ordered me to acquire chicle from the bodega and chipped in a dime for Now and Later payment. When my early-bloomer feet grew to size sevens, Vivi laced me into her skates and hollered about oncoming sidewalk cracks. They all had inner-sanctum ways of lacing off-brand kicks—spiral and macramé that elevated bargains to street art. They never revealed methods, boosting my admiration through mystery.

Season by season they peeled away. For Cuca, it was college. For Nuchi, it was having kids young. For Flor, the constant chase of the next bump or line. It's hard to remember why Vivi peeled away, but the stoop hangs were a long-past memory when she took that bullet. Vivi disappeared into the witness protection program and mom had nothing further to say on the subject. Not how it went down nor who pulled the trigger. *Wrong place, wrong time. Case closed.* The bullet entered Vivi's skull and never left and her survival, mom said, held the grace of one crucial centimeter.

Despite the awkwardness of a few years apart, when Vivi resurfaced on Abuela's porch my relief was real. "Guess who's out front?" mom asked. And through the banged-up door I saw an adult who half resembled the stoop girl. "Vivi!" Running outside to say hello, our greetings caught between gears. Did our old multistep high-five make sense now? A cheek kiss became the compromise. "Is that Qui Qui?" Her volume was brash, over-projected, and I wondered if her hearing had been affected by the gunshot. Vivi's face had filled out. Her jaw was wider now, almost square. There was enough gel in her cropped curls to repair a broken bowl, and her eyelids were painted thickest electric blue. Before, she had been an au naturel stoop kid. She removed her sunglasses, inviting me to look. Her eyes wandered. Blue contact lenses did their best to cover milky-white irises. Before, she had the same brown eyes as the rest of us.

Our conversation took place on Abuela's threshold. We were neither outside nor in, and I propped the door with my foot the whole time. It was as though we couldn't choose who we were now, where we belonged. Our small talk was clipped and her loudness jangled me. We tried to fill awkward silences without seeming overeager. What tapes was I listening to, what was my favorite subject in school? Did I still play piano? I returned the courtesy. Where was she living now? How was Florida? I heard rumors that she'd gotten a bachelor's. "Yup, top of my class! They do all the textbooks in braille, or give you an assistant to read it aloud to you. Gurl, I'm fixing to get my PhD next!" Finally, she asked if I wanted to talk about the incident.

"How fast did it happen?"

"The bullet blinded me instantly."

"Was anyone with you?"

"Nope. It was a hit and they waited till I was alone. I was lay-ing for a long time in a pool of my blood." An accidental assassi-nation, Vivi explained. Dealers had a hit on some fulana de tal with the same name.

"Do you believe in miracles, Qui Qui?" The question was far too chipper, with the rehearsed lure of a sales pitch. When I didn't respond, she tried again. "Do you believe in miracles, Qui Qui? Because we're not supposed to be having this conversation. I felt the gun on my skin, that's how close they held it. Then left me for dead in my own blood. The surgeons couldn't remove the bullet, so it's stuck in me forever. Want to feel?" She guided my finger to a small round bald patch above her ear, smooth as a penny's edge. I hugged Vivi. Burying my face in her crunchy hair, I could almost taste the bullet's metallic scent. It all seemed the opposite of miraculous, but Vivi was floating, inches off the ground. She began again. "Do you believe in the Bible, Qui Qui?" I was unsure what she knew of mom's Lukumí path. Puerto Ri-cans could be judgmental as fuck—Catholics and converts of fair complexion often hated on Ifá with particular finesse. (*Oh no, we're not that kind of Puerto Rican!*) And while I had begun attend-ing Quaker meeting, admitting it might come off as affiliation—I wasn't there yet. Smiling, Vivi awaited a reply. My silence suf-ficed. "Whaaaa? You mean to tell me you don't believe in the oldest book ever written? Gurl . . . !" Lowering to a sultry bari-tone, she assured me the pages were a riot of drama and intrigue. There was incest, murder, revenge—and wasn't I a literature and drama fiend? "You've got to read it, Qui Qui! Te juro, it's a page-turner!" Returned to me in her fresh-scarred incarnation, my cousin hadn't lost her wit.

One more notch on the tally: Vivi was the latest bead in a necklace strung with disappearance and decline. Roll call at family affairs grew threadbare. Maybe best to ignore who was missing any given holiday and why. Best to hope they were stuck on the couch, barrio-depressed, or that their secondhand tire blew out on the expressway. Alone, each case study's dull ache allowed room for a joke, like Vivi's literary sales pitch. But seen as a whole, the grim panorama began churning my stomach acid. During Wednesday assemblies at school I began to lip-synch "I pledge allegiance." I wasn't bold enough to stop right-hand-to-hearting, but I was pissed, too grief-swamped for the actual pledge.

Had we done something to merit the havoc? Or had the vampire crossed our threshold uninvited? I'd visited enough Center City friends, spent enough time with dad in the burbs to know that this shitstorm, this run-on tragedy, was not everyone's America. Seeing my cousins suffer was anguish enough. Seeing the disproportionality slayed me.

"Are we cursed?" The question had looped in my mind once the Perez deaths gained steam, but I'd never voiced it. Mom and I were driving home from Abuela's, Vivi's miraculous return weighing so heavy that potholes double-jangled the car. Mom shot me this look like *why ask shit your gut already knows?* Like *why conjure vast complexities when I'm merging onto 676?* She rattled off vaguest mumblings about certain of her sisters who fucked their karma, about children inheriting parents' cursed fates. It was vague, purposefully diversionary, and all she could muster. Maybe mom felt the language problem, too—that no words could purge the maelstrom, no matter how fluent the speaker or how armed with facts. She'd spoken on Latina medical crises at Harrisburg's dome, served on mayor-appointed health boards, so she knew the disproportionality down to hospital intake rates, blocks hit hardest, deaths per capita. But she didn't say any of that. All she said was, "It's worse being the titi. I changed Vivi's pampers, Quiara. You never changed her pampers. Or Mary Lou's. Or Big Vic's. Or . . ." And the outspoken advocate, the bang-down-the-FOP hell-raising megaphone, fell into silence because when the zeitgeist sits on your doorstep, what good are words?

In October 1992, the AIDS Quilt went to Washington. I carried my dinner up to mom's room, where the only TV was, and ate on the floor as Channel 10 covered the story. Grave-size rectangles of fabric stretched from the Washington Monument all the way to the National Mall. My family's secret was a countrywide spectacle. What relief, what terrible grave solace: it wasn't just us. I was not alone. For the first time, nightly news became my habit. I began reading Pop's turned-over *Inquirer,* listening to KYW, using microfiche to explore periodicals archives and out-of-prints. There was mounting proof that others were bereft. Evidence that my cousins had a context beyond hemmed-in North Philly. Giovanni's Room, a queer bookstore on Pine Street, became a regular after-school stop, and though I couldn't afford the stock, they had beanbag chairs and lax browsing policies. It was there I first read Audre Lorde and *Bitch* magazine. I skipped lunch and bought a *No Glove, No Love* pin, a *Silence=Death* necklace. At Central, I became president of Peer Education Against Contracting HIV (PEACH), an after-school extracurricular comprised of zealots and the grief-stricken. The Red Cross trained us in STD prevention and we marched into health classes rolling condoms onto bananas. Doing dental dam and vaginal sponge show-and-tell was a great bit of sanctioned classroom rebellion. My PEACH friends told me of fallen family members. We raised three thousand bucks for the AIDS Walk and marched wall-to-wall with all hues of Philly queer folk and allies. We chanted in unison, no shame or apology, with joy and purgation. After completing all twelve kilometers, we headed for the water coolers at Eakins Oval. The small circular park faced the art museum steps where years earlier mom had let slip the possibility of Guillo having AIDS. My PEACH friends and I removed our sneakers and peeled socks from tired feet. Some were hippies with attendant foot funk, others were rich kids with new socks and fresh Pumas, still others athletes with sole-worn trainers. We let the autumn air caress our tired feet. In the wake of loss, we formed a barefooted community.

I had this big idea to organize a Central High AIDS Quilt. Central had twenty-four hundred students, so the pool was big. No way, statistically, it was just me and the PEACH kids who'd been touched by the virus. After a few bake sales, I purchased a garbage bag of felt scraps from one of mom's fabric stores. Everyone in PEACH had to bring in sharpies, glue, scissors, sequins, buttons, yarn. "Search your parents' junk drawers," I instructed. Pipe cleaners? Cool. Feathers? Game on. Come lunch hour, we piled all the stuff on the floor. People stopped, asked what was up. "If you lost a loved one to AIDS, honor them by making a square." For a week, people came and worked on their patches every day. Twenty squares or so. Each one with a name. All sorts of colors. Arranged into a grid pattern, the vibrant fab-

rics resembled mom's altars. Trimming, scraps, and baubles stolen from her closet found new life. There was a little Ogun in that
quilt, a dash of Babalú Aye.

Problem was, none of us sewed. So how would we combine
the squares into a quilt? Until we found a seamstress, all we had
were AIDS patches. Mom was to a needle what Ben Franklin was
to a key, but she worked nonstop, was perpetually exhausted, and
the family ethos was that I took care of myself—homework,
commute, piano, activities, all on me. The notion of parents
helping with a school project was foreign, a sitcom contrivance.
My adolescence had become pretty unsupervised, so that some
days I hardly saw mom at all. But even more than that, I was
afraid to show her the felt squares with Guillo's and Big Vic's and
Tico's names. Our family silence around HIV felt consecrated, a
matter of honor, the only part of our narrative we controlled.
Being the megaphone felt risky. I worried that, to mom, these
fabric squares might brand me a turncoat. En el barrio, the shame
and silence surrounding AIDS was stunning, complete. I knew a
guy, a neighbor of Abuela's, who thought if you go in a room
with the disease, you get the disease. He skipped his own brother's funeral, and they had been close. And yet, hadn't lack of in-
formation caused the regret he carried with him and spoke about
for years? In telling our family's story, I sensed, for the first time,
the possibility of healing, of forging love from affliction's ore.

The Central High AIDS Quilt never got sewn together. Disconnected felt squares, that's the best we could do. The principal
gave us a bulletin board and we thumbtacked them in a grid,
where they hung for a few months. The last day of school we
packed them alongside our Red Cross manuals and leftover rainbow condoms in a closet. Returning to Central years later for an
alumni event, I learned that the fall after my graduation, PEACH

was disbanded by the Board of Ed. As ordered by the chancellor, after tremendous parental pressure, our archives and club materials had been disposed of immediately.

Tico's was the loss mom and I spoke of least because while living with us, he became one of us. There was no emotional distance caused by separate homes. He was my second or third cousin who left PR to rake it in as my live-in nanny. I was a teen and required no childcare—mom was just helping a family member who needed cash and a change of scene. That side of the family was conservative, mom explained, and Tico deserved a place to spread his wings, *tu me entiendes?* A half-generation older than me, Tico was a party on legs. Despite being in his early twenties, he was a kid at heart with an easy laugh. The West Coast Video guys were on a first-name basis with Tico and provided a good opportunity for his wobbly English to improve daily. We scoured every coin jar and pants pocket in the house until the $2.99 rental fee was acquired. Tico's preferred genre was stand-up, best for mastering American slang. *Eddie Murphy: Raw* and *Whoopi Goldberg: Direct from Broadway* became English 101. I sat by the VCR and pressed pause on command. Then he would repeat some phrase by Eddie or Whoopi and go, "Yes? Did I say it good?" Tempestt Bledsoe's workout became an obsession. I owned the VHS, so if we couldn't cobble $2.99, aerobics was our backup. With a chestnut fro and slender-cut physique, Tico actually resembled Richard Simmons. Except his tan didn't come out a can. Sometimes we raided mom's closet and drawers to improvise trendy workout gear, like slipping on a bathing suit over tight jeans. And sometimes we straight-up turned my bed into a trampoline, bouncing for hours, trying not to hit our heads on the ceiling light. "Can you do a back flip?" he asked. "No!" I shouted. Then he looped his feet over his head, nailing a perfect-ten landing.

Tico, like myself, ate a lot. "Who needs plates?" That was his motto. So, two spoons dipped into the applesauce jar. Two forks plunged in the SpaghettiOs can. A full box of Kix was tossed, one by one, into open mouths. And when the pantry was low, Tico got creative. We studied the various microwave times for Cheez Whiz to melt, bubble, char, and explode. Once we ate ramen off the floor with our toes, laughing till broth ran out our noses. Mom had no clue of our antics because Tico was an exceptional cleaner. Her clothes were always returned to their drawers, the kitchen floor wiped to sparkling, Cheez Whiz scraped from the microwave ceiling.

He wasn't out—gay was slander en el barrio, gay put a target on your head—but Tico was at ease in his skin. He didn't temper his mannerisms or modulate them. That made him tougher than all the machos combined—his unwillingness to front, how he didn't mask selfhood.

One day after school, Tico wasn't home. Next day, same thing. No word, no note, no explanation. After a few weeks our panic subsided—he wasn't a child after all, he could take care of himself. "He's young, he probably wanted to go have fun," mom said. "Anyway, he was too vibrant to be stuck working as a nanny."

Months later, the New York coroner called. Tico had joined a pilgrimage of infected men who found, in New York, a place to die shame-free. When the test results said positive, Tico peaced out. Later we heard, through the grapevine, he died alone on a mattress on the floor. What's worse than a funeral, I discovered, is none at all. Mom was never given the chance to accept him (since he hadn't come out or shared his diagnosis) nor to mourn him. Our family's and community's silence surrounding his queerness was all the info he needed. It literally equaled death.

Mom held an umbrella above me as I stood at a podium before City Hall. It was a rain-drenched October morning, World AIDS Day, and I'd won *The Philadelphia Inquirer*'s student essay contest. Earlier that week, my speech had been published as a short-form essay. There was my name, on the *Inquirer*'s op-ed page. A published author at fifteen. Mom was making coffee on the stovetop when I handed her the newspaper. She read in silence. Then looked up from the paper in tears. "You used your middle name," she said.

The day of the speech the emcee asked about pronunciation. "Quiara Alegría Hudes," she said correctly, and I took my place at the podium. My remarks would precede the mayor's, which Pop declared a big deal, so he thumbed out some fifties for an outfit and haircut. In the end, my new look was sheathed beneath a single-use poncho. Fat raindrops fell in sheets. My pages grew damp and the ink began to blur so that mom had to adjust the umbrella above the paper. I looked out at the crowd. It was hardly the hundreds they'd prepared me for. Fifty or so people stood around the plaza, shielding their hair with newspapers and briefcases. Folks don't come to World AIDS Day out of curiosity. They come because HIV was their reaper, too. With a respectful hush, they waited for me to begin. "Good morning," I said, and the words entered a vacuum, then bounced back at me with eons of delay. Dear god, I thought, just let them hear me. Slowly and loudly, I began. I named Tico. I named Big Vic. I described a brief memory of each, eulogizing them in fondness. It had been harder to write about Guillo. Rumors of his temper made me avoid him in early childhood, and I'd never spent quality time with the man. Still, if I didn't have an anecdote about Guillo, I could name him.

Because of the umbrellas no one could clap, so when the speech was done I just waited in silence, then accompanied mom to a wet bench upstage. As the mayor took the podium, mom leaned my way. Her hot whisper stood out in the October chill. "I love your middle name," she said. "It's about time you bring it back. Because how can you name all those family members, Quiara, if you won't even name yourself?" Then she slipped her hand beneath my poncho. Her thumb stroked my closed fist over and over, as though my knuckles were rosary beads.

17

UNWRITTEN RECIPES

When I asked Abuela for cooking lessons, it was an excuse for one-on-one time, a way to hear her stories. As an oral historian, she came alive at the stovetop's blue flowering flame. Isn't that how cavemen did it? Told it all around the campfire? Anyway, cooking itself was my lesser concern. These lessons happened informally for my cousins, but I felt the need to make an appointment. To formally ask, thereby signaling my curiosity. Side dishes like serenata and sorullos could come in subsequent years but white rice was the ABCs, the 101. If you sprinkled pique on her grains, Abuela's arroz blanco was a satisfying meal. Her rice glistened, with a toothy bite. We settled on a Saturday but no particular time, so that when I arrived, she was just coming out of the shower. She had no qualms about nudity, but she sprang for her teeth as I came upstairs. Her uppers and lowers laughed in a water glass by the bed. After slipping them in, she grabbed the tortoiseshell comb: a hefty, wide-toothed thing with mother-of-pearl inlay at the handle. Unlike most of her stuff, this comb was no dollar-store purchase. Abuela sat naked on the edge of her bed, combing her hair in long, patient strokes. Though she didn't have much of it, each strand was thick and straight, and it cascaded down her shoulders, past her breasts, and over her belly like a brook's gentle waterfall, ending in a silver pool on her lap. In the end all those long strands were swirled into a bun no larger than a Dixie cup. It was rare to glimpse her hair down, because she cooked every day and had to protect it from the flames.

Then we headed toward the Bustelo can in the kitchen, and once coffee was ready, she began.

Step one: After measuring the desired number of handfuls, rinse the rice in a colander, picking out any stones.

I craved the accuracy of measuring cups but Abuela didn't own any. They lacked the intention that makes a meal burrow deep. A good dinner starts with a handful of dry rice. *Como asi,* she said. *Feel how I cup my palm.* When I touched Abuela's hand, I touched ten thousand yesterdays. Her skin felt like parchment: thin, smooth, and crackly. My hand was smaller, I said, hers was bigger. What is the exact amount of rice to put in? I asked. She just laughed. *Poor Qui Qui.*

How you cure the pot is important. Mom's old adage came to me. Stone masons could behold a city block with pride, thinking, *I cobbled those streets, I laid those bricks.* A good home cook could serve her neighbors and think, *I made this pot. It's cured by my hours in the kitchen.* Mom bragged relentlessly about her cookware's patina. She could afford new pots, but woman was loyal to the old. Abuela couldn't afford squat, and if she was proud of her oil-stained pots, she never let on. That's how it went from first generation to second. Workaday tools for Abuela became bragging points for her daughters.

Abuela was suspicious of my Spanish. No sooner had she launched into a story than she paused mid-tale and asked, "Repeat what I just said." She wasn't gonna waste a good climax on half-ass comprehension. So, I paid close attention and earned what I had come for. I memorized her sentences as she spoke them, ready to repeat whenever asked. Always mentally translating, filtering her history through English's roughness.

Obdulia Perez. An old-world name, bien highbrow. Born to a Spaniard who hated Spain and a Taína who shared the sentiment. Her parents both detested colonialism, albeit from flip sides of the coin. They lived in Lares, right next to Jayuya and Utuado, a regional hotbed of the underground independence movement. Obdulia's musician father and midwife mother often traveled for work. Perhaps participating in the island-wide resistance network. What is certain is that during a demonstration, the midwife's breast was injured. Either blown off entirely or partially grazed. Obdulia never saw the wound firsthand. Had it been El Grito de Lares, that historic day Puerto Ricans armed themselves against Spain? The timing was possible, but the revolution also spanned another fifty years. After El Grito, the whole region was on fire. Details of gory persecution abounded. Obdulia's family fled to Arecibo. Her parents grew afraid to even say "We come from Lares." A fear they instilled in their daughters, until the instinct to hide became ingrained.

In Arecibo, Obdulia and Ramona—notoriously beautiful

sisters—were nicknamed Las Españolas for their clear blue eyes and Canary Island roots. As a descriptor it was fine, but as a "compliment" it held colonial undertones, racist code: light-skinned Puerto Ricans jockeying for status, mentioning distant European origins. But Abuela was no parlor Boricua and the nickname La Española chose her, not the other way around. She married the most Taíno motherfucker in Arecibo. Juan Bautista Perez, aka Indio. Straightest profuse hair on his head, not a strand on his body, gorgeous square teeth: diente de pala. From his rich mahogany skin, mom and Titi Ginny got their trigueña hue, while the older sisters, Toña and Margie, were fair.

At thirty-two years old, Juan Perez was twice Obdulia's age. A respected laborer, the man was proud to a fault and was rumored to have a lover in every neighboring town. He was the kind of worker on his land by sunrise, harvesting the earth till sundown. The kind of laborer who, in the off season, headed to his second job at the power company. For years he hung electric wires on the streets so Arecibo could march into modernity. When he lost two fingers on the job and got disability, he asked for payment in land; his small farm expanded. Still, on weekends he set up shop on the roadside and sold carbón—handmade natural charcoal—dressed head to toe in white linen. In the early sixties, Obdulia left Juan Perez—the father of her five children—and Puerto Rico, the only island she'd known. She loaded four girls—two daughters, two adopted grandkids—on a plane for Los Bronx. There are many versions of why she left. In the simplest, which she told me as we plucked pebbles from hard rice, she discovered Juan Perez humping her cousin on the sofa.

·   ·   ·

"No!" my mom protests twenty-three years later while cooking rice in her fancy new kitchen. I'm only relaying the story her mom told me. "That's not what happened, Quiara."

"But that's what she said!" By this time Obdulia had long left the earth, and mom's cheap old caldero sat on an eight-burner chef's stove.

"Well, I don't know why she told you that," mom said. Her refusal to engage was uncharacteristically prudish but typically cagey. I mean, sofa sex? It at least merited discussion! Arecibo was a sweltering valley town. No one had electricity for fans, let alone AC. I imagined sweat-drenched bodies glistening like rice. I imagined Juan Perez thrusting, his lover seated on the sofa, knees skewed wide. Did they have plastic-covered cushions in PR, or were those a Philly thing? Had their sweat soaked the fabric? They surely must have fallen to the floor when Abuela discovered them, fumbled for zippers and belt buckles. But mom U-turned to her theory before another word was spoken on the topic.

Mom's benign version began when Toña, her older sister, developed a rare cancer. "Now, Toña was a kick-ass businesswoman. She had a gypsy cab and drove it any hour of the night. She was very successful for a woman in those times. So, she could pay for the best of the best. But even the top doctors in Arecibo couldn't identify the cancer. The real experts were in Nueva York. Bueno, she headed to Los Bronx. Mami was devastated. She had never been apart from her girls. And she couldn't take care of Toña during the treatment because she had to stay in Puerto Rico with us younger kids. Anyway, Toña was selected for an innovative clinical trial. Her health improved overnight. But months after the treatments ended, she remained. Mami begged her to return, pero her treatment had been outpatient so she spent all that free time finding new hustles, me oyes? She went crazy for the city. She wanted to stay and make more money than was possible in Puerto Rico. Entonces, Abuela was not gonna let her daughters be split up. So she brought us all to Nueva York. Verdad, Cuca?"

My older cousin was standing above the caldero "tasting" mom's rice out the pot. Cuca was one of the adopted grand-daughters on that original plane ride. She couldn't cook—not a grain of white rice or a piddling kidney bean—but Cuca was great company in the kitchen and did the dishes. "I mean, yes, that did happen with Toña," Cuca said, "but that's not why Abuela left."

Cuca's was my favorite version of how the Perez girls ended up in Philly. But I denied knowing the story because she'd tell it better if it was my first hearing. As Cuca spoke, mom grabbed the serving spoon and took a turn "tasting."

"Bueno, you know Titi Ginny was an athlete, right? And not some chippy-choppy sorta thing, she was the best of the best. Javelin and discus, those were her specialties. Verdad?" Mom nod-ded with a mouthful of rice. "By senior year, Ginny had beat every girls' and boys' record in Arecibo. Well, she heard there was a competition to go get Olympic training. The slots were limited, so it was a long shot, but Luis took her to San Juan for the competition."

"Wait, Luis, mom's older brother?" I had never met him. He had died while mom was pregnant with me, and she was so near my due date, the midwives forbade air travel. Mom never at-tended her older brother's funeral.

"Right," Cuca continued. "So, Luis took Ginny to the compe-tition in San Juan. It was very hush-hush. Because Papi was strict, he would've never let Ginny go. Ginny cut school and they went knowing they had to be back before dark, before their papi returned from the farm. Well, Ginny won each round. She kept getting passed to the next level. And it's getting later and Ginny and Luis were like, oh shit, what are we gonna do? They hadn't really thought through the timing. Way after dark, she was one of the last girls standing." And here, Cuca squeezed my arm for emphasis. "She was selected from hundreds to fly to the States for free summer training, and a potential spot on the Junior Olympic track team! And that's not all," Cuca said. Mom poured a glass of Cuca's favorite sweet moscato. Cuca sipped, then continued. "It gets better. La Universidad de San Juan Rio Piedras had sent coaches to watch the whole thing, like, for, como se dice, recruitment. They offered Ginny a full scholarship starting in the fall!"

I had never heard that part before. It was a moment of potential transformation for the family. Their first college degree. Obdulia had left school after second grade. Juan Perez's farm skills were based on Taíno tradition, not schoolhouse education. But, Cuca told me, Juan Perez said no. A girl's place was on the farm: cooking, cleaning, providing childcare. Ginny would labor like the rest of them. Stubbornness had already cost him two elder daughters, both of whom eloped with men he deemed unworthy. Juan was not about to relinquish Ginny to adulthood, too. The day of Ginny's flight to training camp came and went, as did the deadline to accept the college scholarship.

If Ginny was devastated, Abuela grew determined. A combination of family tragedies, natural disasters, and agrarian realities had forced Abuela out of school, but no man would deny Ginny what Abuela had only dreamt of. Obdulia had secretly bought Ginny a suitcase, a congratulatory gift for the journeys ahead. The suitcase had gone unpacked and unused. Now Abuela bought more suitcases and filled them with summer clothes and determination. Juan Perez, the proud Taíno, sneered his denial. "You'll never leave!" Even as Abuela exited onto the porch, girls in tow, weighed down by heavy luggage, he yelled after them, "You'll be back!"

In a way, he was right. Tía Toña, daddy's girl number one, returned that Christmas with a rose gold pocket watch for her papi. Twenty-four-karat proof of her Nuevayol flourishing. Titi Margie, not to be shown up, visited on Three Kings, with a matching rose gold chain. Their father-gifting became a civil war. The two sisters would visit the stubborn Taíno, bringing suitcases of flip-flops, leather sandals, summer linens, electronics. But as long as Juan Perez lived and breathed, Obdulia, La Española, would never again return.

> Step two: Coat the bottom of the pot with oil and turn on your flame. "How high should the heat be, Abuela?" "High enough to cook it," she says, smiling.
>
> Step three: Empty the rice into the pot. Now stir, coating each granito with oil.

Landing in the Bronx, Abuela saw concrete stretching toward the horizon. A far cry from the curvy water hole where her daughters had learned to swim, and where the strong current had strengthened Ginny's athletic core. They moved into a noisy apartment on Jerome Avenue. At seven stories, it was the tallest building Abuela had ever seen. For a front yard they had four steps, and instead of roosters, pigeons head-bobbed at their ankles. Their small windows looked out onto brick, so that the only way to see sky was to stick your head out and crane your face upward. Within weeks Virginia, the youngest at eleven, was coming home late from school. She developed a habit of hiding in the hallways long after the final bell. And until the janitor kicked her out, she would stay there, hoping that the gang had grown tired of waiting. But many nights they were ready, rocks in hand. In the mid-sixties, gang wars between Puerto Rican girls and Black non-Latinas came with turf rules that Virginia couldn't decipher. In Arecibo, Black girls spoke Spanish and were Boricua same as mom. But in Nuevayol, she learned, there were Black people beyond Puerto Ricans, and the gangs signaled that separation. Luckily, Virginia had some of her sister's speed and most days got home intact if winded. But her head was bloodied more than once. Until the rock crew was greeted on the stoop by Obdulia, machete in hand, her body fixed in the stance of a farm woman who knew the blade well. They didn't bug mom after that.

Shopping had a whiff of heartbreak, too. Walking half a mile in the stinky heat to buy a hard avocado for a dollar. Just months earlier, soft avocados rained down if you shook a branch. Half-spoiled chicken was now an indulgence—gray meat with an off-smelling odor. Just months earlier, little Virginia chased hens through the yard, snatching at them, the hens eluding and pecking her. Trapping and defeathering those birds was her least favorite chore, but she did miss the sopita's fresh flavor.

A visit to Obdulia's sister would surely be medicine. Years earlier, Ramona—the other Española—had set up on Callowhill, a Puerto Rican enclave in Philadelphia. There the buildings were only three stories tall. Low enough you could see sky out the window. The Callowhill oaks and chestnuts were no twiggy affair like the stunted Bronx trees. Sturdy wide trunks burst toward the clouds. There was a century-old poplar, Ramona boasted, outside her living room window. There were gangs, to be sure, but they were concerned with men's turf wars, not stoning little girls. To speak Spanish in the bodega, to hear música jíbara out a fresh-waxed Chevrolet, to see Boricuas waving out windows and sidewalk domino games—Obdulia savored her brief time in Philly. She missed that sense of belonging, chores and conversations done out of doors. Used to the island's open air, she had not yet adjusted to life behind Los Bronx's burglar bars. Philly felt a tiny bit like Arecibo. When Obdulia and her daughters returned to the Bronx a few days later, they walked into an empty apartment. Furniture, gone. The chest of drawers had been stolen along with the panties inside it. Obdulia and her four girls turned on their heels, piled into the car, and moved to Philly that same day.

After some years on Callowhill, Obdulia and her girls migrated to Mt. Vernon Street, another Puerto Rican enclave, just north of Spring Garden. It was also lined with old-growth elms and handsome brownstones. These were spacious apartments on well-kept blocks where neighbors, pastors, and grocers spoke Spanish. At the end of the block was a public garden, playground, and ball field—a sanctuary escape amid the urban hustle. Sartorial jobs were walking distance—laminating fabric, manning the sewing machines, being a bundle boy. Softball leagues recruited the buffest mamas in town—they welcomed Ginny's radiant laugh onto the position of third base. Lassie, Abuela's life-size statue of a collie, stood at the door welcoming guests with a ceramic grin. With a chipped tongue draped from his open mouth, even the statuary smiled. Shortly after they moved in, a new mural appeared on the corner. It was two stories high, covering the entirety of a row home's side wall. In it, the Statue of Liberty's proud face stared at the onlooker, her crown threaded with the Puerto Rican flag.

Though Boricuas were busy integrating into Philly's economy, the Fraternal Order of Police hadn't gotten the memo. The mandate in those years was: if a Hispanic stepped to a white person, round up every brownie you can find. A single-suspect crime might yield fifty or a hundred arrests in one night. The Philly police got prolific: elderly men, preteen boys, any spic in sight. A reverse crime spree. Neighbors developed networks to spread the word quick: *All men inside! La policia are doing roundups!* Viejas calling viejas, girls running block to block whispering warnings into windows. But still there were boys coming home from ball practice (*You've got a bat? That's a weapon*), there were viejos coming home from factory jobs (*Walking with a cane? Weapon!*). Eventually the FOP sweeps galvanized the community. When a roundup took place, the Boricuas raised hell on the precinct steps, drumming pots and pans in a loud two-three clave. The syncopated ruckus continued till news cameras came and detainees were released. Who led many of these party-protests? Tía Toña, the Perez family's eldest daughter. Abuela's firstborn hustled for pocket watches and against police brutality.

Abuela had a softer strategy and never joined the protests. The local beat cops—all white—grew to adore Abuela's open table. Their lunchtime visits originated the day they kicked in the downstairs door, then banged at her apartment, threatening arrest. For what, Abuela had no clue, until she recognized the word "marijuana" and saw them pointing at her window plants. Abuela didn't speak a lick of English but somehow made clear: those cops were to sit and eat before any arrest would go down. Using gestures and demonstrating knife skills, she convinced them, correctly, that the herb in her window box was recaito, not cannabis. That's why the beans tasted so good. Because she smashed the leaves in the pilón with garlic, for sofrito. By the following week her table was their hearth. The rice and beans were always warm during lunch hour. As the cops ate, she taught them bits and pieces of Spanish, rejecting their reciprocal attempts to teach her English.

On Abuela's turntable, Héctor Lavoe traded spins with the Doors. But by the time Juan Luis Guerra hit the charts and cassette tapes were ubiquitous, judges and lawyers had taken over the brownstones. The new six-figure residents restored the homes to their original single-family design and the Puerto Ricans migrated deeper north into cramped, cheaper row homes. Poverty, it seemed, followed Abuela from the island and held fast even when she fled the Bronx. Only the flavor of the poverty changed. Their new block on American Street had no playground or murals, nor a single tree. There was no farm out back to harvest dinner from, no roosters to kill when the pantry got bare, and more mouths to feed than ever. Abuela adopted two more grandchildren—their mothers M.I.A. to addiction and domestic violence. Now she was raising Cuca and Flor, plus Mary Lou and later Candi. Virginia shacked up with a white hippie in West Philly, sharing a block with Vietnamese, Ethiopian, and African American families. Ginny moved in next door and the two sisters were the only Latinos in the neighborhood. Ginny's slate of coursework at Community was short-lived. Like her sisters before her, it was time to earn a living, to organize community gardens in a concrete jungle, and to lay foundations for the next generation—for us.

Step four: Add water. Hear that sizzle? That's what you want. The ratio of water to rice is one to one, plus a chilín, a splash extra. "But, Abuela, the bag says use twice as much water as rice." Her face turned quizzical. "There's instructions on the bag?"

Step five: Salt it. Half a handful will do.

Step six: Stir and cover.

"Hola, Qui Qui!" As the lid nested onto the caldero, Ginny shouldered the screen door open and threw her purse on the sofa with an *I'll be hanging for a few hours* vibe. She inspected my ass—yup, it's still flat!—and pinched and slapped it in confirmation. Now Abuela passed the baton to her daughter. Waiting for the rice to cook, we drank sodas around the table as Ginny painted her own Philly canvas. Her memories, a generation more proximate, began to mingle with my own, till I couldn't tell if I had experienced this part of it, overheard that part of it, or built a memory from an old polaroid.

American Street is where the bloodsickness tapped the Perez shoulder. Ginny, whose fast legs led the family to Philly, discovered health problems in her athlete's body. They surfaced in the form of an ectopic pregnancy. Her uterus was swollen from PID—her first husband was in the Navy, *y ya tú sabes, all those overseas prostitutes* . . . The fertilized egg implanted outside her fallopian tube. When it burst she lost so much blood medics needed three pints to fill her up. The transfusion had been tested for HIV but not much else. Doctors gave her hep C to save her life. Ginny was grateful. *If you want your garden to grow, you gotta feed it. Even if some of it is manure,* she told me. "We're losing her! We're losing her!" was the last thing she'd heard before making peace with the world. And then, she woke up. She woke up.

Her uterus and ovaries were a jumble after that. Pregnancy was off the table, but Ginny became a sentinel. Woman slept with shoes on. God had other plans, she told people, and she'd be a parent. You just wait and see. So, when addiction ravaged Flor, when it Jekyll and Hyde'd her to an unrecognizable place, when Danito's skull rang out on the bathtub like our family's own Liberty Bell? Ginny was downtown the next morning, filling out the foster-care paperwork. In a matter of months Ginny was taking JJ and Danito, her nephews-turned-sons, to Hunting Park and teaching them to throw a softball. Or bringing them to the gardens she'd made of empty lots, where she taught them to harvest calabaza and oregano brujo. (*Illegal child labor,* JJ used to complain with a grin.) It was rigorous work rooted in her dad's Taíno methods, and the local gardens she began with her sons continue as nonprofits today. With her legs buckling from base-running, her voice hoarse from calling her sons to home plate, her palms cracked from hoeing and sowing, Ginny would get home late and set the flame on high. Ginny perfected arroz con gandules for her adopted boys, JJ and Danito. Just like mom perfected arroz blanco for Pop. Just like Abuela perfected home cooking for her girls. Indeed, if I swung by Ginny's late, after dinner ended, she turned the flame high beneath the "empty" rice pot. Then JJ, Danito, and I would hunch over the stove, scraping the burnt stuff from the caldero. Ginny's pegao was Boricua potato chips—crunchy, salty, fatty, irresistible. Whatever was left after that was placed out back for the stray cats. Not a single grain wasted.

Step seven: When the lid is tap-dancing from steam, lower the flame.

Step eight: Watch a telenovela or study a psalm. Maybe call Puerto Rico, see if Tío Jelin's pneumonia has let up.

Step nine: Stir to fluff before serving. The rice should gleam.

18

YORUBA VOCABULARY

The Norton Anthology slid onto my desk like a pancake from a spatula. I opened the paper brick, fanned its tissue-thin pages, scanned the tiny print of a few random poems. Then wrote my name in number two lead inside the back cover. Above it, in different ink and pencil tones, were the names of students who came before. It was AP English, senior year. I assumed Dr. Phillips's bow tie and sweater vest were ceremonial attire, first-day formalities. Soon it was clear—this was his unchanging professorial getup. He was bald, slender, and far more groomed than any teacher I'd seen at Central. He told us to find Wallace Stevens and read "The Emperor of Ice-Cream." Silence filled the room. After a few lines I grew annoyed. The second reading confirmed my initial response: arrogant nonsense. Wallace Stevens mocked the elegance of Dickinson and Frost. He purposefully eschewed readability. My mind was off at the races, arguing voraciously with Stevens, interrupted only when Dr.

Phillips read the poem aloud. In his voice, the words were music. The lines had no logic but soared with cadence. The contradiction disoriented me. How could a poem be harmonious and rude?

> Call the roller of big cigars,
> The muscular one, and bid him whip
> In kitchen cups concupiscent curds.

I had not heard a poem read aloud since the horse farm, and Dr. Phillips's respect for the spoken word rivaled mom's. He never took a breath mid-line. I had been taught to phrase piano in that manner, lifting my hand from the keys only at a melody's completion. Dr. Phillips ran out of breath on the longest lines, and still pushed forward gently. Reaching the line break, he inhaled and began anew. He read the poem like he loved the poem, intoning phrases as though they cast spells. In his voice, language was erotic and voluptuous—and he lingered for a moment in delicious places. I thought, I want to belong somewhere the way that stranger's voice belongs to those words.

As to fiction, Flannery O'Connor was first on the agenda. Previously I'd been taught to read for plot and theme, but O'Connor was all landscape. I had never been to the South and now here it was, grotesque and monstrous. In her paragraphs the air tasted of molasses and smiling strangers exposed invisible fangs. In O'Connor the devil lurked in all corners, most especially the pious and proper ones. This author wrote blunt and with hell on her mind, odd and unwholesome and bad to the bone. The day of our first exam, the students clumped outside the room before class, whispering of Dr. Phillips's reputation. Some older siblings had gotten C's. Dr. Phillips single-handedly ruined kids' Harvard birthright, consigning them to a fate worse than death: U Penn and Penn State and Temple, oh my! But that was the AP set for you. They talked peace, love, and equality but were dog-eat-dog when discussing college admissions. Test sheets lurked face-down on our desks. I flipped mine over and was astonished to find only two sentences on the other side. "Flannery O'Connor uses the theme of fire in her work. Discuss." Fifty-three minutes. Go. Extra sheets of paper were at the front of the room. I stared at the test sheet.

"Flannery O'Connor uses the theme of fire in her work. Discuss."

Fire. Mom used candles in her altars. She placed them by clear cups of water and photographs of our deceased. I had lit candles for her and watched, over a week's time, as the wax diminished and the flame descended.

Fire. One minute down, fifty-two to go.

There's a moment when the pen moves of its own volition. When an outside voice borrows your ink for its own swift work. I shook like I had in Quaker meeting. My hand struggled to steady itself against thunder. Was it an inner scream I had never let loose or some external tempest that tapped me? This was the opposite of un-speaking AIDS, of holding a tongue, of observing from the steps. This felt how Tía Toña sounded at the funerals and rosaries: a wailing, a thrashing, words to knock crucifixes from walls. At my fluorescent-lit desk, a magmatic eruption threaded itself through my pen tip. Minutes passed, lactic acid thrashing my fingers. Vertigo and nausea carouseled my mind. Still my hand would not slow its course. I would later learn I had gotten up eight times, filled eight loose-leaf sheets in fifty-three minutes. I would later learn that I'd trembled so violently that Dr. Phillips approached to check if I was okay. I had nodded yes.

When the fifth-period bell rang, I was vaguely aware of being the only one left in the room. I put down my pen midsentence. Having no sense of what I'd written, I handed the essay in like that, incomplete. Afterwards, a friend approached me in the hall. "What was that? What happened to you in there?" she asked. Still caught in the aftershocks, I calmed my breathing sufficiently to answer. "I don't know," I said. Central High sounded echoey and underwater. There were my classmates huddling, whispering outrage. *What about multiple choice? Where were the short-form questions, the true-false, the vocabulary fill-ins?* They had studied the character trees and town locations in O'Connor's novellas. How were they to demonstrate their mastery in such a loose format? I heard it all through a tunnel. They stood at the mouth, ten thousand miles away, as my eyes adjusted to the darkness.

I felt subterranean and animal. I had moved the pen despite a mounting resistance. My words were dirty, my sentences stank of gut and had mineral claws. The things I wrote sought no approval or permission. They were raw and disgusting, riots of assertion. I was at last corporeal, like my cousins. I'd always assumed that learning to dance, to move without thought, would be joyous, but no. Sitting in a lefty desk in Dr. Phillips's essay test, learning to dance was an awful initiation. For years I had felt aggrieved by mom's Afro Rican path, by her aggressive refusal to assimilate. For years I had wished she would worship a little bit whiter. But now I had accessed the heavier-than-me, the thicker-than-me, the dormant beast. And it had been unlocked not by a drum, not by blood sacrifice or Juan Luis Guerra, but by a southern white woman who wrote novellas and an English teacher wearing a bow tie and sweater vest.

As senior year progressed, Dr. Phillips had us turn to new pages in the Norton Anthology, discovering new poems in its tis-

sue trove. Each new author was a deflowering. My first Ralph
Ellison. My first Dante. Each essay test, I waited for the beast to
return, but it proved an unreliable visitor. It came only once—
that first time. The rest of AP English was about diligent reading
and sustained curiosity, and the humbling realization that
others—Dostoyevsky, Coleridge—had grappled with the world
in a manner much deeper than I was yet willing to.

"Mom? Do you have a book about Santería I can borrow?"
Though explanations never came easy, mom was a collector by
nature. Stacks of *Architectural Digest* and auction catalogues
crowded our coffee table. Secondhand art books whose pages
smelled of vanilla piled on our rugs. Mom spent that afternoon
searching her shelves, cabinets, and stacks, discouraged to find
that her books on Ifá, the Santos, and the Orishas were all in
Spanish. They were advanced practitioner's manuals whose vocabulary exceeded my conversational ability. Like most collec-
tors, mom had a shopper's appetite. Any excuse for a last-minute
drive to Robin's Bookstore or Garlands of Letters, she'd leap.
Plus, my literary habit brought her great pride. Before I began
kindergarten she was already bragging about my inevitable college degree. Collector plus shopaholic plus bragging mom. I was
aware, when I made the ask, that mom would embrace it as an
invitation.

One day after school I discovered a book on my piano bench.
Spine glossy and creaseless. Unwrapped, unmarked. It appeared
with no ceremony or announcement, like a stray cat at my sunset door. Unlike with the Norton Anthology, I was the book's
first owner. *Four New World Yoruba Rituals* by John Mason. I squirreled it to my room with a pen and began to underline, highlight,
and star every sentence. The first pages offered an explanation of
los Egun, the ancestors. "In constant watch of their survivors on

earth . . . They collectively protect the community against evil spirits, epidemics, famine . . . ensuring the well-being, prosperity, and productivity of the whole community generally. The spirits could be invoked collectively and individually in times of need."* An army of benevolent ancestors stood at my side, the book assured me. And it was welcome assurance, the notion that Mary Lou and Tico were in my court, had my back in higher realms.

I wanted to savor each paragraph, to read slowly and let the concepts sink in. So I paused after the introduction, to practice piano. I appreciated the tactile world of fingertips on black keys, the familiar lick and slide of Chopin nocturnes. Then I opened the book again, reimmersed in the thick and thorny cosmos of my deep history. Located precisely at this sharp turn, at this hairpin pivot between Chopin and the ancestors, was a place that felt like self. I was home.

In detailing four religious ceremonies, the book included invocations in their original Yoruba plus translations into Spanish and English. Such blunt poetry. Cadences that cut with linguistic force. "Death give way. Evil move."† "Yes! Salute and touch the ground to transplant his spirit."‡ "We create the crown of advantage."§ Words like a drum, thoughts like a blade. Phrases dripping with intention, meant to enact change upon the speaker and thus the world.

Weeks later, mom asked if I had read it. I nodded and confirmed that I had. It was our only discussion of the matter.

One day after practicing piano, I climbed the steps and found a new book on the landing. Placed like a love note at my bedroom door. Its matte cover was smooth to the touch. I fanned it

* Mason quoting S. O. Babayemi, pp. 28–29
† p. 68
‡ p. 50
§ p. 70

open, sniffed the earthy pages. *The Way of the Orisa* by Philip John Neimark. The foreword described the tactical genius of those who survived the middle passage. After Boriken's Taíno population had been enslaved, mass-murdered, and significantly depleted—though not fully eradicated—Spanish colonizers needed a new source of labor. Their Yoruba captives smuggled a system of worship and wisdom to the New World right beneath their captors' noses. Quiet and secrecy, I discovered, were not always indicators of shame but were proven strategies of resilience and resistance. I saw mom's altars, and the hush surrounding them, in a powerful new light. She, like her forebears, had taken great risks in her spiritual exploration. Syncretic codes protected such risk-taking.

We rarely ate meals communally. Mom was always coming, Pop always going, my baby sister Gabi, a new arrival, stayed at Abuela's house late, and I was the latchkey kid. One night I was eating dinner alone, hunched over homework, flash cards in one hand, spoon in the other. Mom came in, too tired for anything beyond a "Hi, mija." She tossed down her keys, placed a book by my soup bowl, and trudged up to her room. *A Short Account of the Destruction of the Indies* by Bartolomé de Las Casas. It was written in 1542, fifty years after Columbus set foot on Boriken and thirty years after Ponce de León met Taíno insurrection with a one-two punch of bloodshed and smallpox. Las Casas was a bishop sent to the West Indies as a Spanish Catholic ambassador. The book was his letter to "the most high and most mighty Prince of Spain," in which he anatomized the massacres he witnessed firsthand. Reporting the mass slaughter in detail and describing the humanity of Taínos he'd spent years with, Las Casas urged the Spanish throne to discontinue its violent campaign immediately. He anticipated the disappearance of an entire people and Spain's consequent downfall by a just and mighty God. Las Casas advocated for a kinder, gentler colonial project focused on Christian conversion. I left my soup unfinished on the table, though it was my job to clean the kitchen after dinner. Turning pages as I climbed the stairs. Though it wasn't about Lukumí per se, the book painted a picture of what greeted the Orisha on the shores of the New World. The Taíno blood already swallowed by the soil and an empire perfecting its acquisitional pillage. The phrase "wild dogs" looped in my gut, so proliferative were mentions of this cheap effective weapon. Trained and unleashed against children, women, cacique chiefs. There was no mention of the seaside petroglyphs that had culled my longing that windy day in Puerto Rico. No, in this book, Taínos were the expired, not the enduring. But I had seen the sun rays etched in stone. The fact of me visiting those seaside caves was proof that Taínos lived on. Carrying my grandfather's blood, I embodied a survival that Las Casas warned might become impossible. Around two A.M. mom came into my room, took the book from my hand, and turned off the light.

As I studied the books, returning to highlighted passages, cross-referencing them against each other, I gained a richer understanding of many elements in my own home. For instance, the coconut is used to consult with Eleguá. So that's why it was always thrown by the front door, where Eleguá lived, unlike most other divinations and ceremonies that happened farther back in the house. Of course. But now I knew why. Once, I had sung along to mom's tape, joining the jubilant chorus of "Cabiosile pa' Changó!" The exalting energy had been clear, but now I knew the precise meaning. It was a way to greet Changó's source energy by saying "Hail the king!" The religion required and rewarded study. Things I had once half intuited now had vocabulary, words offered material confirmation. We existed. I was learning to describe my world.

Ofrenda a los Orichas arrived alongside a Spanish-English dictionary, hardbound in blue leather. Mom had exhausted the English-language books she could find on the subject. After that, gifts were often in Spanish. Each new book appeared like a secret message, its receipt acknowledged only when it vanished into my room. The silence of her gifts felt curated and intentional, like anything I might say mattered less than how deeply I dove. In this way, mom and I developed a clandestine exchange, ever respectful of the other's private worlds.

19

A RACIAL SLUR

My senior year, *The Bell Curve* was published. When the school bell rang and lockers started slamming, the buzz was palpable. A vocal subset of guys applauded its publication, relieved that someone had spoken up on their behalf, saying at last what they had all, apparently, known: whites were smarter than Blacks. (Other racial categories seemed altogether excluded from discussion.) The book's argument connecting race and intelligence emboldened certain Centralites to assert that the poor were irreversibly doomed, that affirmative action contradicted the destiny writ in our DNA. Inequality wasn't the workings of the privileged or the systems they engineered—it was biological imperative. Lunch breaks, guys read passages aloud. They'd become overnight intellectuals. The bestseller gave permission to state their superiority, no apologies required.

As an academic magnet, Central High brought in the top test-takers from every neighborhood. It was a microcosm of the city's white and Black demographics. Split fairly evenly, the two groups made up ninety percent of the student body.* At Central, kids from Grays Ferry and Chestnut Hill crammed for math quizzes. Kids from the Northeast and Germantown napped on homeroom desks or sold soft pretzels between periods. Some walked to school, others commuted two hours from the city's farthest corners. Peek into our hallways, you'd have no clue that Philly was among the most segregated cities in the nation.† But after the seventh-period bell rang, students took the Broad Street subway and various SEPTA buses home to separate worlds. We were sorting blocks—taken out and mixed on the playroom floor by day, returned to our distinctly shaped holes by night.

Latinos were underrepresented by half, so most of us huddled together when chance allowed. Miguel was good for a hallway chuckle. Ana, Rubi, and I shared a table in physics. Willie and I checked each other's Spanish worksheets. He was the better speaker but the teacher gave him hell about his dropped *s*'s and *r*'s said as *l*'s. Plus Willie couldn't spell, he got the vowels all scrambled up. So, despite his fluency, I got the A and he got the D. But mostly Central's Latinos befriended other ethnicities or became socially aloof. In a graduating class of five hundred, fourteen Latinos walked across that stage. Our cohort had been bigger when I'd arrived sophomore year, but many had peeled away. You don't notice erosion when it's happening.

A year later at Yale, my Latino classmates were surprised to meet a Philly Rican. "Cool, never heard of that before!" They were Boricuas from Los Bronx, Hartford, or Chicago. I was ex-

* Census data on Philly from www.pewtrusts.org/~/media/legacy/uploadedfiles /wwwpewtrustsorg/reports/philadelphia_research_initiative/philadelphiapopulation ethnicchangespdf.pdf. Central High data is based on me counting senior photos in the yearbook—so, a flawed method but it's what I had on hand.

† fivethirtyeight.com/features/the-most-diverse-cities-are-often-the-most-segregated/

cited to inform them (based on no evidence) that Philly had one of the largest Puerto Rican communities nationwide. It wasn't until I wrote this chapter that the 1990 census schooled me on the real numbers. During my adolescence, Latinos were five percent of Philly's population. A sliver. Residential segregation had given me a warped view of reality. Sure, other communities existed. West Philly (where I lived), South Philly, Chinatown, Rittenhouse Square. But if those were neighborhoods, North Philly was, to my eyes, a universe.

Each class at Central had a distinct microclimate based on the kids in the room. Because the teacher encouraged discussion, Government and Politics was a place where you got to know your classmates. There was Avi, a dark-skinned Indian who fashioned himself in Alex P. Keaton's shadow. His striped polos were buttoned to the top. The way he raked fingers through his hair? It was obvious he'd practiced the move in the mirror. Around his liberal female classmates, Avi played the beleaguered conservative to flirtatious advantage. Though he never mentioned faith to me a single time, his yearbook quote was from John 8:12: "I am the light of the world." He wasn't referring to god.

Robin was a volatile, school-of-hard-knocks, I-will-bash-your-face white guy—at least that was his mask. The blond hair above his fire-hydrant neck was buzzed to bristle. You could always see his goatee because he was a head taller than the South Philly Italians he rolled with. Afternoons, in the standing-room SEPTA bus, obscenities flew out his mouth like bats from a cave. Each curse was its own dare for anyone to complain. Making people ignore him was wicked good sport. "Sit on my lap, bitch!" he hollered to his girlfriend, a wispy creature who collapsed onto his legs, giggling away the humiliation. The elderly riders slouched farther into blue plastic seats. "She did it! She listens to me!" Robin announced. He burrowed into her neck and bit hard, as if her hickey constellation needed one more star. One time the driver stopped in rush-hour traffic on Olney Avenue. She turned off the ignition and intercom-announced that we would not be moving until the delinquent at the back got off. "You can't let a passenger off unless it's a designated stop! I'll sue you!" Robin yelled. "This is my bus, child," the intercom replied, "and this is my finger on the police button." Robin and crew paraded out, muttering about being walking distance from home anyway. His yearbook quote was from *A Clockwork Orange:* "I was cured all right."

Pete, unlike Robin, was actually blue-collar white. (Turns out Robin's mom was a professor at U Penn.) Pete's father, a fire-fighter, was Pete Sr. Ten bucks says there were more Petes on the family tree. He was from the deep Northeast—you could practically smell the frankincense from his Roman Catholic breeding. Dude adored his father—the kind of hero worship high school-ers should have long since outgrown. Pete had a gentle-giant slouch, always stooping to your eye level so you could see his kind, melancholy gaze. Broad-jawed and mild-mannered, rugby shirts and khakis ironed with care. His etiquette was textbook. Devoted, honorable, confession-taking Pete. When I visited his health class as part of a safe-sex campaign and rolled the condom onto the banana, I thought Pete would blush right into a coma. After class he asked me, saddened, how I could do things like that in public. Another day Pete looked particularly ruminative. His father had been gunning for that promotion in the fire depart-ment. Pete Sr. was a shoo-in, it was a foregone conclusion, and then without explanation was denied the position. Affirmative action, Pete said, shaking his head, more wounded than angry. His hero had been ready to step into the light, rise into his birthright—fire marshal. Even when disagreeing with Pete, I felt for the guy. "How do you know it was affirmative action?" I asked. "The new fire chief is in pampers. He hasn't put out one-tenth the blazes my dad has." Pete didn't mention the new chief's race—he didn't have to.

These three guys were a motley crew. In a John Hughes film, they'd be at different cafeteria tables. In Government and Politics, their desks were in various corners of the room. Robin in the back, taking up two desks (one for his ass, one for his feet). Avi wherever the girls were clustered. Pete alone in the middle. But when the debate topic was government assistance and someone brought up welfare queens? Their interest jolted the room like lasers. The three sat up straighter. An instant, unspoken alliance formed.

Welfare queen. The phrase was new to me, but its blunt weaponry seemed obvious. As with many racial slurs, there was innuendo packed in tight, a pretend innocence and fake sociological neutrality. Still, the phrase was a kid playing hide and seek with half his body exposed, eager to be discovered. It didn't literally say "Monstrous Boricua Woman" but it had North Philly written all over it.

"What's a welfare queen?" I asked, skeptical. The Three enlightened me: When you're on the dole, you receive a set amount per kid. Welfare queens got knocked up as budget strategy, to score a bigger check. They were running the best grift in the U.S. of A. and they had the three-inch mani-pedis to prove it.

"No one does that," I said. "That's some nightly-news race-baiting *Bell Curve* nonsense. Do you know any such person?"

"Read the paper," Robin said.

"There's new stories every day," Pete said. "Not just in the *Daily News*. In the *Inquirer*, too."

"Give me an example," I demanded. "Name one welfare queen, Avi."

"I mean, I can't just, like, conjure one off the top of my head, I don't exactly hang out with welfare queens in my free time, but they exist." The Three nodded like their assertion was clear as gravity, no additional proof necessary.

"No woman has a baby for that reason. That's a complete mischaracterization of childrearing motives," I said.

The thought of my cousin Nuchi as queen of anything other than a crumbling row home was perverted. Nuchi was loyal as hell, a great dancer, joked with grace about life's bum rap, and made a mean potato salad. But she wore her trauma like a windbreaker in a blizzard. The woman's poverty turned heads. Depression and constant hustle had aged her by thirty years. People saw her and thanked god for their blessings. Nuchi needed a root canal, maybe two. Heck, her dental catastrophe needed a time machine. Nuchi needed prenatal care. She needed talk therapy and antidepressants. She needed a laundromat in walking distance. She needed an exterminator and an address not adjacent to a crack house. She needed taxi fare or—dream big—a car. Cable would've been nice. Her oldest son needed an orthodontist for his overbite. Her tall boys went through two sizes a year—she needed clothes for their telescoping legs. The lights had been shut. The hole in her front wall needed covering before the snow. The bathtub leak was worsening—she needed it plugged before the ceiling caved in. Or at least a bigger bucket to catch the water by the sofa. Nuchi needed roach spray and a mold specialist. She needed duct tape to keep the upstairs window attached. Nuchi needed love. One of these needs was within her ability to grasp, to hold on to. Her kids were seven lighthouses in a hurricane.

The assertion that this human want—to love—was her way of enacting some injustice upon us? That her desire to have a family was a hoax—or worse, criminal—or worst of all, implausible—because its setting was poverty? I wasn't saying it was their job to fix her woes, to plug the patchwork leaks in her heart. But we were not the victims of her maternity swindle. If Nuchi was public enemy number one, if our nation's advancement depended upon stripping her bare—she, who had barely a thread to her name—then we were a soulless people, a cruel nation dancing atop its victims' graves.

I stood at my desk (when had I risen to my feet?) and said these things aloud. I had neither Pete's etiquette, nor Robin's rage, nor Avi's smug rationality. I was a hackneyed salesman for a pariah cause. I had outed my kin, aired her dollar-store laundry. And to fully disqualify myself, I had wept. The Three let me finish without interrupting. Their victory speeches came softly. Robin mumbled something about anecdotal evidence versus scientific. Avi sounded vaguely apologetic. Perhaps Nuchi was an exception, they conceded. Then again, Pete offered, perhaps loyalty clouded my judgment. Either way, the issue was real, they said. Women were having kids all the way to the bank.

"Do you want a breather, Quiara? Maybe go take a walk?" Mr. Lafferty offered.

The water ran in the bathtub, fogging up the mirror, so Nuchi and I had to talk loud above the noise. It was unfamiliar, this chemical assault—I had never dyed hair before. Eyes tearing, nostrils dripping. And yet this toxic process was, incongruously, a platform for intimacy. I squirted goop onto Nuchi's scalp and swirled it in with my fingertips. "Don't forget my hairline in the back," she instructed. The nape of her neck was soft. I pressed the gel in tenderly. A vulnerable place to massage a woman, at the small boneless trough between skull and neckbone. My fingers swirled there for a long moment. Nuchi accepted the touch and then nudged me onward. "Don't forget my forehead and temples." Every so often Nuchi wiped a condensation circle from the mirror, but it fogged up too quickly for her to see. So she instructed me blind and trusted my progress. Through thin rubber gloves, I felt my cousin's skin, its warm elastic tenderness. I knew this sort of touch well—fingers in firm circles, thumbs asserting pressure. The summer before kindergarten I'd developed a nasty pneumonia, and mom shiatsu-massaged my back ribcage to break up the phlegm. Her left and right rotated in gears, until I could feel the pneumonia break loose a bit and my lungs came unburdened.

"I'm done," I said after double-checking Nuchi's roots. "What's step three?"

"The shower cap." I slid it over her head. "Now we wait for me to be a blonde."

"For how long?" I asked. She told me to check the instructions. But they had been left by the sink, out of reach. Since my hands were dripping with dye, I didn't want to stain the bath mat. So, I asked her to check the instructions while I rinsed off in the bathtub. Nuchi was reticent, which baffled me. It's not like I was asking her to run a marathon. She finally grabbed the instructions and held them before my eyes.

"How much time does it say?" she asked. I was now washing my hands beneath the tub's spigot, watching the gel swirl toward the drain, craning my neck toward the instructions' tiny type.

"You tell me," I countered. Finally, I turned off the tub and the room plunged into quiet. The only sound came from towel-drying my hands. It seemed Nuchi wanted me to intervene, but I hadn't a clue how or why.

"I thought you knew, Qui Qui. I can't read." It was said with neither shame nor malice, just pragmatic resignation. I had backed her into a corner, till she had no choice but to explain. The weight of her statement settled in. I filed through all my memories of Nuchi—dancing, talking, hanging with her kids. Yeah, I guess we'd never read together.

"But . . . didn't you graduate high school?" Even as it left my lips, the question felt unkind. What right did I have to demand her credentials? And yet, I needed to know the score. This was seriously fucked. It didn't seem possible.

"They just pass you," Nuchi said. "I just stood in the back." We were two cousins connected by today's beauty ritual, by Abuela's sofa and countless family gatherings. But in my magnet school, commas in e. e. cummings poems were debated. In her zoned school, invisibility was lauded as life skill. My loud-mouthed cousin shrank herself to a crumb and the school rewarded her compliance with the prize of a diploma.

I set the egg timer. Forty-five minutes. We rebounded with a deck of cards and a game of War. But I wanted to break free from my living room, from that card game, to run screaming through the streets of Philly, past the monumental art museum, past glistening brownstones, past the white-gloved doormen of Rittenhouse Square, all the way to the Free Library of Philadelphia, to hop up the stairs two at a time and into the stacks and ask James

Baldwin or Pablo Neruda: "My cousin can't read and I can. What do I do?" Except that now, praying in the temple of my literary saints was revealed as its own sick privilege. Still, I needed Baldwin and Neruda now more than ever, to make sense of one nation, one family, in which two cousins could walk such different paths.

The timer rang. Nuchi kneeled at the bathtub and bent over its edge, her wet hair like tentacles slinking on the tub floor. I peeled off the shower cap, filled a cupful of water, and poured it over her head.

"Did it stain my skin?" she asked. "Cheap dye does that sometimes."

"No," I said, rinsing the dye away, "no stains."

I accepted Mr. Lafferty's invitation to leave class early. It was a few moments before class let out and I savored the temporary privacy. Of all things, I hated myself most for crying during the debate. They would never take me seriously—the girl who blubbered when reasonable young men simply spoke. They hadn't allowed for the possibility that Nuchi loved her children, but if I screamed and cried, they won on sheer optics.

I wondered if Nuchi would've been mad at me for discussing her poverty in such detail. She was strong, a survivor. She hardly needed a weepy schoolgirl to protect her from a world whose cruelty she knew well. There was shame attached to being publicly poor and here I was, spreading the news.

Had I seen Nuchi dance since that Fourth of July? Four years had passed since I'd spied her hips in motion. Four years of grief had been rent upon her—first a father, then a little brother, then a younger sister felled. Obituaries she would never read—she was, instead, her brethren's living flesh-and-blood eulogy. Nowadays, Nuchi either avoided family gatherings altogether or sat in a corner. Despite her frailty, she still had the physical capacity to dance. Her stillness was, instead, evidence of a protest abandoned. Nuchi's stillness was the ultimate, final precarity.

The bell rang and students filed out from classrooms. Locker doors slammed open and shut, open and shut, open and shut.

20

A BOOK IS ITS
PRESENCE AND ABSENCE

Every book, a horizon. A world I had no prior access to. An eye-opening.

Books from Dr. Phillips's class.

Books from Giovanni's Room, Borders, and the Free Library of Philadelphia.

Books from mom's favorite botánica.

Books purchased by skipping meals for lunch money and walking home to save SEPTA fare.

Qui Qui became two readers, split down the middle as if by an axe. There was real Quiara who read the book, same as ever. And there was What-If Quiara, who would never unearth the revelations in its pages. Each book became its presence and absence, its voice and its silence.

Who would I be without Ralph Ellison? Without the battle royal's electric brutality? Without five words strung together: "I am an invisible man"?

Who would I be without reading *Beloved* on the El, North Philly zooming below? If I'd never known Sethe's back scars? "He would tolerate no peace until he had touched every ridge and leaf of it with his mouth."

Who would I be without *The House on Mango Street?* "In English my name means hope. In Spanish it means too many letters. It means sadness, it means waiting."

I'd be more reticent, less bold, lonelier. My inner music would thrum more quietly. Those books were definitive experiences. Their impact on me felt unquantifiable yet certain as Abuela's palm cupping dry rice. They were recipes for my inner life's feast. They implicated me, demanded much of my consciousness, and thrust me into an American conversation.

Books on the southbound 5 to the eastbound 42 on piano lesson Tuesdays. On the northbound Broad Street Line heading to Central. Books on 49th and Baltimore during trolley delays. Or on an Independence Hall bench, in the Saturday morning hush. Each one a stone on my path, guiding me one step further from Nuchi's reality. And yet as I read with double vision, thinking of her often, each book had the strange effect of binding me to her. The more I learned of our divergence, the more I paid it attention.

21

MOM'S ACCENT

My non-Latino friends always had a comment when mom answered. After she handed me the phone they'd be like, "Her accent is decent!" "I don't hear it," I'd say. They'd be like, "Stop playing, yes you do." Old friends found comfort in her vowel-rich "Hello?" New friends just got confused. If mom answered they'd be like, "Yo, are you a jungle fever baby? I thought you was white but your mom sounds pure Spanish Harlem!" Mom's cadences were invisible to me, with a few exceptions.

When mom said "obnoxious," it rhymed with "precocious." Precocious, obnoxious.

When mom said "Home Depot," it rhymed with "teapot." Teapot, Home Depot.

When mom said "realm," it rhymed with "stay calm." Stay calm, re-alm.

I corrected her in the car. I corrected her in the living room.

No cash register or playground was too public to fix her blunder. Sometimes it was embarrassment, which I pretended was charity, others it was the know-it-all cockiness of youth, and still others to tease a mystical giantess. Her numinous ass needed reminders that I was down here in the plebian realm. She never once said, "Fuck you, child, stop colonizing my ass." But she never changed her pronunciation, either. We went to Home Depot a lot, so she was definitely asserting her right of mispronunciation.

I wonder what it's like. To grow up in Arecibo, Puerto Rico, learning English in first grade, starting with songs like "Pollito, Chicken," to bring your papi his coffee on the farm, your papi who doesn't speak a lick of English, made by your mami, who speaks even less, to leave Arecibo at eleven, come to Los Bronx as autumn breezes take hold, to have girl gangs mocking your spic accent and hurling rocks at your head, to wait until the janitor is done mopping and the floors are dry and he turns off the lights and is like "Out kid, I'm locking up," and still the gang is there with the rocks, to have a Philly guidance counselor deny you a college conversation because *I mean let's be real,* and anyway there was no money for college and anyway your parents didn't make it past second grade so simmer down, to advocate for immigrant moms who can't afford cereal or prenatal care, to be honored by the National Organization of Women for getting those immigrant moms cereal and prenatal care, to be hired by state senator Hardy Williams and while drafting his legislation to write in backdoor deals so your Boricua brethren aren't left with crumbs, to do all that off a high school education and a hunger for books, and then to have your love child from a white hippie correct your pronunciation when she's six years old. Then when she's nine. Then when she's seventeen and should fucking know better.

As if the words I write are my language and not hers. The

woman who taught me English. The woman who gifted it to me and I now drink ten-dollar prosecco and pay my river-view mortgage and take vacations off the English language she nursery-rhymed in my ear before I had words at all.

I eat my words. I eat my corrections como una comemierda. Mom, if you ever read this book (and make it this far without disowning me), I ask you one favor: break this English language today and tomorrow and the day after and bestow it new life with each breaking. Endow your fullness upon this cracked colonial tongue. You language genius. This is your English. You earned it. I am only a guest here.

PART III

———————

How Qui Qui Be?

22

DAD BUYS ME A TYPEWRITER

Soon after the horse farm wedding, dad and Sharon had left for Carroll Lane. A zip code over, the backyard woods were sliced in two by train tracks. Only one or two trains came through every hour, and the slick silver rails made good balance beams. The trees bordering the tracks were kind company, and though I never spoke to them directly as I had on the farm, their fellowship was preferable to the lonely shroud of my bedroom. Night sickness took hold, and I became well acquainted with the cold bathroom floor, the brown-tinted faux terra-cotta tiles. I would wake up to crickets and the moon's blue-glow blanket, then sprint out of bed, the day's meals spilling forth. I would quake and tremble, an elbow on the toilet for ballast, waiting for the next eruption. A few hours later, the bile would be spent. The first time this happened, unsure what was coming over me, I had made a mess of it: some sickness on my pillow and the brown tile floor. An internal voice said *Learn to clean up after yourself: this is the way of visitors.* If I didn't ask for help, dad or Sharon would not get to deny me care. So I taught myself to hand-soap the sheets and ajax the bathroom floor. A small independence that put me, at three A.M., behind the wheel. It was early days after the separation. Custody was a biweekly matter, and my weeks at mom's meant an hourlong commute from Philly to the "good school" near dad's. It was the same daily trek, in reverse, that had once turned mom vacant and angry. Now I was latchkey of the highest order: training alone for two hours daily, too young for such voyages, my imagination now my one constant companion. Weeks at dad's were logistically simpler—a fifteen-minute school bus rather than an hourlong train—but mom's affection was a phantom limb. I had never gone a day without her touch, so I had never understood it as lifeline. Now there was no hand slapping my ass, no fingers raked through my hair, no cooing and expectation I would dance to her lullaby. I was an island, a castaway. I begged out of the biweekly home swap, moved to Philly permanently, and eventually transferred to a city school.

Siblings were born and grew to toddlers, and dad moved to a rental with vaulted ceilings, wooden rafters, and abundant bedrooms. The tall sloping roof was handsome, with a steeply raked back lawn that echoed the architecture. I got no bedroom there, just a mattress on my brother's floor. Finally, they purchased on Tinker Hill Lane: the very house where Sharon had spent her girlhood. Her parents gave them a good deal, which was apparently an insult to dad's hopes and dreams. Still, they were ascending in status to proper American family.

I visited the suburbs monthly now, like one visits a zoo, ogling a species through glass. The suburban nuclear unit: Oh, how their YMCA pool gleams! How their hair doesn't frizz in August, how their thighs don't touch! See them apply sunblock before going in water! See them cook different dinners for each family member's preference! Oh, how they shuffle to gymnastics and rehearsal! Can we push back your visit three weekends, Quiara? So many birthday parties this fall!

Compared to my North Philly cousins, they seemed normal. Over and over, the word tossed like a stone. Normal, normal. The mom and dad under one roof? Normal. The five-minute time-outs and weekly cash allowance? Normal. They had egg timers on their toothbrushes. Two minutes, two minutes! Even glimpsing the loneliness in Sharon's insistent smile and the bitterness tossed in dad's junk drawers, my envy of their whiteness chewed me like acid. Even preferring the Perezes' corporeal, sometimes criminal parenting to the well-mannered masks of dad's new living room, still the chorus sounded: normal, normal. Filmmakers loved capturing this polite sort of hell. The Free Library's shelves sagged beneath the picket fence canon, so that even the dysfunction at dad's was fucking aesthetic. They were an art-house genre. We, the Perezes, merited no novels, films, or dramas. I craved what they had: the routine, the constancy, the ubiquity of stories that explained them. Back in North Philly, mundane routines were fleeting. Everywhere lurked precarity, disruption the promise of each sunrise. The Perezes were in a constant state of mourning or preparing to mourn, because love was a synonym for tragedy. In North Philly, when we protested, did homework, or took on extra jobs, bedtimes were forgotten, meals skipped. In North Philly, no one invited the whole class to a birthday—there was a fifty-person family to host. In North Philly, when we danced, we pressed our shoulders against tomorrow's surefire grief.

.　　.　　.

Still, I favored dad and thirsted for his affection. I wanted him to shower me with countenance and attention, or to call every now and then and say hi. Everywhere I looked, a dad-shaped hologram shimmered. His froggy whisper. *Keep your eye on the ball. Go read a book.* His grip steadying my hold on the archery bow. How he let go of the bike seat and I stayed upright, balanced for the very first time. His patient breath, encouraging a campfire's reticent flame. How he delicately licked the tissue-thin rolling paper and patted the joint closed. The cracked-open window of his pickup, sucking out the exhales, as January frost hammered me. Memories.

At some birthday, back in grade school when I still spent weeks at Carroll Lane, when I still had a bedroom and dad still remembered my birthday, he made an event of driving me to Circuit City. Together we mazed through television aisles and surround-sound displays to the most extraordinary corridor in retail history: word processors. "Give 'em a spin," he said. I typed my name on one machine after another, all the way up and down the aisle. One model could do italics and bold. One had built-in memory and could print copies. One did the accent in Alegría. Another could erase words or even sentences: I pressed delete and Quiara vanished from the page. Each had a three-digit price and I knew money was contentious between him and Sharon, but dad said choose anything. He bought me paper, ink ribbons, font inserts. Happiness tickled us in the checkout line. It was levity by the time the register guy called *next!* I was dad's first child, the only one who knew his long hair and twenty-something laughter. If he had since pushed me from the airplane, the typewriter was a parachute made of our composite dreams. I set it up that same afternoon, typed in a frenzy. Treacly poems, fan essays about teenage heartthrobs, short stories. There was no connective aesthetic or topical focus, simply the act of imagination as a way to pass lonely days. When I wrote, I soared. If I ran out of ideas, I typed Top 40 lyrics to keep the jubilant racket going full-tilt. Dad took pride in the clatter: noisy proof of a fatherly triumph. He'd peek into my room, *keep it up kid,* then disappear again.

Eventually, I took the typewriter to mom's where I could use it more frequently.

Now I was a senior with a Yale acceptance letter. Before leaving, I trained it out to the burbs. One last trek to dad's. The trips had become intentionally rare. Overnights provided manifold chances for the word "guest" to rear its head. I'd lie in a bed not my own and a cavernous loneliness would swallow me till sunrise. A pillow borrowed, a blanket scrounged. Not one photo of me lived on a fridge layers-thick with their happiness. Honor roll certificates, team photos, and school portraits gleamed on end tables and sideboards, none bearing my name. By senior year I quietly vowed: day trips only. I wanted to see my six-year-old sister and four-year-old brother while honoring the house's implicit instruction that I stay at arm's length.

Dad cranked the parking brake and my siblings ran up the path, begging me to build an obstacle course and play indoor HORSE. My little bro had a ringer where he tacoed himself, butt-first, into his hamper and hit a "backboard" shot off the ceiling. They were smart, lively, impeccably behaved children whose affection thickened a cord I wished to cut. How I yearned to set that daddy wish sailing. *Love me, choose me.*

The horse farm was a distant memory, but Malvern's whiteness remained intact, uniform as rolled-out grass. Whiteness as landscape. There were no sidewalks—an omission that thwarted any potential mixing. In the 215, I strolled many blocks with ease. Between Central High, Quaker meeting, and piano lessons, I knew my way around white spaces, but Malvern's homogeneity was chilling, complete. No wonder my kindergarten peers surrounded mom the day she brought cake. No wonder, years later, my four-year-old brother's eyes sparkled at the sight of some Black hotel workers on the train platform. "Where did they come from?" he marveled aloud. Then, adopting a movie-trailer voice, he said, "They're a secret gang who travels at night." "They're hotel employees at the end of a shift," I said. He deflated at the crumpled fantasy.

After traversing obstacle courses made of couch pillows and throttling me at HORSE, the kids washed their hands for dinner. It was this household's nod to corporeality: handwashing. Otherwise hugs and kisses were kept to a minimum. The kids pushed buttered noodles around cereal bowls while we ate our adult dinner. Sharon tried her honey-voiced best to hide the unhappy marriage, and dad escaped his haiku of rage on occasion to laugh at one of the kids' clever puns or jokes. Dad and Sharon had cultivated a civil enough rapport to mask their mutual hatred. Then Sharon nuked a Pepperidge Farm frozen cake, which had been pre-sliced for added convenience. The scene felt reminiscent of Duchamp's *Étant donnés* . . . Realistic and pastoral, bordering on eerie.

I planned to take the last R5 back to Philly but my siblings begged for a longer visit and I relented, promising a treasure hunt in the morning. I read them a bedtime story, then joined dad and Sharon in the living room for grown-up talk. Dad poured Coca-Cola into an etched tumbler and swirled ice cubes till they chimed like soft bells. The conversation turned from President

Clinton to libertarianism, a new word to me. Were income and property taxes unfair? Not the particulars of implementation, but the very existence of enforced communal funds? It had been on Sharon's mind. I leaned in, curious. "Say my neighbor has a child out of wedlock who she can't afford to feed. No father in sight," she began. "I see her at the mailbox, her belly's looking pretty round. My taxes already support school lunches for her first kid. Now they'll pay for prenatal care she can't afford. Meanwhile, I pay my kids' way. So I'm being penalized for her poor choices. How does that incentivize her to do better? How is that fair to me when I've been working hard?"

"Which house does she live in?" I'd never seen the woman in question. Then again, I had spent very little time at this house.

"It's hypothetical."

"You don't believe in helping your neighbor?"

"Not in being forced to. Of course, I can choose to, but that's my personal prerogative." This was my opportunity to yawn, claim sleepiness, and pad off to bed. But they had apparently decided I was an adult now, prime for grown-up conversation, and the phrase barreled in before I could escape.

"It's the inner-city problem," dad said. He had been making Sharon-doesn't-know-shit eyes up till then, but now this seemed a rare point of alignment between them.

"What does that refer to?" I asked. What I meant was *whom* does that refer to, but he didn't catch my implication, and I didn't have the courage to say what I meant.

"Take public education. Teachers are the worst-paid employees in this nation, when they should earn more than doctors. And schools need up-to-date textbooks. No one's questioning that. But no budget can replace actual parenting. Values come from the home."

"Values like . . . ?"

And so it began.

Values? Here's one. Graduate high school. Without getting pregnant. Create a two-parent household. Marry.

But you never married mom, even though she wanted to.

Put a hundred dollars toward books instead of Nikes.

So Nuchi's boys don't deserve a nice thing?

There's Air Jordans that cost three times that. But people let their kids starve to buy sneakers.

Like Flor? It's fine if her pantry's bare, but she better not have good shoes.

Eat less McDonald's. Your child is obese.

Okay, stop. Please?

I hate to say it, because it's the children who suffer.

You mean Danito, JJ, and Candi? I bet it keeps you up at night.

But at the end of the day, I tend my backyard, so go tend yours.

Ah. The English word "my." Now I remembered. My backyard. Right.

It's a shame . . .

Because there are children involved . . .

But having compassion doesn't mean there's no accountability.

Inner City was some kind of code all right. Culture of Poverty had a lofty ring. They couldn't mean the Perez family, no no, surely not. They might as well have been talking about a rodent infestation at an upscale department store—surprisingly *kind* rats, to be sure. They took great pains never to call them nasty creatures—though if a rat grazed Sharon's ankle she would've leapt up onto the nearest chair. Hey, dad *felt for* the rats. But the real conundrum, of course, was which department store would provide a better shopping experience next time.

Clink clink went their ice.

Man, I started having this fantasy . . . *A van pulls into their drive-way. This occasions some concern because on Tinker Hill Lane, where there are no sidewalks, you don't touch someone's property unless invited or to pull a three-point turn. The van pulls all the way to the garage, then the engine goes quiet and car doors slam. By the time the doorbell rings, my entire Puerto Rican family's gathered out front. "Hey, we hear you're talking about us. Can we join the conversation?"*

Who were dad and Sharon anyway? King and queen of Shit-Don't-Stink Land? Where were my child-support checks? Not in our 215 mailbox, that's for sure. Someone needed to check them, turn on the houselights and stop the show. Probably, I should have. But I stayed quiet as a confidante, a nonconfrontational good girl, the dutiful eldest, cooperative and diplomatic, every unvoiced retort piling up and burning. Once I had ajaxed the bathroom floor, now I ajaxed my mouth and I hated myself for it. Any onlooker would think me their ally.

Clink clink as the ice cubes melted into Coca-Cola.

Did I, in truth, have more compassion than dad and Sharon? Hadn't I once seen mom mounted by an ancestral spirit and another time slicing the blade across a chicken's jugular—hadn't I beheld she who lullabied me with repulsion? Toña roared into mind, her church-floor wailing at Big Vic's funeral, her corpulent limbs pooling on the marble floor. Hadn't I stepped around and past my elder's valley of darkness, vowing not me, dear god, I will never be so grotesque. Hadn't I witnessed the aunt I claimed to love and reeled, thinking, *beast, swamp creature, ghoul, monstrosity.* From all angles, it was I, not dad or Sharon, who hosted the horror show.

Drip drip went the condensation down dad's etched tumbler.

And the memory came . . . *Oh god, unremember it.* (Drip drip pooled the condensation at the base of dad's tumbler.) And boom: I was thirteen again, in Sharon's minivan after she met me at the train. She asked how things had been, I mentioned highlights from my week with mom and my baby sis, Gabi. The van fell silent. Sharon's eyes left the road, pinning me till I met her gaze. "Please don't talk about Virginia around me. Or Gabi. I don't enjoy hearing about them. It makes me uncomfortable." Then she turned her gaze back to the road. Banishing mom's name was ask enough, but Gabi was a damn baby. I told myself, *That's it, this is my last visit to dad's.* I told myself, *How 'bout I mention mom and Gabi in every goddamn sentence for the next twenty-four hours?* She will regret the day, I swore. She will suffer my wrath, I vowed. *I will never, ever love you.* I hurled the thought from the back of my head, eyes fixed out the window. *Say anything,* I begged myself. *Say no, at least.* Instead I bit my lip. *Really? Not one word? Traitor.* I removed mom and Gabi from my mouth for every visit, for years.

Clink clink went the ice on the sitcom soundstage. Clink clink went north on the wholesome American compass. Innocuous and jovial, all in good fun. Sure you don't want some soda, kid? They left me two options that night in the living room: be white or be Puerto Rican. Their rules. They forced my hand. Fine. My heels dug further into North Philly. My soul took a side that lasts to this day.

If I'd had Ginny's cropped afro or Nuchi's walnut hue, this dialogue would not have happened in my presence. It was disquieting, how my fair skin provided familiarity, how it gained me access to a conversation that blistered my heart. Around light-skinned Qui Qui, Malvern held forth with impunity. My silence was their playground. I was accomplice to the slander and to my own uneasy awakening.

Part of me, to this day, remains in that living room, hearing the ice clink and swirl. Quiara is the sentinel who never took the R5 home. That after-dinner chat, and the fury it ignited, are as much of a birth as I can claim in my life. A picket fence of civility gleamed around me. I didn't have the language yet to tramp it to the ground, but I swore to eventually find one.

I boarded the R5 in the morning after the treasure hunt was over, telling myself *day-trips only.* No sleep came on the ride, though I tried. I'd have happily woken up in Delaware if it meant forgetting the visit for an hour. Disassociation wrapped me in its mist. This always happened on the train home from dad's. The weighted blanket of numbness. Life as a blur, ten million miles away. A comforting, cool-to-the-touch hazy blue from which no tears need spring. I pulled Yale's course catalogue from my bag. Underlines marked classes I might take, dog-ears marked disciplines I'd not previously heard of. I was firmly on the path to assimilation, wasn't I? The kind of bootstraps American who rises above and gets out. During the overnight visit, Yale had hovered, shimmering, above the proceedings. While serving microwaved cake, Sharon even invited me to participate more fully in my sister's life. *Perhaps a campus visit? An overnight in your dorm?*

Out the train window, the Main Line's manicured lawns gave way to gravel. St. Joe's Prep's freshly painted ball courts, fifteen minutes later, were milk crates on wood poles. Electric wires swooped, water towers stood firm, and graffiti whipped by in a here-and-gone blur.

23

SHE SAID NORF PHILLY
AND ONE-TWO-FREE

That same summer Gabi ran in naked. She had four years to my seventeen. Her hair and body dripped from the bath. It was a high-speed chase wrangling her into pjs. Her pouf of curls, typically bouncing in a cloud, now slithered down her back like wet snakes. Taunting me, she circled the room. Any time I got close wielding the towel, she shrieked and darted away. It was our usual game but today she froze abruptly, shocked by her reflection in the full-length mirror. She ogled the chubby nude reflection. Experimented with poses: forward-facing, profile, hand-on-hip. She poked her butt cheek so its fat jiggled. She smooshed her abundant belly into a volcano whose tip was the navel, then sucked in Mount Gabi till her ribcage protruded. Finally came a grand proclamation: "My belly is round as the earth!"

Here was big sisterhood: watching a child discover herself. At four, Gabi had no reason to doubt her life force—planetary in scale. Girl held the cosmos in her torso. Immediately, I was improvising a refrain to DMX's "Party Up." *Y'all gon' watch my belly curve! Up in here! Up in here! Y'all gon' watch my jiggle butt! Up in here! Up in here!* Naked, she busted some one-leg moves, a hopping flamingo to my serenade. She would dance a loop around the room, then pause before the mirror and palm her stomach. "Round as the earth!" she would shout, before repeating the orbit.

When she was two days old, I thought Gabi's crying would be the worst, best, and only part of my adolescence henceforth. On the ride home from the hospital, her howls were earth-shattering and unstoppable. The tiny life in the contraption beside me hit a high note to decimate a rabid dog. Pop eyed me in the rearview and chuckled, *Get used to it!* Later that afternoon, other sounds would emerge. A nursing gurgle, a sleeping purr. But her distress, I knew quickly, would become my own. By the time we turned onto our block and carried her up past Eleguá, the baptism was complete. Reborn into sisterhood.

Mom had labored for eighteen hours and Gabi's head, blocked at the cervix, finally burst forth and ripped mom like paper. Hollers drummed the birthing suite as Gabi exploded toward us, and a flood of crimson and murk drenched the linens beneath mom's knees. The wriggling newborn was gooey, a messy ordeal, a weird wet relative. Then the midwife laid the baby atop mom's breast, which throbbed from anticipation. I couldn't believe mom's boob was visibly enlarging, and she wept at the baby's first drink.

The Baby. Long after bottles then pampers were outgrown, that was her name. Mom, can I put The Baby to sleep? Mom, can

I take The Baby to Clark Park? Mom, can I nuke The Baby a Cheez Whiz sandwich?

Because "Quiara" catches in a young mouth, my name became Ra Ra.

Ra Ra and The Baby. The Baby and Ra Ra.

By Gabi's side, I regressed to a childhood more playful than my original go-round. She was my do-over youth. Not once did I sit on the steps and observe her from a distance. I never wondered what size batteries made her go nor did I crown her a god, lying prostrate at her magnificence. More accessible than my cousins, less towering than mom. I dove in headlong to the mire of playtime. We danced together daily. Inhibitions were dropped like old school clothes. I had a body now, because I had a sister.

My bony hip was The Baby's throne. Before she could walk that's how we rolled to the corner store, the pizza place, the cheesesteak counter. My back went numb before I'd put her in the stroller, and when feeling returned, she'd be back on the hip-throne.

From the get-go we were Odd Couple Extraordinaire. She said Norf Philly and one-two-free. Her past tenses were runaway locomotives. *We played-ed-ed in the park then biked-ed-ed home!* She was made of exclamation points. When I got her dressed in the morning, the diva threw fits. "No, Ra Ra! Socks and skirt gotta match! I been told-ed-ed you that every day!" My fair skin and freckles offset her matte tan. My gross bony kneecaps a punchline beside her ample thighs, dimpled and rippling. So rotund were her nalgas that from the bathroom she'd holler: "Ra Ra, come wipe me!" Girl's butt was too plump for a full reach-behind. But if the word "sister" confused people, their confusion became our game.

Since she took herself as the scandalous half of our duo, I

endeavored to surprise her with boldness. Like when we walked to Purple Fox for fish hoagies and a man called out the driver's side, "Hey, baby, smile!" "I'm not your baby," I hollered. The Baby's jaw dropped. "You sassy!" she sang, highest praise.

And when, senior year, I had a stomach so full of butterflies I nearly choked on their wings, I sat The Baby down on the front porch. A talk was to be had. Sister business. Not even a best friend, my same age, had earned this ceremony:

"I need to tell you something."

"Is it a joke?" she asked.

"No. Why?"

"Because you smiling funny."

I tried to fix my face.

"Whaaaa? Tell me, stop being weird!"

"I like a boy."

"He likes you, too?"

"I think so."

Then she nodded, like *he better.* And she gripped my knee like an elder implying *good luck, kid, cuz love makes a mess of things.*

When the boy in question met Gabi, she threw herself on our Scrabble board. It was a tantrum for the ages. Her limbs became windshield wipers, sent the Z tile beneath the kitchen stove and the S ricocheting upstairs. On his second visit, we were careful to pay her more attention. She sat on his lap, chitchatted about Ricky Martin's cute smile, then farted and asked if he would leave cuz it stunk so bad. On his third visit we made clay snakes from a kit. When his snake was complete, she lifted it gently. "You did the zigzag perfect." Then she smooshed it in one squeeze. Before he came to get me for senior prom, Gabi dressed for the event in pink overalls, pink-trimmed socks, and a soft-serve twist with pink baubles. The big event, no one had told her, would happen off-site, making our front porch photos simply the sendoff. "Why can't I be your date, too?" she wept, big tears falling, as the boy slid a corsage onto my wrist and mom snapped photos.

Having a kid on your side like that? There's no hurdle you can't leap over. It's narcotic to be a girl's whole universe, to have tantrums thrown in your honor. You forget about that daddy wish for a day. The bloodsickness that nipped Tico's heels fades away. You lose track of how long Flor has been M.I.A., and you visit Cuca less because girlhood lives right there in your home. The conundrum of mom's worship recedes when Gabi's telling stupid knock-knock jokes on the hammock out back.

One night after tuck-in, after Czerny and Chopin had been exhausted and AP Spanish flash cards had been studied, I wanted one more whiff of the girl. Her sleeping purr was the same as on day one, though she was nearly five now. I nuzzled into her neck and inhaled youth's perfume. It evoked Cheerios mornings, swing-set afternoons, mosquito evenings in the alleyway hammock. Then I noticed a string coming out her mouth. A choking hazard. But when I tugged, she clamped her jaw down. Now I looped the string around my finger and pulled till red shone between her sleeping lips. I leaned in close. Yes, there flowed the tiniest ribbon of blood, like the first swirl of yellow from a punctured yolk. The Baby was bleeding. Alarmed, I plunged a finger into her wet mouth, searching gums and cheek, realized the string was knotted around a tooth. I had nearly pulled the thing out. I startled backward so that my head hit the bathroom door. How could mom and Pop fail to mention Gabi's first loose tooth? How could they dare try removing it without me? As if she was theirs and not mine. Gabi gnawed the string dreamily, then turned over and continued purring.

It had been close. I had nearly torn a piece of her body. The world, I knew, stood ready to do such things to girls, chubby Norf Philly ones especially. Tie strings around their wobbliest bits and begin the demolition. The day she sang in the mirror—round as the earth!—while palming her big belly, I had wondered: *How long, this utopia? When will the belly become a source of horror?*

And so as Yale approached, it became less a horizon than an abandonment. I was in deep for two Philly souls. A sister and a boy. I ached from the thought of a day without them; four years was torturous, an impossibility. He left first for college in Minnesota and I cried into my pillow, sure the college girls would be blond and a Boricua crush from West 50th would be forgotten. It was the noisy pillow cry of a million teen movies. The kind I had never let loose during childhood conundrums. Not during mom's possession or blood sacrifices, as I needed to remain undercover. Certainly not during dad's slow fade to stranger, which was omnipresent as air, too everywhere for tears. Now my snot and howls were tributaries in the swamp of teenage heartbreak.

I didn't cry when mom and Pop drove off the freshman quad and Gabi craned back for one last wave. But betrayal's heavy veil descended when they turned onto Elm Street, out of view. I was a sister-leaver. I was cold-turkey in an indifferent world. College meant abandoning Gabi midcourse, entrusting her flourishing to sinister hands. My fears, it turned out, were dead-on. Mean teachers would taunt the Norf Philly in her cadence, declare her remedial, put her in an ESL class. Four years of schoolyard fat jokes would pummel her. And I would miss it all, offer no nightly antidote. I knew Gabi was live bait in the Skinny Pale Cabaret that called itself America. I wanted to whisper in her sleeping ear, to vaccinate daily against the slander: *You are mother earth, sis, don'tcha forget it.* But she was gone.

Inside my dorm room, I taped her photo to my desk: in pampers atop my hip, a mess of curls, her eyes pure electric joy. Seeing it, I could almost feel Gabi's skin against mine, along with all the possibility that her warmth implied. Abuela's and Toña's and Nuchi's heartbreaks predated me and therefore won on chronology: I could offer no balm or protection to my elders. As to the mysteries of our Perez lost, the secrets of our deaths and disappearances? Well, maybe a four-year-old sis was a remedy, if not an explanation. Imagining her on 95 South, mile markers tallying our growing distance, I saw now the once-in-a-lifetime opportunity she presented me: a chance to foster a self-loving, not-disappearing Perez girl. A shot at building a language beyond my own internal purposes: words that would become instructions to the next generation. Gabi would flourish. She must. Now each folded T-shirt placed in a dorm room drawer became a vow. I would earn my physical distance from my sister. And since she had taught me to dive into joy's deep end, I would make a wild ride of it and come home for Thanksgiving with stories to tell.

24

ATONALITY

My naïveté surrounding college was a blessing. I saw no reason why Yale shouldn't be my oyster, and not knowing what to fear, I opted for boldness. First day of shopping period, when students tried out classes before formally registering, I went to Composers' Seminar, a 400-level course with extensive prerequisites. I had taken none of them.

"Wait, are you the girl who sent the tapes with her application? 'Three Piano Preludes'?"

"Yes."

"You have a memorable name. Those were great. But have you taken music theory?"

"No. But I learn by ear. I'm a quick study."

"Play the preludes, will you? Wait till the stragglers find a seat."

Yale seminars were capped at twelve but these professors accepted only half that. Judging by the greetings, here lay the inner sanctum. "How was that Boston Pops apprenticeship?" "Any headway on your thesis?" The students were boys, the teachers men. No females in sight, and the room's whiteness rivaled Malvern's. But its gleaming wealth added an unfamiliar edge, a new code for me to learn. Racks of digital music gear gleamed, supercomputers stood like installation art, sweaters and slacks looked costly though casual, and at the center stood a six-foot Yamaha digital hybrid.

I adjusted my stool at the piano, coaxed one deep breath into my trembling fingertips, and began. The dynamic range surprised me. Loud became majestic, soft became tender. It was the best instrument I'd ever played. On it, my preludes sounded magnificent. I had composed the first two a year earlier while avoiding piano homework. My teacher had assigned Scriabin; while practicing, I'd made a note mistake, then gone down a rabbit hole chasing the cool sound. The third prelude had come a month later, as I grappled with some low-register Gershwin stuff. Because of my composition's fungible meter, I hadn't figured out how to notate it in manuscript. Some measures were an obvious four-four, while others seemed to lack time altogether. But when played, they flowed like sentences. The chords crunched and resolved, journeying through dissonance to dreamier soundscapes. Ethereal legato traded with witty staccato, and you could hear the Scriabin and Gershwin all over it.

No applause came at the end. Brows were raised, legs crossed, arms folded. These were not the type to express affirmation, it seemed. And yet, I had a sense of having survived the hazing. To be the only girl around and yet hold center like that, it was ballsy. My hands had hardly trembled after the first few notes. I was twice as bold, I told myself, as any of these boys.

"Questions for our guest?" the longer-haired professor asked.

A tall golden boy in cashmere leaned forward. "Most important influences?"

"Celina y Reutilio." Until I said it, I hadn't realized mom's morning tape was especially meaningful. She had warped it after hundreds of plays, an ebullient Lukumí score by which to trim Pop's hairline. She would sing-yell above the clippers: "Que viva Changó!" Celina's voice was twangy as the tres, with the güiro and bongo cutting right through. This was folkloric stuff, campesino to the core, but with chromatic solos that would've turned heads at the Blue Note. Their songs were rough joy, dirty praise. And their songs were influence. I had said it aloud for the first time.

Then we were diving into the syllabus, the professor introducing our semester's first two composers: Schoenberg and Ruggles. One was German Jewish, the other anti-Semitic American. One was a sought-out public intellectual, the other a cantankerous hermit. But both were pioneers of the atonality that had come to define Music Today. This was news to me. I jotted down *atonal* and *twelve-tone row,* vowing to look them up later. Then it was time to listen. Out of state-of-the-art speakers came the most inharmonious, nihilistic note combinations I'd ever heard. There was no rhythm at all, neither a pulse to steady nor a syncopation to pull. These were sonic inkblots, not songs. If my cousins had heard it, they'd have laughed the Cola Champagne out their noses. But I looked around at a dead-serious room: most brows furrowed in serious consideration.

I had already begun craving an uglier language, one that expressed the Perez resilience and maelstrom. North Philly's too-young death and mucky girlhood and gorgeous dance were eager to key their way out my cage. There was a poetics I longed to share with mom at home and the world at large, one messier than dainty Mozart, more syncopated than Chopin, more gut-tural than elegant Bach. But I hadn't yet found it. Schoenberg and Ruggles were too bleak. I needed a dissonance that spoke of love, too. A turbulent woman's tongue. Seated amidst all that spotless machinery, I worried that eight semesters of such exalted noise would sprinkle the wrong breadcrumbs on my path, that this laboratory would not lead me to my language. That, in fact, a four-year detour lay ahead and I would emerge off-course, lost. Having come here to study music, though, I resolved to proceed and learn all I could.

Then the listening was over and the boys analyzed it with mind-numbing lingo and impressive facility. Taking notes was hopeless; I couldn't spell the dang vocab words. But dropping the course was off the table. Not after surviving the hazing.

Girl, I said, *you are in over your head.*

Scholarships and loans had been generously offered, but I still owed the bursar a couple thou each year. Work-study jobs maxed out at twelve hours; I needed twice that for books, tuition, and Amtraks home. Day one, I huddled with other freshmen before the Career Center corkboard. (My roommates were not among us; I couldn't fathom how they'd make tuition or buy books with no income.) It was a grid of half-sheets, each the key to a campus job.

School of Medicine Library. Shelving & front desk. $7.25 @ 5 hrs.
Morse College Dining Hall. Service & cleanup. $8.50 @ 7 hrs.
School of Music Recording Studio. $10.50 @ ___.

That last one caught my eye. The wage was high, the hours left blank. I ripped off the posting and sprinted for my dorm phone.

The studio recorded every School of Music concert, in the same way that the library housed every PhD thesis. Advanced degree recitals, Yale Symphony Orchestra performances, faculty concerts. Guest artists like Bang on a Can crowded the busy internal schedule. The hours were rigorous, my interviewers intoned. How committed was I, five upperclassmen asked. Extremely, I responded. Sure, sure, but could I work twenty hours a week, they asked. I'm certain my irises transformed into dollar signs, and I'm certain my interviewers saw them, because I was hired on the spot. The hourly wage had a good two bucks on most campus jobs because turnover came with a steep price tag. Each microphone was worth thousands of dollars. Newbies dropped them; trained staff didn't. I was hired on Monday and started Tuesday.

You'd never know the place existed had you not been in the Career Center that September morning in '95. The studio was housed on the third floor of Sprague Hall, atop a small dusty staircase, behind unmarked and always-locked black doors. If an audience member wandered to that tiny landing and realized the bathrooms were not there, they'd likely think the doors led to janitorial closets or electrical panels. But open the one to the left and the Fred Plaut Recording Studio's massive console eclipsed the door frame. A mothership of buttons, faders, sliders, and knobs. It was *Star Trek* for music geeks. Vintage analog captured the warmth of an oboe's wail, the breadth of a Steinway's thunder. Digital's compression couldn't compare. Even the buttons seemed of a different era, a time when plastic rivaled concrete for strength. The console was kept in impeccable condition. Gene, the boss, kept a steady stock of air spray. He'd go around pulling off a fader, puffing the dust away, replacing the button. Knob by knob, spritz by spritz, the console's sound remained flawless. A speck of dust would mean cracks and pops in the feed. Not under Gene's watch.

The console consumed over half the studio's footprint. Chairs, mixing racks, a desk, and a tool cart surrounded it—planets crammed too close to the sun. A cascade of wires streamed between devices, like overgrown weaving, a giant's macramé.

Sprague was one of two main concert halls at Yale, the austere sibling to the gold-leaf ostentation of Woolsey. Its brick facade, white walls, and wooden seats echoed the Quaker meeting I'd attended. Seen from the ground-floor audience bank, a white bandshell enveloped the stage. Seen from the second-floor balcony, the cherrywood stage was a warm glossy pool. No matter where you sat, the eight-foot Steinway was a regal gorilla. Years of trial and error had allowed Gene to perfect mic placement. He was uninterested in the compression that was industry standard. He wanted to capture a live acoustic experience, in crystalline pianissimo and rafter-shaking fortissimo. A musical journey was not about its average.

Yale's wealth was of a magnitude I was only beginning to fathom. Most kids had no jobs at all. Others quit when the work got tedious or the fraternity tapped them. People cashed checks written by parents, dropped daddy's Visa like corner store pennies. Over a late-night call, my long-distance boyfriend spelled it out to my confused ass. "They're rich," he said. "Sure, some of them are," I responded. "Not some," he corrected, "most." I remembered the pie chart in Yale's recruitment brochure. I had focused on the forty percent slice: students receiving need-based financial aid. That portion had informed me Yale was fiscally possible and worth applying to. But I hadn't considered the flip side of the coin, the sixty percent with a small fortune on hand—

enough to write four years' worth of full tuition, room, and board checks. Now that I lived amongst them, that just about blew me away.

Stepping into the studio was welcome escape. Instant relaxation, my muscles unclenched. And not just mine. All the studio crew left their armor at the door. We were in the same boat—paying our way. You wouldn't hear any of us fronting about poverty, though outside the studio, classmates with Tahoe ski habits insisted on the modesty of their estates. Not us. This was our third or fifth in a string of jobs since our first paper route or babysitting gig—we knew we'd struck gold. Having steady work marked many of us as the fortunate amongst our extended clans. We got paid to hear Bach's C-major cello suite, how it peaked on that crunchy modal tone. Once, we ordered midnight pizzas thanks to Willie Ruff, double-bass faculty, who called and said, "Gene, set up your mics now." An arrangement of "Amazing Grace" had come to him in a dream, he had to get it down before it slipped away. It was a short session. Three live takes. He plucked his double bass and sang the melody atop it. His voice had the rasp of reveries. I got paid to catch the serenade.

Each microphone had a dedicated attaché. Inside, foam cutouts gave the impression of a manger. Wrapping the cables was done with precise methodology. Coil them loose, draped over the shoulder, so as not to kink up the cable. Never drop them on the ground, place them down. Never yank them out by the cord—use the plug as a handle. Blue cables, fifteen feet. Red ones, twenty-five. Green, fifty.

Then we'd go upstairs, adjust levels at soundcheck, and hit record before the concert began. If we had set up correctly, there should be nothing left to do but enjoy the show. Maybe the slightest downward adjustment if an agitato hit the red. Beethoven required a close watch. Wagner, for sure. Bach's Italian Suites meant a laid-back evening. Some evenings I studied. Others I listened to the concert. Still others, I swapped jokes with coworkers, or taught them Spanish curse words in exchange for the German, Italian, and Trini patois ones they had been raised with.

There was a late-night session with only one piece scheduled: Schubert's Piano Sonata in A Major, D. 959. Elizabeth Parisot from the piano faculty was on deck. Because it was a studio session rather than a concert, we started late, after Sprague Hall shut down. The closet-size room adjacent to the main studio had a smaller analog console and just a few rack components. Its focused sound was best for solo projects. I placed the mic at the bell of the piano. Gene checked it with approval, then watched me set levels. He pressed the talkback button and spoke into the console. *Whenever you're ready.* Then came an inhale and two opening chords that swung heaven's left and right gates open. Simple A majors but when they dropped, those fuckers left mushroom clouds. In their ringing wake, a legato minor-key arpeggio ran the length of the ivories, top to bottom. Professor Parisot destroyed the Steinway that night. WWE on eighty-eight keys, seismic as warfare, elegant as ballet. I didn't know any Schubert so beyond sonata form, I couldn't anticipate the piece's direction. Its unexpected turns and dynamic contrasts had me exclaiming aloud in spots. Mm-ing and ugh-ing like the AME back on 48th and Kingsessing. Gene gave me the good headphones—my ears cupped in their plush nest. The first movement, the allegro, is twelve minutes long. In sonata years, that's a quarter century. Mozart's first movements clock in at five. Beethoven's range from six minutes to ten. Twelve is tantric. Plus, Schubert uses false recapitulations so you think the piece is rounding the last bend, then you're in a different key with the melody in the top octave. The final A chord was gentle as the small of a back. A pianissimo that dribbled down your chin. I pulled off my headphones and looked at Gene, flushed. Needing a cloth to pat away the sweat, craving a postcoital ciggy. "I know, it's magnificent." He chuckled. "That happens sometimes." Then he pressed the talkback mic. "I think we got it." We heard Professor Parisot's footsteps on the Sprague stage. Gentle and echoing, she paced atop the hardwood, no doubt preparing herself for the next movement.

25

FANIA EVERYTHING AND
SALSA OUT-OF-PRINTS

Midway through sophomore year, I grew cold to the major. I hopped to Yale music thinking horizons would expand, curiosities would deepen. That's how the best piano lessons made me feel back home, and the best dance parties, too. En el barrio, music was air. There was no funeral, no graveside visit, no praise ceremony, no after-work hang, no morning shower or roll-by without it. Music meant Nigeria and Senegal, Cuba and Brazil, PR and DR, and Harlem, U.S.A. Music is why driver's-side glass could descend, why kitchen windows got jimmied. It was the front door and the linoleum floor. Volume knobs lived well above medium. Every Philly Rican I knew had an instrument in the cabinet—a güiro, maracas, bongos—so that a stop-n-chat might become an all-night descarga. On occasional weekends I fled for Aunt Linda's, from dad's side, and we'd hit up SOB's or the Lone Star Cafe, or climb to the bandstand where her rambunctious rock was on tap and she'd let me be keyboard-side page-turner. I expected that from Yale and more, four years of awakenings, but that late-night Schubert was a rare gem. Many dictionaries live in this world, and at Yale, "music" came from a different Webster, with a different definition. The word meant a particular type—Western classical—without even having to specify. "Music" was a synonym for "white."

The ethnomusicology corner of the listening library was a half shelf of grainy field recordings. As if most of the globe had not yet encountered recording studios. There was a smattering of unattributed Kenyan tapes; some of Alan Lomax's southern recordings. Unlike the strict rules governing most of the collection, non-Western musicians didn't merit attribution. Certainly, no music major would be caught dead at Toad's Place, the local rock joint. That was a lower rung than the field recordings.

Music was for dissecting, a forensic pursuit in which the human body was checked at the door. The only true audience sat in a concert hall. The stuff of dancing? Maybe, if Merce Cunningham or the Joffrey was involved. But the stuff of dance halls? Nope. Atonal theory and twelve-tone rows got prime bandwidth. Bleak stuff, but profs and classmates laughed—out loud—when I once dared to mention Stevie. I would imagine my cousins as flies on the seminar walls. They'd have a field day. *Yo, they call that music? Fuck outta here, I got farts with more melody. How much Yale costs again?*

English 129 offered imaginative escape. After the densely packed Greek and British readings, Ntozake Shange rocketed straight to my core, the syllabus's final offering. Like e. e. cummings, whom I'd read in high school, Shange broke all the rules of capitalization, punctuation, and spelling. But the rule she broke most beautifully was who merited a page and a stage. In her choreo-poem (woman was a genre unto herself) Black and Brown wom-en's heartbreak set the table for a distinct form of communal healing. Here, celebration and suffering cohabitated within the feminine divine, and the piece's ritual structure felt to me like an awakening. It was a baño, a limpieza, in literary form.

The cycling team offered physical escape. We'd pedal thirty miles along New England roads, past orchards and quarries, far from campus. I didn't feel fraudulent or freakish pedaling past the autumn foliage. The cyclists were mostly European grad stu-dents with accents disparate as the Perez family's skin tones.

El Coqui, a cuchifrito joint that rivaled Philly's greasiest, was another get-me-outta-here. The bus picked me up a few blocks from campus and hissed away from the stonewalled fortress, past increasingly Spanish store signs, to a corner where ten bucks meant arroz, pernil, and whatever fritura was under the heat lamp.

That summer, I came home sweaty and salty after days teach-ing Inner City camp songs with no AC. I'd allow myself ten min-utes of sofa collapse, then head to the stereo and continue my project. I would dub mom and Pop's entire music library while home. I returned sophomore year with a duffel of tapes like I was ready to set up shop on Kensington Ave, all I needed was a folding table. And one more thing clattered inside that duffel—my old Circuit City typewriter. Yale's campus was full of clusters—posh labs, dungeon desks, cubbies with dogwoods out the window—but my erasable typewriter in the privacy of my own dorm room, I knew, would be another escape. I scored a rare single. There was room for a cot and a bookshelf, my sixty-one-key Casio, and a tape player. The mattress doubled as my desk. That cubbyhole privacy became my artist's retreat. There,

on a self-guided stroll through my past, I began to study the
music of home.

First came Ramito's *Parrandeando*. The record was out of
print, despite being the best in Ramito's oeuvre. His catalogue
was massive but vagaries of licensing and archival sloppiness
meant that inferior Ramito was all Tower sold. So I worked off a
tenth-generation dub, dissecting songs that would soon disappear. The cassette ran for eight or ten seconds before I paused it.
I'd hum and plunk out notes, sketching in lightest pencil. I'd re-
play when necessary to check a tricky run. The ten-bar phrasing
was counterintuitive to the eight-bar DNA of Schumann and
Haydn that filled my classes. Chunk by chunk the melody filled
out, in darker pencil. When the cuatro part was done, I played it
on the Casio's synth guitar, feeling its arc in my fingers. A busy
line, showy notes. Then I rewound the tape and began again with
the bongo, the trumpet, the vocals. I didn't know the low notes
were a guitarrón; I had never heard of the instrument. So, I transcribed what I took to be double bass. Some parts, like the cuatro,
were intricate and dexterous. Others, like the güiro, were simple
but required mind-boggling consistency. Each song took at least
a day, plus extra to learn to play what I'd transcribed.

Next came Celina y Reutilio. A Santa Barbara's piano solo
took me an entire afternoon, and it was still a rough facsimile. It
was full of chromatic notes that crunched against the root chord.
I was confident my Schoenberg-loving professor would be impressed, so I brought my transcription to Composers' Seminar,
year two, and played it for him. His eyes widened during that
bewitching solo, but the song itself was folk music, *basic stuff,* he
said with a wave of the hand. Dismissed. Moving on.

I craved an intellectual home base, a richer conversation with
peers. One that didn't blindfold itself to my culture, that didn't

other entire hemispheres of art. A music professor took pity and slipped me a flyer after class: there was a fellowship for students of color across disciplines to form a two-year scholarly community. The blank field at the top of the application form read "Brief Project Description." I pondered it while walking home, then grabbed a pen and jotted a phrase: *salsa musical*. Thus began two years of faculty mentorship, interdisciplinary peer review, and summer funding—twice as much as I'd made teaching summer camp. There was even separate money earmarked for research expenses.

That's how I bought three months of piano lessons with Elio Villafranca, an Afro-Cuban expat who'd come to the 215. Elio taught me to tap a clave with one hand while playing a montuno with the other. Swap and repeat. Finger independence—I'd learned that playing Bach fugues. Left-right independence—that had come with Czerny exercises. But rhythmic independence was a beast, and I gained newfound appreciation for the rigor syncopation demanded. I tensed up, accelerating through difficult rhythmic passages. Elio would shake his head, snap the pulse, and refuse to let me pull away. Mas lento, mas lento, as his claps insisted on slow. Every lesson began with "El Manicero," a simple seven-note melody. Elio made me play those seven notes all summer, looping them until my shoulders relaxed into the polyrhythm. Tension and release. Release and tension. Under Elio's tutelage I broke old habits, stumbled toward new ones, and learned how contradiction—syncopation—can feel smooth over time, even natural.

Come August, when our lessons ended, there was $276 left in expense money. I took a Greyhound to New York and searched the bowels of the Times Square 1/9. I'd heard of the legendary kiosk. They specialized in Fania everything and salsa out-of-prints. I laid my cash on the counter. "What are the thirty CDs I gotta know?" Héctor Lavoe, Ruben Blades, Mongo Santamaria, Celia Cruz. Cultural pillars my parents knew well. I had to seek them out, buy them, study 'em ground-up. Just like mom claimed her old pots were some kind of merit badge. She had put in the time and I would, too. I wanted to disassemble those songs like a vintage engine, lay all the parts on my front lawn, reassemble it from scratch. To master the mechanics, to get at the crux of my hometown tunes.

That Celia montuno became a song in scene one.

That Mongo Santamaria jam, the cold-ass shekere? That became a dance number mid-show.

Two- and four-bar patterns, in my hands, got flipped, switched, and adapted into new music, with new lyrics and a story.

It was called *Sweat of the River, Sweat of the Ocean,* and yes, it was as earnest as it sounds. In the story, a Santera dies and her agnostic daughter has nine days to properly dismantle mom's altars. This disassembly must be done according to strict ceremonial mandates—it is no task for cynics. Scene four included a coconut divination. In scene five, characters constructed a throne for Yemayá. There were lyrics about cowrie shells and cascarilla. To immerse myself in the poetics of Ifá, I studied anew all those books mom had given me. *Four New World Rituals* and *The Way of the Orisa* became late-night reading once again. My old underlines were compass needles, guiding me to powerful passages.

I schlepped my Casio to the casting room, where I'd accompany vocal selections. Amber Cruzado walked in and sang "A Boy Like That"—what else was a Boricua Yalie gonna audition with? Felix Torres hadn't prepared a song. Tone deaf, he claimed. This is a musical, I told him. I know, he responded, but there's a play with Puerto Rican characters so what was I gonna do, stay home? I requested "Happy Birthday" or "Amazing Grace" a cappella. His voice trembled and a timid "How sweet the sound" emerged. He was not tone deaf, just shy. Amber and Felix landed the roles. Three more left to cast.

Out in the hallway, waiting for names to be called, were campus Latinos of all hues and backgrounds. Unfamiliar faces mostly. Cats from American Studies and Psychology. All us Latino undergrads scanning the room going, "How do we not know each other?" Perhaps we had crossed paths at one of La Casa Cultural's holiday parrandas, but Yale's campus was diffuse. Here were aspiring Latino performers, squeezed on a few benches in a hallway, united by a script and some very rough demos. My doing. Cuz I had written a story. Just being in a room together felt, at Yale, like a statement. It almost resembled American Street. Except the host of today's gathering was not Abuela, but me.

Nick Chapel was a forty-five-seat black box. No backstage, and a playing space too small for musicians. Karaoke tracks would be the only way to pull off a musical. Gene gave me the keys to the studio. I had to wait till cover of night, when Sprague Hall closed, and I was under strict orders not to tell my coworkers. I was entrusted to manage the session alone.

Aunt Linda, from dad's side, and Uncle Rik drove up from New York. They would be playing piano and trumpet respectively. According to family lore, Linda had laid my bassinet beneath her keys so Bach's Italian Concerto would be my first language. I couldn't corroborate, but I did remember at five how she stacked two phone books on the bench and dropped the needle on Champion Jack Dupree. Play along, she said, and left me alone to figure it out. On weekend trips to New York, she had snuck me into pot-hazed dives where Steel Pulse and Etta James brought the night to its knees. Queen Etta even put me on blast between songs. Girl's too young, get her out, this is grown folks' music. But I stayed. The exquisite populist music that Linda and Rik gifted me made Yale's insularity all the bleaker. Now, for tonight's session, they would be professional anchors to a mostly student band. Our Peruvian percussionist was getting a PhD. He was apparently monstrous on the timpani but when I told him the first song required a cáscara beat, he looked at me like, huh? I had to write it out for him, as Elio had for me. Our Spanish guitarist was another pre-doc. I had recorded his all-Bach recital and recruited him, assuming he had a Fender or six steel strings at least. Not so. The cat was a dedicated nylon-stringer. Nylons have a ruminative timbre ill suited to rhythmic parts, but you work with what you got.

Setting levels was tricky. The mics were engineered for classical instruments in concert halls. They could pick up a mosquito in the third row, but bass amps and cowbells threatened to blow them out. After conducting the band through a take, I ran up to the third-floor console to check if we'd hit the red, which we often had. I adjusted the levels, ran back down, fixed microphone placement, ran back up to hit record, and then back down once more to conduct the next take. Balancing the sound was a game of whack-a-mole. For the nylon strings to be audible, I had to max out the mic level. But that meant catching a lot of bleed from the congas, even when they were exiled to an upstage corner. How to marry these disparate instruments, create cohesion from chaos, fix it in the mix?

On opening night of *Sweat of the River, Sweat of the Ocean*, New Haven tasted a little like North Philly. Nuchi never traveled, Flor was on the lam, Abuela was frail, and Toña's weight kept her close to home. But cars full of cousins and tías headed north on

95. The Perezes descended on Yale. Danito's cheeks still were round from baby fat. A few whiskers waved hello on JJ's upper lip. The boys had never stayed in a hotel room. "A hundred dollars a night, Qui Qui!" they said outside the theater. I took their tickets and handed them programs. "Yo, mom and Pop went all out! There's two huge beds and free breakfast plus TV! We brought Sega and we about to play all night after the party!" Gabi could congratulate me in my actual name now: "I'm proud of you, Quiara!" I was no longer Ra Ra. And the boy came, too. No college girl had stolen him yet. Ginny and George purchased a few cast albums. In addition to being librettist, lyricist, composer, conductor, and sound engineer for *Sweat of the River,* I was box office, usher, and merchandise, too.

I was also audience. Lights faded and a hush fell. Mom patted my hand. The room experienced that brief interstitial darkness where the day is over but the show has not begun. That ceremonial bit of suspension. I realized, in those few seconds, how the piece was saturated with mom's influence. Her poetry and cadences unmistakable in the dialogue. Her morning tapes woven into my melodies. Lyrics inspired by Orisha books she gave me. Homage and grapple in every scene. Mom had sewn some costume pieces over winter break—a skirt for Yemayá, a gorro de Orisha ceremonial hat. But beyond that I had crawled into an artistic cave, losing contact with her as I wrote and rehearsed the show. Mom didn't know what she was about to see. Nor, perhaps, did she know how closely I'd been watching all my life. The first few notes rang out—my spin on a traditional aguinaldo, played on nylon strings rather than the typical cuatro. But it was close enough: música jíbara filled an Ivy League basement. The cast sang in unison.

Cowries para Yemayá, cowries para Yemayá
In my altar I bring you treasures
Te traigo tesoros en mi altar

The numinous world of Ifá burst onstage. Rather than apologizing for the Orisha, as I'd done many times, rather than insisting they were not black magic or ignoring my friends' disturbed gazes, I had created a space where the Orisha required no explanation. Where the Afro-Boricua could be hilarious and true, contradictory and complicated. I hadn't fully clocked the implications while creating the thing. It had felt, in process, like following curiosity's thread: longing to know the difference between danzón and son, between guaracha and guajiro. I had only meant to escape Schoenberg, for Christ's sake, and spend a few summer months with bomba y plena on loop. Perhaps also to run toward my elders' lexicon rather than away from it, to outgrow my inner escape artist. Perhaps, even, I'd gone rooting for a narrative complex enough to carry my name. But watching the show as mom grasped my hand, I understood the event as more than curiosity or personal reckoning. I was no longer an Ivy imposter. I had invited Yale to our family table and it had joined the feast, ready to break bread. In that way, I had bettered the institution.

Mom squeezed my hand over and over, a Morse code of connection, wiping tears, mouthing thank you. That is, until scene four, the coconut divination. When the padrino character lifted his palms, mom gasped. "Is he going to throw the coconuts?" "Sh." "Quiara, he can't do that!" "Mom, sh!" "Stop him now, he has to be consecrated!" "Mom, be quiet!" "Quiara, those aren't energies you just toy with—" The actor opened his cupped palms and the coconut pieces toppled to the stage. All four landed fruit-side up. "Aláfia!" mom gasped. The highest blessing. She laughed up at the lighting grid, exultant.

Trumbull College hosted the after-party. North Philly Boricuas were pulling sparkling ciders off silver trays. Mom made a show of praising the student actors in Spanish; they relished her cariño. Our faculty host had even asked my input on catering. No question. "El Coqui on Grand. Here's what to order." I wrote down the proper dishes and there they were—arroz con gandules, guineos en escabeche, pollo guisado—in glistening buffet trays. The host had made one woeful addition—salad. Boricuas don't eat salad at parties. No disrespect, but Puerto Rican salad makes the iceberg wedge look sophisticated—we just hack up cheap lettuce, spritz white vinegar on top, and let it wilt as we fight over pork cracklings. Cuca and Ginny praised the tostones. The crispiness-to-garlic-salt ratio was spot-on. "Qui Qui! How far is this place?" We made plans to hit up El Coqui for breakfast. I was psyched they'd hang in my favorite cuchifrito joint. There were murals of El Yunque on all the walls, plus El Coqui's Chinatown plates added to the experience. Arroz con pollo tastes better when it's served on Year of the Pig melamine. Danito shoved catered alcapurrias in his face till Titi Ginny scolded him for embarrassing the family. "But, mom, dem jawns beat the bricks they be giving out at Porky's Point." And we had to laugh because Porky's Point was responsible for half of all Gas-X sales in North Philly.

There was no DJ so I got full rein on the CD player. For the first hour it was all Cachao—old-school, midtempo, loosen up the vibe. Now I popped in Celia and "No Me Cambie Camino" busted out with that saucy opening montuno. Cuca began pulling my roommates into salsa spins and I wanted to find mom, to dance with her, but I realized she had left the party.

I found her in a powder room far from the action. Past the caterers in the kitchen. Tucked beneath a stairwell. The door was cracked open and mom was talking to herself. "Mom, are you okay?" "Sh, come inside." Her palms cradled four coconut pieces like baby birds. "Mom! Did you steal our props?" Rather than answer, she closed her eyes and recited mantras over the fruit. Finally, she kissed the coconut pieces and handed them to me. "I slipped them in my pocketbook after the show. Now at least they have the proper intention attached to them. Keep them in water so they don't dry out." Felix Torres, the actor playing the babalao, threw aláfia at every single show.

26

THE SERENITY PRAYER

lor reappeared Thanksgiving junior year. An unannounced comeback years after the bathtub fiasco. I keyed through our heavy front door—delicious how it turned with satin ease, one of the original set, grooves well worn. Familiar click of the bolt, truest welcome. There is no colder homecoming than a new finicky lock. My duffel parked on the sofa and no sooner did I holler "Guess who's baaaaack?" than Flor danced at me from the kitchen. She salsa-stepped past the table, hips in a Celia Cruz fast-forward. The radio was full-tilt—important to ensure delicious pasteles. Thanksgiving meant blowing out the subwoofer for two days of meal prep. Flor held her hands above her head—No me toques! My fingers are covered in masa!—and an assault of cheek kisses was upon me, with squeaks, sniffs, and mews for emphasis. She nibbled my shoulder, smelled my neck. She smiled that Flor smile so warm and innocent it made her tattoos seem like Sunday comics.

"Qui Quiiiiiiiiiiiiiiiiiii! I bet you're surprised to see me!"
Instructions flew my way. I was to describe Yale's campus.
Then play my latest Chopin. Was I still with the blond, el gringo,
from high school? Ay thanks god, Abuela loves that boy, I gotta
meet him! Will he come for Thanksgiving? Qui Qui, grrrrrrrrl,
we got catching up to do! So I was a music major at Yale, huh?
Did I teach them to salsa yet? Are they real conceited there?

Flor scrubbed the masa from her hands—two squirts of
Palmolive—and was hungry for details. Her white turtleneck
looked very L.L. Bean, a surprising style choice, but the sleeves
were rolled for food prep, showing more tattoos than I remembered. Her skin was bronzer than last time, cheeks downright
supple. Her butt was juicy and filled her jeans with confidence.
Good signs. "I really missed you, Flor." "Me too, Qui Qui. We'll
talk. We'll talk." We mashed plátanos for pasteles, found the
porcelain in the basement, searched for matching cloth napkins,
played an old parranda tape. It wasn't Christmas yet but we were
singing "Dame la mano paloma!" to some scratchy cuatro riff.
Through it all, Flor reminding me: "We'll talk, Qui Qui. We'll
talk." When the lasagna was baking and the arroz soft to the
bite, she led me to the upstairs couch. It was ceremonial, sitting
together like that—the formality of a confession, the eye contact of a friend. She began by reaching into her shirt and pulling
out a gold nameplate. It didn't read *Flor,* but rather *N.A.* Narcot-
ics Anonymous. To honor her anniversary of being clean. She
spoke softly, with pride that weighed little more than a feather.
There were keychains for each sober month, goalposts in a marathon. But she had run a mile and treated herself to a necklace.
I want you to know, she said. *I ain't proud of things I done, but I
ain't ashamed neither.* She painted sobriety's landscape, detail by
detail. Cocaine's lovely high, the loneliness of cravings. She quit

booze, too, so no more Bud Light in Titi Ginny's backyard. Newports and Kools still lived in her purse. Tattoos helped. The twelve steps were a work in progress. Lots of amends still unmade. Lots of damage done, zero time machines. No Band-Aids big enough for the wounds inflicted. Perhaps her children would forgive her one day; for now they were battling their adolescent demons.

Accepting god in her life had been the hardest part, and pivotal to her turnaround. Not going through the motions like a kid at Sunday mass—praying, genuflecting, grape juice and wafers. An actual reckoning. Removing the self from the solar system's midpoint. Flor was futility, Flor was failure, Flor was not behind the wheel. "People try to do the twelve steps and skip the god stuff, they just mumble the prayer to get to what they like. That's shortcuts, you gonna relapse. When they were the one in charge, they fucked up. Surrender or it don't work."

She asked permission to say the serenity prayer. Not to proselytize, not to freak me out, but to share something that helped her be a better self. Same as me playing Chopin. I said of course, but as "god" left her lips my toady little cynic was turning somersaults. I was the Muppets in the balcony, sneering at the artists. *God? Really? REALLY?!* And yet Vivi's bullet and penny-smooth scar pricked my conscience. Mom's five-year-old premonitions jangled my memory. And what of my own knees throttling during Quaker meeting, or my pen-in-hand blackout in Dr. Phillips's essay test?

> *God grant me the serenity to accept the things I cannot change,*
> *The courage to change the things I can,*
> *And the wisdom to know the difference.*

Words familiar as the hiss of a kneeling bus or a car alarm two corners away. Background noise, the soundtrack of Philly. But in Flor's embarrassed delivery the lines trembled with solace. To be better today than she was yesterday, that was her new North Star. Every bit mattered. The little bit may be all you get. She laid her flaws on the sofa cushion, as though my witness were medicine.

Her success would receive no departmental honors. There would be no leather-bound degree in Latin, no brass parade. But which accomplishment ran deeper? Every string quartet I'd composed at Yale, or every night Flor fell asleep sober? Her life was a pebble skipped across a stream—a brief event whose ripples were real.

Then mom was hollering *Come dust the gravy boat!* and *There's nine matching napkins pero necesitaba sixteen, carajo!* Flor slipped out to the alley for a smoke. I searched the closet for the missing linens, my cousin's testimony throttling my brain, tilt-a-whirl. A full hour of explanation, of this-is-me and here's-what-happened. Of I-speak-the-beast, I-put-the-beast-between-my-teeth, I-name-myself-aloud. Flor's story as communion wafer. The opposite of silence.

I did find the napkins, but it wasn't little Qui Qui who laid them at each Perez place setting. Qui Qui was the kid who lost her cousins. Quiara was the woman who got one back.

27

STERLING LIBRARY

There were a hundred ways to spend a Yale afternoon, and all of them came with an unparalleled setting. An emerald lawn, a modernist dining hall, mahogany wainscoting on the seminar wall, an Olympic pool. Sterling Library was the crown jewel, its Gothic spires poking the clouds. Numerous slate walkways converged at its facade so that Sterling's majesty was a part of almost all daily foot traffic. En route to the dining hall, seminar, studio. Heading to Ashley's Ice Cream or back from the practice rooms. The cycling team gathered at its wide shallow steps before pedaling toward scenic Connecticut. Student tour guides barked its pedigree to hopeful high schoolers. "Half a city block!" the work-study sophomore would declare. Each of its three thousand stained-glass windows was unique. It housed millions of volumes. Cracking the door an inch required half your weight, heaving. Peek into the cavernous nave, you'd see columns uplit like a scene out of *The Godfather.* A brooding, shadowy, amber darkness antithetical to reading.

Venture farther in, it would come clear that the treasure chest had been abandoned. Sterling's labyrinthine stacks were rarely visited. None of its sixteen floors had computer labs or viable napping sofas. Students visited on a transactional basis. Get your book and go. All the more reason I loved it. The cavelike reverb and concrete floors in late spring. I'd sit with a book and let the cement's cool kiss jolt my thighs. Corridors smelling of old paper and metal bookends. Dust hovered in what meager light permeated the stained glass. The time was always one breath before dawn inside those dim glowing passageways. Wandering aisle to aisle, often without goal, I raked my fingers along cellophane spines. I tried the religion section, poetry mimeographs, gardening books. Such meandering might lead to a song lyric, a line of dialogue, a term paper idea. The less related to my project, the better. Staircases between shelves secreted me to vaults of epistolary folios, military ledgers, nautical maps. Sometimes I pulled a drawer from the card catalogue simply to touch its well-thumbed edges. As if the past, and my place in it, were a simple matter of touch.

Summers were for the other Quiara, the quantum Quiara of the parallel universe aka Philly, aka home. Half a block of Sterling versus half a block of North 2nd. Whiplash contrasts bordering on absurd. There was a haunting indulgence in my freedom to wander, to pick a book from a shelf, to read. So many aisles Nuchi would never roam. So many pages she would never turn. Nuchi would not be dumbstruck at the climactic lines of *for colored girls* . . .

> *i found god in myself*
> *& i loved her / i loved her fiercely*

Nor would she arrive at those lines by way of these, a few pages earlier:

> *i waz missin somethin . . .*
> *somethin promised . . .*
> *a layin on of hands*
> *the holiness of myself released*

Pages that might talk her off some spiritual ledge, as they'd done for me. Narrative armor, safe places to land, instructions for survival sent to future generations. That is, if we in the future could decode them.

With each passing semester, Nuchi occupied more real estate in my imagination, as did Yale's monstrous beauty. Senior year it got bad. Graduation was a beast roaring at me, its approach magnifying my four-year remove from home. Soon I'd be back in Philly with my cousins. We would dance, no doubt. My stiff hips had loosened with age, my inhibitions shed. There would be a laying on of hands. But my cousins knew the raw score as did I—my ship had set sail. Toward what, to where? I didn't know, and Yale hadn't shown me the answer. But somewhere other than the Marines, nursing school, the corner—paths my younger cousins had already begun walking. The snag of resentment hooked and caught. Yale's opulence became a mean sort of mockery until a bitter kernel implanted in my gut. I stopped visiting Sterling. Averted my gaze when I strolled past. A question on loop, taunting: *Why do I get Sterling Library and Nuchi doesn't?* It roiled and implicated me. I was troubled by both extremes: Yale's affluence, Philly's scarcity, but more so by the divide separating them. Truth being: the divide was where I had made my home. Until I became a bridge, if such a reconciliation was possible, there would be no peace.

And what of Gabi? Kindergarten went fine in my absence. It was a bilingual pilot program in the heart of el barrio. Latino kids, half English speakers, half Spanish. Then for first grade, mom advocated her into Greenfield, a magnet in Center City. Amongst a whiter population, Gabi was labeled different. Remedial. Grade levels behind. A report card came home with the word SPANISH stamped across it. A real *Looney Tunes* image. The red-ink letters might as well have read DANGER or FRAGILE. Mom didn't understand its significance, and when she asked, Gabi spoke fondly of her new ESL classmates. She was with Latinos again! Mom was floored. Thought she was telling stories. Had to march into school and ask the damn deal. English is her first language, mom told the administrators. Her Spanish is conversational at best, mom would say.

Summer and holiday breaks were too short to cram in four years' worth of tutoring. Thanksgiving break my sophomore year—Gabi was in first grade—I had pulled her to the couch, cradled her close, and plunged my nose into her nest of curls. I missed her smell, her soft embrace, the dimples bracketing her rascal smile. I missed being the center of her saucy world. Smooshed arm-to-arm on the cushions, I had opened a simple board book. Pointed to the first word. The letters were random squiggles, she said. They don't pair with sounds, she insisted. Let's memorize it, then, I responded. A straight line with two semicircles, that makes B. Can you find another B on the page? And seven-year-old Gabi pointed to a B, rankled and shutting down. I'm not like you, she whispered, tears welling up. For you, it comes easy, she said. It became her go-to armor against my impatience.

"Try again, Gabi. What sound does *B* make?"

"I don't know! I'm not like you, remember?"

And I would close the book and we'd play hide-and-seek till the tears were forgotten. By my senior year—her third grade— she could read to the end, but not without painstaking effort or shutting down or crying.

Is this what had happened to Nuchi? Had no one discovered the proper intervention, or bothered trying in the first place? Had she been dismissed to the back of the room or from the room altogether? Sayonara, kid, go be someone else's problem. I wasn't there to witness either childhood. Not Nuchi's, which preceded mine, or my sister's, which continued regardless of my absence. Providing homework help from far-off Yale was impossible. I couldn't even counter all these new Gabi narratives with the heft or pace at which they arrived. Couldn't insist daily: girl, you a gat-dang genius. Couldn't say, mark my words, I know smart and you're off the charts. Couldn't promise over Cheerios, we'll fig- ure this out, matter of time. Or wrap her in the bath towel with a melodic reminder: your belly holds mother earth, Little Shake- speare.

One thing I could do, though. Feel the sisterly-cousinly love plunge knife-deep as I walked past Sterling and looked away.

28

THE FORAKER ACT
(ON BORIKEN'S—AND THE
DIASPORA'S—LANGUAGE HISTORY)

"Do you believe in god?"

All the other Yalies in the car had taken their turn with the question. Unilaterally, their answer was no. They were white or, like me, white-passing. Secular Jews, nonpracticing Protestants, fourth-generation atheists. They approached the question as a twenty-minute segment of the day trip, half-deep getting-to-know-you talk. Each had a different story about their particular flavor of nonbelief. They cracked self-deprecating jokes about their stubborn skepticism. They lamented having no tradition—there were times it might provide ballast, they conceded—but such was the cost of reason-based existence. Now came my turn, last.

"Do you believe in god?"

I often struggled to squeeze my reality into words that didn't fit, English ill-fitting as a stranger's shoes. As it had so many times, a gulf stretched between me and this language. My language. I clammed up. The heat flooding my cheeks tipped beyond reticence into panic. I was certain they could see my fever rise, sniff a faith that snagged and cobbled me beyond small talk's palatable edges. And the words, which slid off their tongue with such ease—did they not see how the words were inaccurate to the topic?

"You" was a straightjacket. There is no plural "you" in English. But a question regarding the sacred implicated a circle beyond myself. It meant Tía Toña's sopera urns, mom's Lakota prayers translated into Spanish, it meant herb gardens, Yoruba thrones, cowry divination, Abuela's whispered Bible study.

"Believe" struck me as not only irrelevant but almost comical. Back in my Philly living room, god started fires, made sock puppets of flesh and blood. I had seen mom down a whole jug of rum. God played hard with my material world. My eyes had borne witness. What did belief matter?

And which "god" did they mean? Atabey, an Orisha, a spirit guide, los Egun, Abuela's Jesucristo, mami's Olofi Olodumare, Tía Moncha's Virgen Maria? Divinities had crossed oceans to enter my Philly home, and naming them required four languages: Taíno, Yoruba, Spanish, and English. Not to mention the visual language of mom's thrones, the vibrational testimony of the batá drum.

My Yale friends awaited an answer. But English—my first tongue, my mother's second—lacked the vocabulary to describe my concepts. So how could I tell them? How could I name myself?

Finally, I spoke in softest voice. Yes. I whispered it, half wishing they wouldn't hear.

"Really?"

"Wow. So, what does god mean?"

"Like, a bearded man in the sky? The Sistine Chapel guy with the pointed finger?"

I was an oddity, a real curiosity. Qui Qui's primitive beliefs, a throwback, an enigma. This confusion was nothing new. Descriptions of Santería and Changó were often required in my life outside el barrio. Though I didn't love having to explain mom, I was used to it. But amongst this eloquent company, positioned as we were near the levers of earthly power, I worried my bumbling explanation would reduce mom's spiritual genius to sideshow. But how I yearned to share the numinous world I had come to study, metabolize, and respect.

Maybe that's why I began looking away from Sterling Library. Because I was dreaming, instead, of a library I might fit into. One with space to hold my cousins, my tías, my sister, mi madre. An archive made of us, that held our concepts and reality so that future Perez girls would have no question of our existence or validity. Our innovations and conundrums, our migrations and Rashomon narratives could fill volumes, take up half a city block. Future Perez girls would do book reports amid its labyrinthine stacks, tracing lineages through time and hemispheres, knowing that one day they'd add to the collection. A place where we'd be more than one ethnomusicology shelf, but every shelf, the record itself. And future Perez girls, or hell, even Gabi, would step into the library of us and take its magnificence for granted. It would seem inevitable, a given, to be surrounded by one's history.

My Yale friends and I continued driving through the mountains. Foliage flanked the twisty road and blanketed the valley ahead of us. It was calming, how the trees stood and offered themselves to my heart.

I answered the follow-up questions as best I could, fumbling toward explanations of religious syncretism, how the old world folded atop the new out of necessity and invention. They could tell I was rankled, and moved on to other topics. I pondered the view, remembering, suddenly, those two strange moments in which I'd become . . . possessed? Was that the right word? In Dr. Phillips's essay test and at Quaker meeting. Two instances of writing and storytelling when I had lost control, relinquishing authorial power to something deep within or far outside me. During those fleeting tempests, language, meaning, and narrative enacted themselves upon me. A truth was spoken and therefore purged. I had named dissonance, ugliness, suffering, love, and divinity in ways my everyday language didn't equip me to. Rough and raw words had ripped into the world, unconcerned with permission or modulation. English words. Why couldn't I do that with English now, in road-trip conversation with college buddies?

Those particular Yale friends had English-speaking parents. Their grandparents held advanced degrees from American universities. English was a generations-old mastery in their homes. Their upward mobility was enabled by English, their conceptual reality sculpted and limited by it. They thought and dreamed in the language. It was the English-language god whom their families had long abandoned.

My elders had been educated in various languages, inconsistently. At twelve, mom was plunged into English-only junior high in Philly. A few courses at Community comprised her higher education. Pop had left Barranquitas, Puerto Rico, for grade school in Philly. His English had a few years on mom's, but taking over a grocery store—becoming a businessman—at sixteen prematurely ended his formal education. Abuela used her second-grade education to read La Biblia. She scorned the English language, downright refused to speak it. And her schooling, she knew, was more than some got. My abuelo, an indentured servant since childhood in Puerto Rico, never stepped foot in a classroom.

Language was not what connected us as a family. A dinner table ritual, where people gather to discuss news of the day, was not at the heart of how we communicated. Bodies were the mother tongue at Abuela's, with Spanish second and English third. Dancing and ass-slapping, palmfuls of rice, ponytail-pulling and wound-dressing, banging a pot to the clave beat. Hands didn't get lost in translation. Hips bridged gaps where words failed.

I gotta step out of the narrative for a sec. I have studied, at forty, histories I hadn't at twenty-one. Perhaps if I had majored in American Studies, I would've known I was not the first in my lineage at a loss for words. Perhaps I would've accepted my place on the historic battlefield that is Boricua language. Perhaps I would have found context, or even strength, in the centuries-old cultural becoming that now included me. Quizás. But at that time, I thought speaking English marked my profound cultural failure.

Prior to 1493, Taínos spoke various Arawakan languages and dialects in the island's coastal and interior pockets. Then European ships appeared, importing guns, smallpox, and Spanish.

From first encounter, the Taínos refused to assimilate and speak Español. Their words, and the bodies that housed them, were pillaged. The colonizers' vocabulary, in turn, grew. *Hurakan, boriken, barbacoa.* These became Spanish for "hurricane," "Borinquen," and "barbecue." *Hamaka* (fish net) became "hamaca" (hammock). *Batata* and *tabaco* would traverse Spanish toward the English "potato" and "tobacco." *Wayaba* would become the Spanish "guayaba," the English "guava." And of course the colonizers learned *yuca,* for that nourishment rooted in Boriken's soil, which the god Yukahu's fertility made abundant. These weren't solely new words to Spanish occupiers, but new realities, new concepts, new food, a new material world.

After murder and smallpox diminished Taíno slave labor, the Spanish crown approved African chattel slavery in the colony. Yoruba, Igbo, and other West African languages arrived on Puerto Rican shores, mingling with a Spanish that now held whispers of Arawakan dialects. The West African *ñame* and *guineo* were adopted to describe tubers and bananas. The word *merengue* survived the middle passage and centuries later became a Juan Luis Guerra tape played on July fourth in North Philly.

Language loss on Borinquen was not limited to vocabulary, syntax, and sound formation. Names, too, were obliterated. Yoruba surnames, excised and replaced by those of Spanish slaveholders. Recorded family lineage was thusly ruptured. How, then, to track one's kin? Delineate predecessors and forebears? How to know one's sequence in the vast human current? The mass excising of names was a campaign of terror, a violent anti-insurgency strategy. Neither were the names of Native tribes and dialects immune to forfeiture. Simplified in the Spanish record, the descriptors "Arawak," "Lokono," "Carib," and "Taíno" became catchalls for a diverse Native population. Today, debate on the accuracy and appropriateness of those terms rages on.

For nearly half a millennium, words born of three hemispheres mixed and informed one another's music. If language had been an effective colonial tool of violence and erasure, it was contrapuntally a West African means of resistance and resilience. While some prayed to Jesús as told, the tongue behind their tongue pronounced Obatalá.

No sooner had Spain declared Puerto Rico autonomous in 1897 than the island became a U.S. territory in 1898. Language differences threatened the new colonizers' ability to rule. Four hundred years of Puerto Rican literature, history, laws, and business records were in Spanish, but neither the U.S. government nor American sugar corporations hungry to buy up land spoke it. A few years into the acquisition, the Foraker Act foisted English, virtually unknown on the island, onto every level of the culture. Overnight, government departments were mandated to use English coequally with Spanish. Nonresident white men— English-only aliens—were appointed to govern by the U.S. president. School days now began with the United States pledge of allegiance and national anthem. Students learned both phonetically, oblivious to their meaning. Teachers and students were forbidden to speak Spanish in schools. English-language textbooks were imported from the mainland without adaptation, imposing a curriculum of U.S. history and culture. Island holidays were erased from school calendars, replaced by the Fourth of July and Thanksgiving. English-language nutrition lessons recommended fruits and vegetables that didn't grow on the island. Without them, course materials asserted, good health was impossible. Students were cut off from Puerto Rican arts and letters, the international Spanish-language canon, and the island's self-created historic record. English enforcement (for the ease of stateside governors and sugar corporations) was justified as moral imperative. New leaders touted their will to bestow the blessings of enlightened civilization on the island's masses. English was not simply a language, but a betterment project.

I imagine that in this setting, speaking one's heart and mind in public becomes dangerous, and necessitates strategy. I imagine that Native history, in order to survive, necessarily goes underground. Indeed, it was considered seditious when the 1930s Nationalist Party platform included the stipulation that Spanish be reinstated as the island's primary language. For their nonnegotiable demands, party leaders were jailed, tortured, and murdered.

Confusion and disenfranchisement reigned in the schoolhouse until primary instruction returned to Spanish in 1948. English was demoted to the secondary language of instruction. But the damage had been wrought. Two generations had fled formal education. School was the place you went to fail, to be misunderstood and deemed stupid. A fifty-year rift in the cultural record, and those empowered to contribute to it, now existed.

In 1966, Obdulia Perez brought her daughters first to the Bronx then Filadelfia, where she settled next door to her sister. The racial slur lobbed at Abuela and Tía Moncha mocked their accent. I no spic English. Mom's generation, after girlhoods en Español, became bilingual as they studied, protested, and paid rent en Ingles. At clandestine Young Lords meetings, mom and Tía Toña studied Black Panther methods, so that African American revolutionary phrases were adapted by Philly Rican rebels. Perez women married or mothered with Afro Boricua, African American, and white men alike. In hoagie joints, jazz clubs, and late-night love beds, Black Philly's dynamic speech patterns folded into the Perez tongue. In Center City workplaces and hippie communes, white articulation allowed the Perez women to pass. My cousins and I, we flipped the equation, with English-first kindergarten and Spanish-second oral histories and Sunday chatter. Spanglish's ever-shifting syntax and double-rich sonority became the common tongue of Perez generations. It was a dialect capable of tremendous calibration depending on who was on the front porch smoking a Kool or at Abuela's table for some bistec encebollao.

You are a child of three catastrophes. You are born of three holocausts. The Native. The African. And the Jewish. You are a descendent of the survivors. It's in your blood. The resilience. The deep memory and experience of survival. Mom had, in my youth, cornered me to whisper this incantation. The bloodsickness that nipped at our Perez shoulders, that clung to our heels like shadow, was so historical as to be, essentially, unfathomable. All the language loss—and creative repurposing—was one facet of my inherited catastrophes.

But did I not, with my particular racial and cultural makeup, also inherit the perpetration of those holocausts? Had I not committed the very crimes I sought to heal from? Had I not pillaged the mother tongues I also aimed to honor? Yes: I was—I am—both sides of the coin and the edge. This inherited trauma, this epigenetic memory. How to name myself with lucid precision, compassion, and unyielding rigor—I, the inflictor and the inflicted? The mother tongue robber and the mother tongue holder?

When my friends asked, "Do you believe in god?" heat lashed

my cheeks, seared my throat. My perimeter went on lockdown so that what lived inside—divine spark, spiritual curiosity—could not escape and find voice. I did not yet grasp the magnificent and fraught language history I'd inherited. I hadn't heard of the Foraker Act or known Abuela's early schooling arrived in meaningless phonetic *een-glush*. No, instead I cursed my incorrect mother tongue, certain it was my deepest personal failing.

29

GIL SCOTT-HERON ASKS
ME A QUESTION

M usic was the only language I'd chosen. It offered safe harbor to feel confused, depressed, lonely, alive. At the piano, both fluency and blunder were rewarded. Wrong notes became new compositions. Its constancy was infallible, its role in my life uncomplicated. But I didn't know if, as a language, it could say everything I needed it to, if it held the vocabulary to parse, wrangle, and reveal all that I'd dammed up inside.

My musical loves, like my family tree, branched wide from the get-go. Aunt Linda snuck me into CBGB for her neo-romantic punk gigs—a Puerto Rican preschooler primped in velvet and lace. She was the only chick instrumentalist in sight. Coltrane's *A Love Supreme* and Stravinsky's *Firebird Suite,* both discovered with Tower headphones cupping my ears, were loaded into side-by-side decks, trading late-night plays when I should've been sleeping. When Uncle Rik scored tickets to Steel Pulse, I got preteen high off secondhand reefer. The last number in the set ended with a minutes-long ritardando. Phrase by phrase, steel drums slowed to a standstill, leaving me dumbstruck—a finale, a climax, made of space and silence. Adimu Kuumba, with gray-streaked locs and high-proof breath, played beneath the 48th and Baltimore traffic light. His African instruments were all sculpted from trash. Man could hypnotize you with his Bustelo kalimba. One day I stepped off the 34 and he called, *Come close, I've been waiting.* His boom box's volume knob was busted, Bobby McFerrin whispered so low I had to press ear to speaker. Mom gave rent money to Joaquin Rivera, a barrio trovador, to bolero-serenade us graveside at the cemetery. Aguinaldos for the dead. She hired batá players and our living room became a dim sweaty speakeasy: motherland polyrhythms making the cobwebs quiver.

At Settlement Music School, Dolly Kraznapolski assigned me Scriabin preludes and frowned when, come Tuesday, I played original music. Donald Rappaport, a theory teacher down the hall, took over weekly lessons when she was at wit's end. For my last year of high school he encouraged and critiqued my compositions, never charging a dime. He showed me dissonance in less than ten seconds: Play a C major in your left hand. Now an F-sharp major in your right. Now, go compose, bye. When I brought in the resulting piece, he declared it better than Scriabin.

In my final lesson before college, Mr. Rappaport gifted me a Music Tree. An eleven-by-seventeen paper flowchart so intricately drawn it resembled circuits. He had spent adulthood tracing his pedagogical genealogy, tracking music teachers over twenty generations, all the way back to Johann Sebastian himself. The man knew his lineage and therefore his soul, and thought the Music Tree would bestow this clarity onto me. "You are a descendent of Bach," he told me. Two days later, I was on 95 North to New Haven.

A month after that, the dorm phone rang and I was informed that his decades-long battle with stomach cancer had ended. I hadn't even known he was sick. Now an actual legacy rested in my hands. Bereft, I taped the Music Tree beside my bed, then left for class. As I tried sleeping later that night, the Music Tree stared me down, demanding more than I felt capable of, and I removed the tape and folded it into my desk drawer, where it remained, folded, till we moved out of freshman dorms.

How could Yale's offerings not feel reductive in comparison? Music had been a window onto humanity, diasporic to the marrow. Rather than going wide, perhaps Yale went deep. But its particular focus felt out of touch and at times arcane. Coursework in my major often felt surreal, like I'd been mistakenly dropped onto someone else's path: someone with laser focus and unassailable skill. I was all grit and romance. I often feared the mix-up would go public any second and the Yale intercom would announce, "Sorry, kid. Head down the hall to English, where you belong."

Senior year, I was accepted into the BMI Musical Theatre Workshop, a well-regarded creative lab for burgeoning stage composers. At twenty bucks a pop, the weekly Metro North round trip to New York meant adding to my studio hours. So be it. New York, far as Aunt Linda showed me, meant soul, rock, and reggae. She had taken me to some musicals, too: Savion Glover's tapping, South African chorales, and American gospel had fueled those stage scores. On BMI day one, I walked into a room of forty white composers and lyricists. "What is your favorite Sondheim?" was the icebreaker. I'd never heard of him, not even *West*

Side Story. They vowed to remedy my cultural blind spot, burning me CDs, listing seminal works to study. But the god to which they unanimously prayed left me cold. I was informed that the stage works that had inspired me—*Sarafina!; Bring in 'da Noise, Bring in 'da Funk; The Gospel at Colonus*—were in fact marginalia, trimmings from the true meat of music theater.

Wynton Marsalis spent a brief residency at Yale, rehearsing a jazz oratorio before its Lincoln Center debut. I cut classes for a week to watch, and he eventually outed the music major in the back row. "Hey! Yeah, you! Know how to copy charts?" "Yes, Mr. Marsalis." "Well, look at that, she can speak!" Sixteen jazz cats chuckled. "Here, Cassandra Wilson threw a fit when she saw her pages," and he handed me some charts that looked decent far as I could tell. I got to it. Ten minutes later, the regal alto arrived and thanked me, in elegant voice, for her cleaner pages. "Now I can rehearse," she said with a smile as Wynton Marsalis put a twenty in my hand. "That looked like the calligraphy of a composer. Am I right?" He told me to bring an original trumpet piece to tomorrow's rehearsal. "You've been eavesdropping on us, now we'll hear where you're coming from." I stayed up all night. Eraser dust snowdrifting atop eighty-eight keys, corner store coffee haloing my treble clefs. Next day, Wynton Marsalis waved to the band. Listen up! He propped my new piece on the music stand, lifted matte brass mouthpiece to lip, and began to blow, fingertips padding the opalescent valves. The piece was all sustained notes, prayerful and sexy. While composing, I had used only the piano and my singing voice. Heard on the trumpet for the first time, the melody cooed like a baby waking calmly from a nap. "Girl's got an ear, huh?" he asked at the end. The jazz orchestra nodded and mm-hmm'ed. "She's bad," said a sax player. To which I nodded a cool thanks, but inside I swooned.

Evan Ziporyn, a founding member of Bang on a Can, taught a master class. He selected my bass clarinet piece for his guest recital. The night of the concert, all the faculty came. Usually a frumpy bunch, the professors dappered up for the evening, headed as it was by New York royalty. Professor Friedman was an elite amongst elites, though he rarely tucked his shirt in properly so it tended to stick out his unzipped fly. Undergrad boys hovered near him, trying to cull favor with Classical era trivia or modal philosophy. I was a pleb, and female to boot, who'd begun piano in high school—Friedman hardly knew or cared I existed. But after Evan Ziporyn played my hypnotize-your-ass solo, full of double notes and harmonics, Friedman approached me and shockingly made eye contact. "That was actually quite good." To which I responded with a string of *gee-whiz-really-aw-shux*es, though regardless of his affirmation—almost in spite of it— I knew that jawn was decent.

After graduation I intended to scrape by on gigs. To spend coffeehouse afternoons composing for stage and Ethiopian res- taurant dinners scribbling lyrics on napkins. I didn't crave much in the way of stability. Mom's income as a grassroots organizer was always sporadic, so depending on the year, shopping meant Macy*s or the Second Mile Thrift Shop. The vagaries of Pop's contracting work meant one summer with Dorney Park excur- sions and another where fish hoagies were shared, not eaten solo. Flush and tight felt the same to me, and in this I recognized artis- tic freedom.

It was Clinton days, jobs were falling like rain in spring. Philly had cheap rents and music for days. My typing straight-up broke the Mavis Beacon test, so I could land desk jobs on a dime when gigs slowed. The boy and I had survived four years of long dis- tance. We moved into a cheap West Philly rental, the row-home-chopped-into-thirds kind, with a huge picture window that let in January frost and August stink. At halftime, we made love on our futon, then, half-dressed, continued watching Iverson turn the Sixers upside down. Reflected in the boy's eyes, West Philly shone brighter. One day while walking past Clark Park he made me swear not to propose marriage. "Allow me that much," he said, pissed I'd long ago asked him to prom.

Tuesday afternoons were my days to get Gabi. She told me how school was on the 42 westbound. I cooked arroz y habichuelas with extra olives, how Gabi and my boyfriend liked, then unfolded the futon and tucked her in. Wednesday mornings we rubbed sleep from our eyes, crunched Kix, sipped Bustelo, and grabbed the 42 eastbound, where I blew besitos as the school bell rang. Gabi disappeared into a sea of backpacks and it broke my heart every time. On paper, I was up thirty points in the first quarter. Living life so full that Wednesday mornings, after the boy left for work and Gabi was at school, hurt.

The Roots had started Okayplayer, a Monday night neo-soul revival at the Five Spot. Jill Scott, John Legend, Jaguar Wright, the Jazzyfatnastees, Kindred the Family Soul. They were all catapulting to fame, an ascendancy that was dizzying to be near. An old neighborhood friend invited me late one Monday. Rashida's voice had been the stuff of fourth-grade legend. When she sang the Kwaanza song, parents wept. The vibe onstage was down-to-earth, its smooth backbeat offset by ferocious female vocals. Two appletinis later, we conspired to join the cause. Over the next few inspired weeks we cowrote some songs, neo-soul with a dash of rock. Soon we open-miked the Five Spot, trying to catch some Okayplayer pixie dust in our hair. Me on keys, she on mic. Testing, testing. The club lights shifted from blue to ninja turtle green, with stage smoke obscuring my view of the front row.

Four bars into my piano intro, the house bassist laid down a reso-
nant lick. We made eye contact to confirm: groove on lock. Two
bars later, the house drummer's rimshot got a few extra hips
moving in the crowd. I had never played with rhythm cats so
refined—such a high caliber of time, touch, and feel. They nodded right back at me, letting me know. Shit felt good. Then came
vocals, and the audience was swaying, hands waving, heads bop-
ping. We played the hell out of our two-song limit.

We expanded our set to a full hour and landed us the headline
at Doc Watson's, a bar known more for dollar wings than music.
But the manager had CBGB dreams for his beer-soaked rugs—
hoping his venue would become for rock what the Five Spot was
for neo-soul. Our first gig had twelve paid tops. Our second, over
fifty. We scored a regular spot.

Meanwhile, dance classes needed accompanists, choreogra-
phers needed incidental music, record companies needed session
players. I'd do whatever asked: keys, vocals, duos, solos, band
stuff. "What's your genre?" bandleaders and engineers called and
asked, seeking last-minute players. "Tell me what you need," I
responded. Thankfully, the piano hid my trembling fingers while
showing my confident eyes.

Moonlighting as a solo performer, I served up dreamy, broody
rock songs. They were darker than the bright neo-soul bops from
the Five Spot. And more sensual, too. Playing the keys, microphone perched like a praying mantis, I sang about my lover's
body as a season, taking me like a storm. I sang about a more
forgiving world in which redemption would be on time. Audience ears perked up. Crowds stayed longer, bought more drinks.
Bookers and DJs asked for demos. Erik Tribbett, Jill Scott's traps
guy, agreed to lay down three tracks. I worked extra hours at a
Center City desk, found the cheapest studio that wouldn't em-

barrass me in front of the prominent musician, and we scheduled the session for a week out, after he returned from Hawaii
with the Roots, where he was filling in for Questlove.

For our demo, he enlisted a childhood friend from deep
Southwest, by Grays Ferry, on bass. They came up playing church
together. Day of the session, Erik comes in with a mass of gauze
where a hand should be. He looks ready to spar, not jam. Living
it up Hawaii-style with the Roots, he caught a wave on his jet ski
and it threw him. Next thing he knew, lava rock found the knuckle
bone. Erik duct-taped a drumstick to the gauze, counted off, and
began. His stick grazed the high-hat. A touch that was more
breeze than beat, like ninjas in bamboo, barely rustling leaves.
His drumming was all pizzicato violin and tiptoes. But he kept a
pocket backbeat. I played low chords on the ones—deep, spacious, sonorous. A few takes and we had a track on our hands,
but Erik's gauze had soaked through with red, horror-flick stuff.
Session over.

A few days after the rough mix, my phone rang. "Erik said I
should take a listen. Swing by tomorrow." Larry Gold was a
Philly legend. Came up in local schools, dropped out of the Cur-
tis Institute—top orchestral pedigree—to become an R&B cel-
list. The Roots or Floetry might be banging up his recording
studio's foosball table any random day. I arrived to discover a
miniature white dude with a shiny bald spot and long silver rat-
tail. He had forty years on the youngsters around him. On nice
leather couches, musicians slouched, laid, splayed, and listened.
The way Gold held forth, man's lisp had authority. Plus, he let
players light up in the booth, so young cats stayed hours beyond
session time. Gold played for the Delfonics back when the Philly
Sound was in pampers. Tales of Teddy Pendergrass and Hall and
Oates sprinted off his tongue. He was walking history. He ges-

tured for me to join the sofa audience. His Erykah Badu track was fresh out the oven. "It's a rough mix." He hit play. Gold's bowed lick anchored Badu's meandering rasp. He played cello percussive as a cajón.

The couch crew was unanimous: the track was ice cold. Even the master was happy for the praise. Then he shooed them away for some one-on-one time. Let's hear what you got, kid. I sat at the white baby grand, played the slow jam Erik and I had recorded, plus two more he'd been too bloody to play through. They were sensual neo-soul rock grooves with watercolor poetry. As if, from proximity, the Roots and Okayplayers' seductive world might reveal my own.

"Here's what I propose. We record two songs here. If I like it, we'll talk about making a whole record. If not, then you got a free demo and off you go. You got this Carole King vibe. Let's see."

The two tracks we laid down were lifetime benchmarks. Down grooves, dreamy Rhodes pads. They were satin sheet jams, dripping with the lust of a cheap West Philly walk-up where two young lovers were finding their way. I came home and played them after another Sixers victory, so the boy was already happy. The songs set a mood, as did the success they hinted at. Our clothes were off before we made it through the bedroom door.

"What would you say your music's about? If you had to put it in words?" Larry Gold was once again waving people away for a one-on-one. It was nearly a month later. After finishing the demos, he had stopped returning my calls. Now I was back on his couch for the moment of truth.

"Wow. Yeah. That's a good point."

"It's not a point, it's a question." I figured sitting in silence would allow the right answer to materialize. This was a test, I was good at those. But seconds into my hesitation, Gold spoke. "You don't know. I can hear it in the songs. Stevie knew what he was about. Floetry knows, that's why she gets my studio keys for a month. I knew. I was the cello guy. That's something to build a life on. Ya kinda gotta know, don't you?"

I nodded.

"I'm trying to get your take, but you're looking at me like I'm supposed to provide the answers."

I stopped nodding, just sat there motionless.

"Maybe you'll figure it out. Most don't. You're smart, and so are a million other people." He snuffed out his Kool. "Anyhow, that aside, my professional opinion: you're not good enough. You're almost, it's close, but you don't cross the line that makes a musician special." I shook his hand. Put on a brave face. Stood tall and pushed my way out the studio's heavy door. But as I moved through the empty parking lot and beneath the 95 under-pass, I had the chastened hush of a kid who'd been caught in a lie.

The Tin Angel called. Tracy Chapman and the Indigo Girls had played between those exposed-brick walls. The club was indie-folk heaven. "Your demo's good. It's been on my desk for months, waiting for the right moment," the booker said. "Want to open for Gil Scott-Heron?" I ran to Tower Records, found him in the bargain CDs, and discovered an unacknowledged source of half my urban idioms. The revolution will not be televised? Gil Scott-Heron's words. I had heard him but never heard of him, quoted him without the proper citations.

After soundcheck, I joined the old poet in the back room. There was time to kill before the house opened. The room was dim and derelict, with stuffing clouding out the sofa. Heron's un-

kempt silver afro and old leather blazer spoke of a guy whose ups
and downs had blended into a cohesive whole. His hips were too
narrow for his jeans, cheeks too gaunt for his beard. He rolled a
joint, toked deep, and passed it to his conga player then flautist.
He always requested local kids to open his shows, he said. They
kept him current, often sampling his work on future tracks.

He held a toke, then spread his lips and let it swirl out naturally. "So, what's your story?"

"West Philly, born and bred."

"Right on. And what are you about? What's your story story?"
His players nodded, approving the question, waiting for their
minds to be blown or simply to meet a fellow traveler. But I sat
there like "story" was a vocab word I'd never bothered learning.
As though I had no name, let alone one that broke its own rules,
let alone one that meant revolution masked as happiness. My
brain felt Men-in-Black zapped. This cat had lost his following,
his weight, and some teeth—poetry didn't pay much—but he
never lost his story, the about attached to his bones. So who are
you, Quiara? Who Qui Qui is? Quien eres? How Qui Qui be?
Who? What? When? Where? Why? How? Grade-school shit, and
the half-breed Ivy Leaguer had nothing.

"You're up, hon." I took the stage. Applause occurred. Keys
were pressed. Notes emanated from vocal chords. But I felt hollow as a tree trunk with upturned roots. I listened to my songs
like an operating room specimen, a spirit hovering above the
bright lights, looking down at her anesthetized body. What char-
acterized my chords and lyrics, I pondered, other than a general
pleasantness? Life is nice. Sometimes a bit hard. Romance feels
good. That was the thesis written all over my music: agreeable
and undisruptive. My songs were a pantomime, a picket fence.

Applause happened again. A body shaped like mine left the

stage. *Next up, put your hands together* . . . A conga guy perched and slapped a groove. A flautist stood and looped a hook. The old poet looked at the Black, Brown, and white faces between brick walls. His disheveled leather blazer brushed against the mic.

"A rat done bit my sister Nell / with Whitey on the moon
Her face and arms began to swell. . . ."

He was funny, if salt in the sugar dish made you chuckle. He was real in a world that liked dress-up. Poor in a city of new glass towers. Unpleasant before a camera that said wave and smile. It bordered on embarrassing, the old poet's lack of adornment. Words that poked fingers in the American socket. Zap, char, spark—you been burned.

The old shame was at me again. The one that visited when I was asked if I believed in god. The one that choked me when ice cubes went clink and I smiled and nodded about the Inner City Problem. The old shame that loved my silence, that embraced me when I clammed up, warming me like a partner in bed. I wanted to be done with it, to venture out on my own. But without shame's evergreen love of my silence, would I speak out and freeze to death, alone in America, with no blanket to warm me?

This is not some rags-to-riches tale. If you skip ahead to the final chapter, you will not find me knocking on Larry Gold's studio door, announcing how wrong he'd been to reject me. This is forty-something Quiara issuing an internal storm watch. This is my warning lobbed right at the mirror: that if you ask for an audience, you best have something to say. That if you have something to say, the clock is ticking on the hours left to say it. These are notes to self on a memoir I am drafting at my desk at 1:48 P.M. It is a late-October afternoon, gray and rain greet me through the window. And I type a writer's prayer with you, dear reader, as my witness: May silence, that evergreen seductress, not turn these pages too palatable. May I stand alone beneath the stage lights, honest and embarrassing as an old poet.

"I'm bored." I didn't mean it in a Victorian way, a parlor problem sighed from a chaise. I meant it like a tickle in my throat, a lump in my breast. Symptomatic of bigger problems.

"Bored? That's unlike you."

"Dad used to say 'Then go read a book.' "

"How is your father? Have you heard from him recently?"

I shrugged. We were in mom's new kitchen. She had moved from my childhood home during college to a historic stone farmhouse. She grew impatient with my slow potato work and snatched the peeler from me. "You're bored with the music? Well, what's your end goal? You're playing with the best of the best. Where do you see yourself taking it?"

"Beats me. Haven't a clue. That's the problem."

"Let me ask you something." Now she put the peeler down and rinsed potato dirt from her hands. "How come you never took writing seriously? Why didn't you pursue it for real?"

"I write all the time."

"I mean professionally. Coño, hija, from the time you came up to my knee, I was sure you'd be a writer." She poured uncooked rice into a colander and handed it my way. I lifted the faucet handle and raked my fingers through the grains, searching for stones and un-threshed bits. "That musical, *Sweat of the River, Sweat of the Ocean*, that was deep shit, man! Nobody is doing stuff like that. Why did you drop it and move on?"

She was right. On closing night we had struck the set, and I breezed on to the next day, skipping-stone quick. Then the next day, then the next, until I'd built myself a haven: Philly jams, the boy, and proximity to Gabi. And yet, there were questions of self that no sonorous melody or tight groove could address, but that syncopation and dissonance—and words—had once drawn me toward. I still believed, despite Larry Gold's rejection and Gil Scott-Heron's question, that I could forge a life out of music if I worked at it. Music had, after all, rescued my younger self in crisis, dragged me from shipwreck to shore. But had it, would it ever, bring me closer to myself? Can a haven, in fact, ever do that?

"You have a story to tell, Quiara. And with that Yale degree, you got the means to tell it. Which is more than most get."

"I never considered it possible. To be that. A writer." And why should I have? I'd never been assigned a single Puerto Rican author, not in the burbs, in Philly public school, or at Yale. Aside from one or two Christmas gifts from mom, Puerto Rican writers might as well have been unicorns.

"Recuérdate a Forest Lane. You spent all day in those woods reciting poems to the trees. Telling your stories to the ferns." And now she plunged her palm beneath the running faucet and grabbed my hand from the rice so that water bound us together. The sudden intimacy annoyed me, but she only gripped more firmly when I tried pulling away. "If I had one favor to ask you, Quiara . . . It's not my place to ask my daughter, who has been the blessing and affirmation of my life . . . After all you've given me, I have no right to ask for anything."

"Ask, mom. Please."

"Don't you know how badly we need you? So much history will go to the grave with Abuela. She doesn't have many years left. This is stuff that's not written anywhere, Quiara. Y recuerdas que, if it's not written down, it doesn't exist. Didn't I always say how much power a library shelf holds?"

She let go, returned to the potatoes, peeling fast. Having laid it bare, her wish for me, she seemed embarrassed, even chastened. I continued rinsing rice as she wiped tears on her sleeve. Mom had never asked for much. I was the artsy adventurer, the straight-A student, self-motivated and self-disciplined without need of outside guidance. When she caught me as a teen smoking pot and being promiscuous, she had hardly even scolded me—the shame of being caught was enough to right my ship. Now, there was no unvoicing the ask. Her subtle call to arms that bent inward to something personal.

Mom was asking me to break a silence I had lived with all my life. Society's silence and her own—and her sisters' and mother's. Silence had been armor for my elders, emotional preservation through public scorn and in the face of deep-seated shame. Mom kept the Orishas secret so her faith could thrive without persecution. My elders kept AIDS quiet, a machismo that ensnared even our radical matriarchy. The addiction was quiet, too, performed offstage like a redacted scene. As was the illiteracy. But perhaps I didn't need their old silences anymore. Perhaps mom's survival had paved the way for my articulation. Perhaps I, of the next wave, faced new burdens and battles, including the struggle to push into the light. Underground, mom had built magnificent thrones. Could I build a throne made of visibility?

I stood at the kitchen sink, a cascade of water blanketing my hands and the rice. In my mind's eye, images appeared: snapshots from a childhood behind eighty-eight keys. Playing along to Champion Jack Dupree before my feet even touched the ground. How kind Bach had been to let me learn that minuet in G, and how he'd pushed me with harder works: fugues, sarabandes. Tuesday visits to Dolly Kraznapolski as she hammered my fourth finger into agility. Aunt Linda four-handing the Dvořák *Slavonic Dances* on her baby grand—the boom of the propped-open lid. Uncle Rik and me at Tower listening stations, swapping headphone discoveries. Copying vocal charts for Wynton Marsalis. The unaccompanied solo I wrote for Evan Ziporyn, the great clarinet experimentalist.

I now felt childish for loving something so unironically, for savoring a meal with no censure or temperance. Music, my first love, my self-indulgence, my life raft—it was, in one breath, no longer enough. Mom had pointed out the slow leak in my vessel; I had to jump ship.

The images gave way to sounds. My first Coltrane. *A Love Supreme*, O holy prayer, O insistent openness. Clumsy mistakes while learning Chopin—dissonances that pulled me around new bends, that became opening notes of my piano preludes. Adimu Kuumba's strong thumbs on a kalimba made of garbage.

Each musical memory blinked before me, a ceremonial kiss, then nodded farewell.

When all the images were gone, a profound stillness stood in their wake. The charge of the air when the storm has passed. A thirsty atmosphere, waiting for its lightning bolt. It was a calm as whole as any I'd known. In a breath I had abandoned what I cherished most, and now a vast nothingness spread before me. My ears opened themselves to silence. Faintly, I heard something. *Why do I get Sterling Library and Nuchi doesn't?* That forgotten question blinked open like a flower. Could this be the same question that once roared, monstrous, at my throat?

"Mija, the rice is clean," mom said. I looked down at the grains. They were rinsed, and then some. The removal of stones and flawed grains, a step I usually skipped altogether, had been thoroughly executed. I tilted the colander above mom's cheap caldero, yellowed and browned from a million meals cooked, and scraped the grains into the hot oil. They hit the pan in an explosive sizzle, a sound that, as any Boricua chef can attest, means a meal is well on its way.

PART IV

*Break Break Break
My Mother Tongue*

30

WRITING'S A MUSCLE,
IT GETS STRONGER

"Hellooo, can I please speak with Quiara?" The unfamiliar voice cut a friendly slice of mischief.

"This is she."

"Did I say that right? Quiara?"

"Yes, thanks for asking."

"It's Paula Vogel."

I paused. Took a breath. Only months ago, deciding to be a writer and realizing I had no training and was woefully under-read, I figured some instruction was in line. While researching grad programs, I had read Vogel's plays and been floored. Her characters were misbehaving women with messy hearts and a freewheeling lack of shame. They were suburban moms who wrote porn to subsidize back-to-school clothes. They were slutty sisters who lost film noir brothers to AIDS. They were agnostic dykes and temporary asexuals. She wrote these fallible females with humor, precision, and a structural creativity that felt like a big middle finger to Arthur Miller's self-important patriarchs. Now, I loved Arthur Miller. But I was not against giving the man the middle finger. Vogel's characters were stupendous contradictions, women with complicated, sometimes monstrous bodies, who fucked, had fun, and put a twisted spin on integrity. She'd been rewarded for such protagonists with a Pulitzer Prize and a professorship at Brown. I could hear in her voice, just from that initial phone greeting, the spark of joy.

"Wow! How are you, Ms. Vogel?"

"Please, you have to call me Paula. Is that okay?"

"Sure."

"Now, your musical. I just finished reading it and ran straight to the phone. Tell me about your process. The language. Where did those words come from?"

"I uh . . . I mean . . . I wrote them all." That's not what she meant—obviously I wrote them. I had submitted them as my original work, for Christ's sake.

"How did you come up with the dialogue?" she clarified, all eager curiosity. I fumbled for an answer, found none to offer. Now I know, looking back, the script I'd submitted featured blunt exclamatory dialogue inspired by Yoruba incantations, as I'd heard spoken in my living room and read about in mom's books. The clear, intentional tonality of the babalao; the declamatory, intense cadence of prayer. But I couldn't parse it then, which strand of my work—of me—came from where. It was too complicated and messy, all the disparate parts coming into and out of me without any clear traffic pattern. My first language was English, my second Spanglish, my third Spanish, and my fourth a bookish rudimentary Santería-Lukumí. But I had no vocabulary for this vocabulary. I told Paula the truth.

"I don't know," I said. She could feel it, too, how she was asking me to describe the whole chasm when I was only midway across the bridge. She was probing an instinct player about mechanics. She broke it down.

"Ogun. Tell me everything. How did Ogun come to be a part of your life?" I began to understand. The musical I submitted with my grad school applications centered around an Ogun shaman. I told Paula a bit about my mother's spiritual path. I was careful not to use the word "Santería," which was still misunderstood and villainized at the time. Lukumí was a ceremonial practice, I told her, whose prayers and stories had influenced me, given me access to a vocabulary of power outside the language of the everyday. Mom had gifted me books, I told her. Books I studied, underlined, and savored with a flashlight after Philly had gone to bed. I had been to ceremonies, I told her, and felt the dynamic interplay of the unseen and seen, the ancient and now, the material and ineffable. Bodies in the dark, breathing in communion—was that not mom's living room? Was that not also theater?

"How soon can you get to Providence?" she asked. "I'll drive you to Horseneck Beach. You must smell the Atlantic soon, while the air's still cool. There's this third-generation Portuguese joint—do you like feijoada? If we have time, I'll drive you up the hill to Little Italy. There's a café with west-facing cast-iron benches. Mafia retirees eat pistachio gelato and watch the sunset. Crash on my sofa for a night, let me convince you to make Providence your two-year home. Listen, I so hope you'll join my workshop. That you'll come teach me how to do what you do." Teach her? When I couldn't yet name what I did, even in casual conversation?

She picked me up from the train station in a sweet little matchbox, clouds reflected on the platinum hood. Not a scratch to be seen on the vehicle. A Honda Del Sol, fresh out the dealership. Inside this two-seater was a woman in a sun-faded Cape Cod tee whose original color was no longer discernible. The neck boasted holes and frays, all unironic. The T-shirt, unlike the pristine car, had been in rotation well beyond its years. It had, no doubt, been unfashionable when first purchased. Her mismatched style put me at ease. "Playwriting can get you this!" Paula said, drumming the dash. The odometer readout was just three digits long.

"Do you listen to music when you write? Here's the playlist for my latest." She spun the volume knob loud—Bonnie Raitt perhaps, but I was hesitant to ask—and sped me through the New England city, heavy-footed, rolling right past stop signs, pointing at historic landmarks, double-parking to sidebar on local tidbits and oddities. She was a lithe conversationalist, lacking in pretension, all curiosity and exclamation points. During anecdotes and townie gossip, she lowered the volume knob. During quiet stretches she turned it so high North Philly ghetto blasters would kneel in homage. She was hell on wheels, decked out in dad jeans, with a kindergarten sparkle in her eye.

"Questions! What do you want to know? I'm sure I'm forgetting stuff. Shoot!" Here I drew another blank, unsure what one ought to ask when choosing a grad program.

"Do we get electives?"

"Take any class at Brown you like. Or take zero classes, just attend workshop, write your plays, and hit the beach all day. Or the dive bar. I've had folks do it all sorts of ways."

Creative Writing was in a new glass box, still under construction, at a prime location across from the historic main quad. It was a source of great pride to Paula. Opening a freshly painted door, she went in search of hard hats, then called me inside. Construction dust filled my lungs. Windowless dark swallowed me as Paula fumbled along the wall for a switch plate. "I thought they put the controls here. Lemme try upstage. Aha!" Fluorescents blinked on and she apologized: "We ran out of budget to get faders on the houselights." Here it was, the new black box built from her fundraising. Brown protective paper still lined the glass balcony partition. Sleek wooden seats awaited their first audience. It was intimate enough for poetry readings, flexible enough for small-scale theater. There was even a narrow backstage crossover and a dressing room, two things my musicals at Yale had lacked.

"Can you see your plays being produced here?"

"Yes, Ms. Vogel," I teased, using her last name.

"Do me a favor," Paula said. "Write a full-length play in forty-eight hours and bring it on day one. Any forty-eight hours you can scrounge this summer. On your honor. It sounds daunting but the freedom will surprise you. Leap of faith. The record holder is Nilo Cruz. A hundred and twenty pages off of two days' work. If you do that, I'll produce it in this space." Writing 120 pages, even without a deadline, seemed unfathomable. "Writing's a muscle." Paula beamed. "It gets stronger."

Labyrinthine unlevel hallways deposited us in the building's historic wing, home to Paula's fourth-floor office. Out-of-print playscripts wallpapered the room's dollhouse angles. Certainly, the office had once been an attic. She found *Night Train to Bolina* and gifted me the paperback. "But it's your only copy." "Bring it back to me." She winked. It was the published play that had resulted from Nilo Cruz's two-day cram session. Paula stacked a few others in my arms—all by former students, all with legit barcodes and Library of Congress numbers. Some even had that natural-edged paper that was, as bucket lists go, the closest I came to dreaming big. "Read them on the train ride home. I'm curious to hear what you think of Nilo," she chimed. Homework was piling up before I had accepted Paula's offer.

There would be no tuition, she reminded me. Workshop participants received two-year stipends, enough to cover rent and groceries. We would get paid to earn our master's. The expectation was that for two years this would be our center, our daily bread and vocation—that we would not only steep ourselves in the mechanics of playwriting but live the lives of full-time writers. A privilege and rarity even amongst pros.

Where to next? Antique shops? The Pawtucket Red Sox served a mean dirty-water dog, should we catch a night game? There probably wasn't time to swing by the Cape. Had I been? "There's a good turkey club across from the Orleans windmill. Then you walk to the public beach and dip your toes in the bay. When's your birthday? Perfect, turkey clubs in September!" We drove north on Hope Street and she ranked the passing Thai joints. "Spring rolls or summer rolls?" she quizzed. I preferred pizza rolls at the Chino Latino by Titi Ginny's. "Ooh, I gotta stop for this!" Paula parked smack on the yellow lane markers, blocking traffic, blinkers on, and rolled down the window. "There's the cemetery where Edgar Allan Poe proposed marriage! But he was a drunk and his fiancée ditched him before the wedding. Are you into ghost stories?" she asked. My life, I told her, was pretty much one nonstop ghost story. "I knew it, I could tell by your writing! Brown is teeming with spooks. Once a year, I bring the writers out to my Cape house and we stay up telling ghost stories and roasting marshmallows."

We decided on Horseneck Beach. On the way, she declared I must be fed. A roadside food truck had a sign whose phantom letters read CREAMERY. Paula was more unguarded than the squealing teens clumped at picnic tables. "You've never had moosetracks? I get to introduce you to moosetracks!" She bought me a lobster roll and an ice cream cone and we listed first shows seen, favorite plays read, poets adored. Formative words were recited from memory. *Whan that abril* from *Canterbury Tales*—I could still remember the first sixty-four lines. I segued into Shange. Fewer words, they cut closer to the bone. *i found god in myself / & i loved her / i loved her fiercely.* We talked smack about ghost stories we might tell and ghost stories still grappled with. Paula named a brother lost to AIDS. She brought Carl to the conversation not as a victim but a beacon. She smiled, youthful and affectionate, recounting his final days. I wondered if she knew about my family. I'd not mentioned Tico or Guillo or Big Vic in my application and became suspicious that she was manipulating me, that she had looked me up somehow. But I realized, no. We'd simply been alive at the same moment in history, tapped by the same forces.

In mind of my cousins so unexpectedly, that old Six Flags trip came roaring back. The sense of anarchy and anticipation as I rode with my idols, wild wise beasts. Their joy was an F.U. to a hateful world. For each ounce of damage, they had two of life force. Paula was like them. If that Providence afternoon were to turn some humiliating corner, like getting my first period in a parking lot, I trusted Paula to joke till I chuckled and buy me the best bodega maxipad around.

"So? What's the verdict on moosetracks?"

"I mean, the peanut butter cups . . ."

"That's the clincher," she said with a smile. We sped off toward Horseneck with the windows down. In the parking lot, brittle seashells gave way beneath our sneakers. Though the spring wind sliced through my fleece, I peeled off my shoes and socks, left them at the car, and dipped my feet in the tide. The Atlantic gulped my ankles. A burning thrill. On the beach, we did not talk. No sound, save the loud ocean and barks from an off-leash retriever. Paula hovered back by the driftwood. High-tide baptisms, she intuited, are wordless ceremonies.

Why do I get Sterling Library and Nuchi doesn't? As I waded in the New England Atlantic, the old refrain was no longer taunting. It held new clarity. Though no answer materialized, the conundrum approved of my current coordinates. Paula, and the ocean, seemed like good places to search.

"Don't worry about it," Paula said as I attempted to clean my feet in the parking lot. The Honda Del Sol had not yet been to the beach. It was high time the passenger side got blessed by Horseneck. So I pulled my legs into her new ride and sand cascaded to the floor.

I had already interviewed at other grad schools. Eduardo Machado, a cantankerous Cuban refugee with a three-day beard, ran the Columbia MFA. As I reached his office, before I made it to my seat, he blurted out "three things to know." One, I was accepted. Two, he might quit any day, depending on what he ate for breakfast. And three, Columbia was no place for me. "There's too many students paying thirty thou a year, these rich kids living in two-bedrooms on the Upper West Side. Sorry if you're rich. Are you? I didn't think so. You don't write wealthy. Anyway, my students invite me over for wine or beer, I can't even go, it's so fucking depressing. Where else did you get in?"

"Brown."

"Go to Brown." He had the look of an underweight sleep-deprived rhino. "Forget New York. Ten years in this city and your veins run cold. Go write your plays. Delay the inevitable. Give yourself a few years, then move here and let the critics slaughter you. You're a Puerto Rican playwright," he said, "unprepared for the hostility you'll get when putting these people onstage. This naïve vibe you got? Guard it, do not squander it. I can hardly touch a fucking pen without breaking into hives. . . . Therapy's not covered by insurance. . . . I couldn't step foot in my own tech rehearsal last night, I just walked around Hell's Kitchen chain-smoking. Then finally, I sneak in the back to see. Five minutes of this abomination and I grab the god mic and yell HAVE YOU READ MY FUCKING PLAY?"

"What's a god mic?"

"The PA system."

"So everyone heard you say that?"

"I'm not allowed back to my own rehearsals." There he stopped. He would discuss the matter no further, except to tell me that I would receive a partial scholarship at Columbia and it was in my best interest not to take it. Unburdened, having gotten that off his chest, there were more important things to chop up. Things like Ogun, things like Lukumí and diaspora. Things like, what was a West Philly pipsqueak doing putting taboo shit out in the open? White audiences would be disgusted, Latinos would be pissed. This gruff Cuban playwright—all machismo, all bravado, storm-battered and down for the count—was thoroughly versed in los santos. Cuba, of course, was the Caribbean fulcrum of Yoruba influence. But to me, this chat was revelatory. It was the first adult conversation outside of Philly I'd had on the topic. Finally, I didn't need the word "Santería" to help a stranger locate my mother. Finally, I did not need to be a tour guide through my life's basic corridors. I loved him for it, this train wreck of an artist. His gruff, brash manner. The bitter air quotes his voice hooked around "Catholic" when he said the word. How my depth of knowledge demanded his attention. It was invigorating, the notion of two years as his apprentice, two years of conversation on things that had only existed in mom's living room or in books. But his math was spot-on. I was too green, he was too bitter. That he told me so is a generosity I'll never forget. He wished me a great career and all at once seemed to curse it, too. Then he saw me to the door.

31

BROKEN LANGUAGE

The first thing Paula Vogel did was dispel me of the notion that I must be loyal to English. Language that aims toward perfection, she told me, is a lie. Shakespeare knew this, she said, and broke English until its dictionaries grew by a thousand entries. Tennyson knew it in 1835 when he, the Great Poet, used one word to express a vastness. Break, break, break. Paula told of a German cab driver who asked his fare where they were heading. To an audition, it turned out. Can anyone go? the cabbie asked. He parked, memorized the sides, landed a role, and grew angry. The theater lied, he decided. Characters spoke in flowery poetry—peasants and judges had equal vocabularies and elocutions. In reality Berlin schools didn't give day laborers like him the tools to express themselves. So he became a playwright, his characters often rendered mute by their misery.

"Your Spanish is broken?" Paula said. "Then write your broken Spanish."

.　　　.　　　.

I was, compared to my cohort, woefully unprepared. I'd read (and forgotten) one Ibsen and zero Chekhov, names they cited with a worshipper's reverence. My classmates had been theater majors and were hard-core literati out the womb. They had professor fathers and journalist mothers. Some had professional productions under their belt. They cited, with self-deprecating nostalgia, the seminal titles on their parents' bookshelves. Which Jane Austen had been their first, which Nabokov they'd read too young. These authors' names were familiar, but I'd never read them. Well into my twenties, I didn't have an excuse for my ignorance of Western literature beyond the twelfth-grade Norton Anthology and three college lit courses. Foolish me, thinking I had mastered English and the Western Canon, all because I could size up one Duchamp, all because I knew which Chopin note required fourth finger or thumb, all because an English professor had once tried to poach me, over expensive lattes, from the music major. At Brown my deftness, which had previously felt accomplished, was revealed to be a sliver view.

I felt newly cagey about the living room I'd left behind. There was no Henry James lying around mom's, so I had no idea why I ought to roll my eyes at mention of his name. I had never chanced upon a salacious chapter of Freud because Pop had neither a room labeled "study" nor bookshelves inside it. Where my cohorts' childhoods were spent peeking into sexual psychology books, mine was spent standing in mom's altar room, lifting a sopera lid with reticent fingers. The things I'd glimpsed too young—my version of Freud—didn't easily cut into the double-dutch game of their chatter.

Most of my classmates grew up making school or community theater and were well versed in popular classics—a fact they admitted with rehearsed embarrassment. They knew which playwrights were déclassé: most. The Greeks merited consideration. Stoppard, fuck off. (I'd read both and couldn't parse that hierarchy.) August Wilson? Purple. Albee? Overconfident. (I'd read neither.) They could barely tolerate writers they full-on admired, like Tony Kushner. The few playwrights I claimed as influence—Ntozake Shange and Arthur Miller—hardly earned me looks of admiration. "Quaint," their tight smiles seemed to say. Gaining theatrical fluency was the reason I came back to school, so I kept a mental to-read list, regardless of their verdicts of worthiness. For four years, I had been beholden to Yale Music's aesthetic hierarchies. This meant unlearning merengue, unremembering that Fourth of July dance party, turning Ramito's seis con décima into a dorm room hobby. At Yale, music was not for dancing (except baroque gigues). Music, furthermore, was not a social or community endeavor. Music, above all, need not sound good so long as its construction, philosophy, and intellectual acumen was sound. For four years I'd compartmentalized bomba y plena while pulling all-nighters on twelve-tone rows. If I repeated that at Brown, giving The Academy a corner office while relegating local flavor to cramped cubicles, I knew I would spend two years resenting playwriting just as I'd spent four in a lover's quarrel with music.

My classmates proclaimed adherence to various schools. Theatre of Cruelty, Language Playwrights. I nodded but in truth knew what neither meant. During workshop, one classmate whined that his dramaturg had caught a misspelling on his playscript. "Misspelling!" he fumed. "That was an intentional stylistic strategy. I do not make typos." As he said it, my rough draft was being circulated for workshop. I stiffened. With Spanglish and

Yoruba braided through my dialogue, spell-check was hardly an ally. Autocorrect sabotaged my sentences daily. Plus, Yoruba words, on their passage across Atlantic waters, islands, and centuries, had picked up various spellings. The one I referred to as Yemayá was also, according to my personal library, Yemonja, Iemonja, or Yemoja. The Orisha of lightning might be spelled Shango or Changó.

My cohort had impressive facility with language. Their rough drafts were sophisticated, with imaginative plots and keen structural surprises. Mine felt naïve by comparison, with melodramatic storylines and on-the-nose dialogue. One day after workshop, a classmate chatted me up in the hallway. I had seen one of her plays produced on a major Philadelphia stage and it was staggering, dreamlike. Her work and career accomplishment awed me. What could she possibly want out of a grad school education? "Can I make a suggestion?" she said. "Your dialogue is grammatically correct. Every line has proper syntax. But real people speak in fragments. Not every line needs a subject, noun, and verb." I forgot right quick about her impressive writing. *The fuck you think you are?* I thought. *Gettin' up in my ass talkin' 'bout how people speak.* But then I remembered the dynamic markings in Chopin and Bach—staccato and legato. Grammar could deliver such variety, too. That night I cut almost every line in my rough draft down to three or four words. One paragraph became a single word. It worked, she was right. My dialogue had been untied from a corset.

Owning my ignorance, not with pride but candor, was the only viable strategy. I confessed my shortcomings to Vogel, who assigned me a bespoke reading list a hundred plays long. Written responses were due by the last day of classes. Managing the workload was on me. So here came a new string of firsts. My first

August Wilson. My first Edward Albee. My first Caryl Churchill. My first Harold Pinter. My second, then third, then fifth Nilo Cruz. Early in Paula's list was *Roosters* by Milcha Sanchez-Scott. It was a little-known play set in the American South, exploring the world of Chicano cockfighting. The dialogue and plot were a tad banal, the characters never fully leapt off the page, and yet the play's stage directions were a revelation. They detailed how the cockfighting scenes (neither possible eight shows a week nor ethical onstage) were to be enacted not by fowl but humans using martial arts. No rooster costumes allowed. This was eye-opening stuff: that one ritual might replace another. That an empty space created the possibility of going double-mythic.

As if horse-whispering my nascent voice, Paula knew which authors to put first. The list was not chronological nor arranged by canonical position. Instead, she ordered it with a sense of where my curiosities lay and the playwriting mechanics I'd not yet encountered. The breadth of Paula's knowledge on contemporary plays was inscrutable, and she was a fervent B-sider. So rather than assign me one of José Rivera's lauded masterpieces, she had me start with *Sonnets for an Old Century,* a forgotten oddity with an ecumenical structure, like a ribald Sunday mass. It was a series of earthbound, ecstatic, and ruminative monologues that proceeded in the way hymns might at church. Except R-rated. After finishing, I flipped to the author bio. José Rivera was Puerto Rican. I had felt it while turning back to reread, re-savor before proceeding to the next monologue. His poetics of the human body as animal—craven, withering, and holy—resonated in my core. Words that spoke Abuela's world. Never before had my schooling and Boricua culture held common space. I turned to page one and read *Sonnets* anew.

Savoring those early plays on Paula's list, I had to force myself to remain seated, to read all the way to final lines, to see "end of play" before bolting to my desk. Each new play an acclimation, an ecosystem. I was digesting a cosmos and building my own.

As promised, Paula drove us to the Cape. I believe it was an equinox, fall or spring, but maybe it simply felt like the moon was perched on some precipice. We arrived after dark and settled in with the ghost stories. Paula spun a ghoulish yarn about disembodied purple toes. We crashed in various rooms on couches and floors and awoke to blinding white sand dunes out every window. "Playwriting can get you this!" she said, lifting the blinds and asking how we took our oatmeal. It was a favorite bit of propaganda: that we need not be starving artists, that writing would afford us luxuries our younger selves had not dared hunger for. A new house on the Cape, a new convertible, Pulitzer money.

But it wasn't the potential payday that quickened my pulse, that opened and dizzied me in equal measure. It was the notion that no single hemisphere or address wore an aesthetic crown, that the task was to put one's world onstage. It was how curiosity saturated and energized the woman. It was her enthusiasm at the next item on the to-do list. How her untired eyes sparkled as she made us oatmeal. Untired eyes—I hadn't known many women with those.

The pot took a good long while to stew. Quick oats, she said, was the stuff of nonbelievers. She placed on the table a buffet of mix-ins: brown sugar, Grade A maple syrup bought directly from the tapper, dried cranberries, raisins, flaxseed ("At my age, regularity is a godsend!"), and cinnamon sticks to swirl it all together. I watched as warm meals were ladled into bowls, listened as spoons scooped first bites. But when my turn came, I placed my hand over the bowl and declined. I was unexpectedly nervous to dig into Paula's meal. Reticent to fall wholly under her spell, then wake up embarrassed, like I'd shown too much skin. Best to take it slow. To not burn love's candle all in one sitting. To not let the oatmeal lower my defenses, nor allow her magic to thrum me into full acquiescence. Though I skipped breakfast, I enjoyed the aroma and the delicate chime of spoon on bowl. All of 195 East back to Providence, my stomach churned and moaned and roared. I was hungry. This was a good thing.

32

ON OBSCENITY

ind your fellow travelers. It was a foundational Vogel teaching.

When a door opens for you, bring another person through. Oft-repeated Paula scripture.

At the start of each semester, the door swung open and Paula bounced into the room, doing a leprechaun bop. We were in for a treat, she assured us, drumming her fingers like some swell prank was in store. She would name the next guest artist and, eyes gleaming, list their accomplishments: downtown rabble-rousers, performance artists, punk-rock opera scribes, founders of theater collectives with names like Split Britches and The Five Lesbian Brothers. Then she'd reopen the door and the guest, who'd been standing in the hall awkward and alone, would make their royal appearance, embarrassed and honored by the theatrics. They were, like Paula, artists with a penchant toward mischief. Her fellow travelers.

One of the people behind the door was Holly Hughes.

In middle school, if I had fellow travelers they were Keith Haring and Spike Lee. They traveled with me all over Philly, SEPTA tokens of my young artistic dreams. My eighth-grade backpack was a kiosk of Haring pins. Silence=Death. No Glove No Love. National Coming Out Day! Skipping lunch was worth it for the two-buck *Do the Right Thing* rental. The long-haired tattooed anarchists minimum-waging at West Coast Video didn't flinch at the R movie in my twelve-year-old hand. So many afternoons those tense Brooklyn scenes played out before me. Radio Raheem shouting at the shop owners, "D, motherfucka, D!" Radio Raheem with that boom box on his shoulder as Chuck D screamed, "I'm hyped cuz I'm amped, most a my heroes don't appear on no stamp." Sal windmilling a baseball bat from behind the pizza counter, pounding Raheem's boom box till the circuits popped like eyeballs. The cops storming in, nightstick at Raheem's neck, his sneakers kicking in struggle, then sputtering in weakness, then motionless. Death as a sneaker close-up. I rewound and replayed Raheem's motionless sneakers over and over, again and again. In eighth grade, the world hadn't fully Radio Raheemed my cousins, but that movie was prophecy on like a hundred fronts. Spike Lee was a wake-up call, a middle finger, barbed wire at the nation's throat.

By 1993, sophomore year of high school, art as *fuck yuppies life is chaos,* art as *I will name my wound without apology,* suffered a setback. Congress threw a hissy and the NEA stopped funding artists. An instant, nationwide defanging. It became a gamble for artists to be too wild or countercultural. Before, if Mapplethorpe got fifty thou, he didn't need an institutional greenlight. He could develop his photos and produce his own opening. After, institutions became the financial gatekeepers of the arts. You might go to the museum or theater and see something that stormed your heart, but good luck finding anything that stormed the gates. Our national rebel-needle shifted toward the palatable, marketable, and sustainable. Art as a renewable subscription.

I learned about this via Channel 1, an eleven-minute Board of Ed–approved string of ad spots masquerading as a news broadcast. Mondays my homeroom teacher wheeled a TV cart to the blackboard and unleashed the brainwashing upon our minds. The episode about the NEA Four was eleven minutes of theatrics about Twisted Sister's front man, Dee Snider, and Robert Mapplethorpe's infamous bullwhips. They didn't show the offensive works alluded to, meaning, of course, I was desperate to get my hands on them. What they did show was Jesse Helms and Tipper Gore pissing their pants about obscenity. These artists were depraved souls who, Helms and Gore asserted, smeared shit on their naked bodies and called it art. Still, that Disneyland broadcast got me hip to the NEA Four, so props are due.

I spent lunch in the library, but the periodicals section was lacking. After school I hotfooted it downtown to the main branch, 19th and Vine. Hell yes, I was gonna check out the "disgusting, insulting, revolting garbage produced by obviously sick minds" that Helms abhorred. Nice sales pitch, Senator! Turns out Holly Hughes, Karen Finley, and company didn't pee or jerk

off on the audience, didn't smear shit all over themselves. I discovered artists who spoke frankly (and in Finley's case, nudely)
about sexuality, queerness, and the body. Yeah, some of it was
definitely obscene (an obvious plus). Some of it was beautiful. All
of it did something my family was unable to. Back then Perez
deaths were wordless dull aches, quiet question marks. If my
family could not bring themselves to utter the word "AIDS" in
each other's company, these artists screamed it, shouted it,
claimed it. The Central High AIDS Quilt, the essay about Tico's
death I read at City Hall? Those happened after Holly Hughes
and her colleagues came into my life. Their work gave me permission to claim my silences aloud.

American History was less dull that month. I wrote a book
report on the NEA Four's foulmouthed poetics. That's how I
mastered the Dewey decimal system, scouring collections for obscene art. I got microfiche headaches thanks to Tipper Gore's
beloved death metal. My poor American History teacher probably had to take confession after grading that book report. He
circled half the words in red ink and wrote notes in the margins
like "not appropriate" and "unnecessarily explicit." He returned
the graded report not to me but to the principal. But he couldn't
deny me an A-plus. The research was impeccable.

A decade had passed since that book report. I was now twenty-
five. Still, when Paula opened the door and Holly Hughes walked
through, I was like *Hell yes, gracias a la vida, this puta was born
ready BEEYOTCH!* The microfiche had captured a sliver of the
woman—her broad toothy smile and tiny stature. But that loud
easy cackle was new. That terrier's jumpy ebullience. Her thought

lines and crow's feet were an abacus of good times had. She got right to business, too excited for name games or warm-ups. "List your identities!" She more screamed it than spoke it. There was a pause as we waited for more. "That's the whole exercise. A list of your identities." "Should we explain them or, like, elaborate?" someone asked. "Nah. Five minutes sound okay? Go!" The task brought me right back to Dr. Phillips's essay test. "Flannery O'Connor uses the theme of fire in her work. Discuss." An ask so terse it's essentially a dare.

Every identity I could think of . . . I started with the chosen ones. *Pianist. Poet. Composer.* There were identities thrust on me, census stuff. *Female. Latina. Boricua. Mixed. Twenty-something.* There were alter egos. *Rock star. Girl who saves the world. Barrio Grrrl!* What else, what else? I loosened up, got playful. *White rice chef's apprentice. Girl with the stiff hips. Hides-on-Abuela's-staircase-during-the-party girl.*

Then it rushed in, jolting and heavy, as though a tap had twisted open or a water main had blown. Tremors coursed through my hand, knees, shoulders. I gulped for air like a toppled goldfish, bowl nowhere in sight. My pen moved, this much I could feel, but of some other accord. The ink was autonomous, it would not succumb to my brain. It had been a decade since Dr. Phillips's essay test, but the same violence ripped me, the same volcanic heat thrashing my heart, lungs, larynx. I was thrumming, asphyxiating. Holly Hughes, gone. Classmates, vanished. My hand lanced the page, an undomesticated thing, a sword slicing through battle. I'd vomit any moment. Half of me pleaded, "Stop! Stop!" while some other half, which sought no permission, thrilled at the precipice. *Ride the wave, grab the reins, mount the beast.*

Then time was up and people were sharing aloud and it was rude, I knew, how rather than listening I was reacclimating. Regaining consciousness felt old and familiar. I knew how to do it. You're trapped underwater, swimming countercurrent toward the surface, daylight shimmering nearer as breath, at last, finds you. Based on everyone's behavior, I apparently hadn't done anything unusual. Had my shaking even been visible? It felt, in the moment, as though I had collapsed to the floor, torso heaving, legs twisting. But no one looked my way. I put my pen down. Kneaded my throbbing hand.

My classmates' lists were ten items long, maybe twenty. Their identities tended toward the accurate and objective: gender, sexuality, age. Thumbing through my notebook, I saw a list that continued for pages. Some of them two or three columns thick. My identities were neither accurate, objective, nor purely autobiographical. Reading them aloud, each one struck me as obvious yet surprising.

Fat ass.
Junky.
Crackhead.
Twelve Stepper.
Yalie.
Illiterate.
Witch.
Welfare Queen.
Righteous Thighs.
West Philly.
North Philly.
Spirit Medium.

Santera.

Quaker.

HIV positive.

I was somewhere in the recipe but not the main ingredient. Asked to name myself, I had instead named my Perez women, my matriarchal family tree. Each Orisha is a source energy, with particular creative and destructive powers. Yemayá for the ocean surface—her ripples, swirls, and tsunamis, her saltwater hips the essence of maternal life. Oyá for the tornado—the winds. The cosmology of my cousins was divvied up, too, into specialized forces of creation and destruction. Flor was wild-me, promiscuous-me, junkie-me, recovery-me, regrets-me, me-on-the-couch-in-a-depressive-coma, reborn-me, serenity-prayer-me, me-who-laughs-volume-eleven-mothafucka! Nuchi was streetfighter-me, most-truth-telling-jokester-in-North-Philly-me, talk-shit-me, illiterate-me, sits-at-the-back-of-class-me, me-who-lights-a-blunt-with-my-teenage-son. Mary Lou was church-wedding-me, laugh-at-the-ceiling-fan-me, strict-young-mom-me, shake-your-ass-like-your-soul-depends-on-it-me, me-who's-gonna-outrun-el-barrio, me-who-died-too-soon. Cuca was caretaker-me, loyal-me, virgin-on-my-wedding-day-me, granny-panties-me. Gabi was planet-earth-belly-me, lotsa-sass-square-ass-me, diva-style-me, fat-bullied-me, dyslexic-shamed-me, sharp-tongue-to-hide-the-tears-me.

My pantheon, my Perez women, my biblical ribs and mud. Out of their rough, mortal flesh was fashioned my tempo and taste. Being three hundred miles from Philly did not mean opting out. Each mile of distance magnified a self I'd always sensed but only newly named. My cousins were that of god within me.

They were not the faith I chose. Like mom's ghostly visitors when she was five, my cousins chose me, knocking on my midnight door, portentous at my bedside. After all my god denying and god shopping. After all my hours in Quaker pews, reading Yoruba books, studying Lukumí prayers. Just so the universe could be cute a decade later and pass me a note in class. *You were born into the church, Qui Qui.*

33

COLD DRINK BECAME A PLAY

Pop spent his early childhood in Barranquitas, an agrarian mountainside in Puerto Rico's interior. The midday sun radiated so heavy it melted afternoons, tempered by cool daybreaks and midnights. All the postcard images of PR— turquoise water, white sand, flat glimmering horizon—that's coastal stuff. Before age five Pop never laid eyes on the ocean. His horizon was a verdant zigzag behind which the sun didn't so much set as ooze. A sunset like a shirt tossed over an armchair. Barranquitas was lush terrain, farmland. Residents could squint ten mountains away and tell you which green patches were plátanos versus ñame. Rush hour sounded like hooves on gravel. Cars weren't uncommon in Barranquitas, but horses were cautious and stayed on roads, whereas vehicles had the nasty habit of toppling over switchbacks. At night the coquí's thunderous chorus was its own monastic silence.

Most households had battery-op radios. Some were blessed

with the occasional ice delivery. But lightbulbs and Frigidaires were not a part of Barranquitas life. Electricity had not yet been poled up the mountain.

Still blows my mind. No electricity. Forget counting sheep, one of my teenage sleeping tricks was imagining five-year-old Pop, no nightlight save the moon. By necessity he lived on a dual-function clock: sunrise, sunset. It's hard for a West Philly girl to comprehend. I'd never been to a plug-free zip code. No TV? No Nintendo? Shit, just do what all of North Philly does when they miss a PECO bill: run an extension cord through the neighbor's window. Maybe cook them chuletas as a thank-you. Me, if an AC shorted mid-August, I ran to the basement and switched a fuse.

"Cold drink! Cold drink!" That story was my video-on-demand before such a thing existed. Pop never hesitated to indulge me. "You not tired of that one yet?" Then his voice doubled in volume. His smile went goofy-wide and his hairy hands started wagging, clearing a path back to the past.

It went like this: Pop was five the day his uncle rolled through. A Sunday, probably, after church let out. "You ever seen the city before?" Pop hadn't. So the uncle said hop in and the pickup coughed north. Dirt switchbacks became concrete boulevards. Slouching bamboo became cast-iron streetlamps. In Barranquitas, bromeliads spidered in little nooks. In San Juan, pigeons cooed in dark corners. So many people and cars in one place. "Wow!" grown-up Pop would narrate, eyes wide, looking five all over again. And the signs on every store! Painted signs. Lit-up signs. Each one a declaration of presence. I want a sign one day, little Pop decided. His uncle found a soda counter near the plaza. "Your first Coca-Cola, enjoy!" But when Pop pulled it to his lips, he yelped and dropped the bottle. "It stung me!" Pop gripped his burning palm. "It didn't sting you, it's cold. That's a refrigerated drink." Back on the farm, the milk served with supper was warm as an udder. Agua de coco came hot, too—coconut husks were nature's thermoses. Pop pulled the bottle from the ground. Its thick glass had survived the fall. Half the soda remained. Now he clenched it, determined, and the Coke went down in gulps. By the time he demonstrated the empty bottle, feeling very cosmopolitan, little Pop had made up his mind. *Wherever that came from, I want to go there.*

Prescient yearnings. Over the next handful of years, his parents and siblings moved to North Philadelphia. A few more siblings were born until there were twelve of them—the Jíbaro Dozen. By sixteen, Pop left high school to run a grocery where he sold cold drinks and had a sign. By twenty-five, he graduated the Job Corps as a machinist. By thirty, his union paycheck was funneled directly into North Philly real estate purchases, setting up his siblings with storefronts of their own. The more run-down the spot, the better. Each ramshackle lot, a future sign. HOUSE FOR RENT. 1 BR AVAILABLE. SANCHEZ BAR & LOUNGE. His signs were many and varied. By the time Pop adopted me, Barranquitas was a place to visit once or twice a year. When he first showed me his hometown, the orchids and striated sky caught my attention, but he was pointing at the power lines and Burger King. "It didn't used to be like this!" He beamed.

Cold Drink became a play.

The Fourth of July dance party became a play.

My bungled Spanish, Abuela's polite disapproval? Another play.

The granny panties Cuca gave me for my first period? Another play.

Once I began writing for real, as mom called it, a lifetime of eavesdropping, secret-keeping, and spying poured forth. After long hibernations in my gut, our silences burst into daylight. Twenty-four hours weren't enough, seventy words per minute couldn't capture them all. Memories shot from my hand like Spider-Man webs. Each line of dialogue was a zipline back to North Philly in the eighties and nineties. Three hundred miles north and decades past the memories, I felt closer to home than ever.

Measuring rice with cupped palms? That became a play.

A woman who can't read the hair dye instructions? That became a play.

Mom's herbal baths to cure my adolescent depression? Another play.

One afternoon, senior year of high school, I collected the mail behind the screen door. Bills, credit card offers, grocery circulars, then a thick envelope from Yale University. The letter began with one word: "Welcome." I'd made the cut. Me. I was in. It made me jittery like a surprise party reveal. Didn't see it coming, caught off guard, but it's good. Mom and Pop were still at work and Abuela, whose past migration had made this future migration of mine possible, deserved the first call. My fingers fumbled over buttons. The call went through. I inhaled ceremonially.

"Jail? Tu vas a jail? Que pasó?" Her voice was panic, a confusion of tears.

"No, Abuela, I got into *Yale!*"

"Pero que hiciste? Cual jail? No hables con la policia!"

"Abuela! Y-A-L-E." She'd never heard of the school.

"Voy a la universidad," I said. So much for my ticker-tape parade.

You got into jail? became a play, too.

The funerals in all their phantasmagoric horror: the pallbearers' footsteps echoing in naves, me fake genuflecting with murky holy water, each sewn-on smile the undertaker got wrong, a shovelful-of-dirt thud as Toña screams. They became a play. Even my hollow gaze, my dry eyes, my certainty that unless I wept for Mary Lou and Tico and Guillo, I had not loved them right. My non-crying became a play.

Mom's spirit world filled every page. My work dripped with los santos. Yemayá entered stage left. Lights rose on Oshun. Ochoosi, the herbalist, lurked behind a garden scene. Sometimes the Orisha were main characters, front and center. Other times they went unnamed, my secret code behind the story.

One play had mostly conventional scenes that I interrupted midway for intentionally awkward "rituals"—sensual, silent moments. In these rituals, an actor moved her body in embarrassing ways when words became insufficient. A ritual to mourn a wife lost to fire. A ritual for a boy's first sexual arousal. Invented ceremonies, the stuff of dreams. But all mom's cleansings and ebós and possessions lurked between the lines, gave me a physical vocabulary to put onstage.

Magic realism, a dramaturg said. The label irked me. *Your Greek and Roman gods,* my classmates said. *Your Romulus and Remus, your Echo and Narcissus.* The comparison annoyed me. Sensual is different than magical, I thought. The Greeks were then, I thought. The Orisha are now.

In my kindergarten days, mom's spirits and Spanish were secrets in her own home. Then she built a living medicine wheel—the circular herb garden—where she could take off the mask and speak to me honestly, without fearing condescension or misinterpretation. When she took my hand and shared her truth, I thought spirits and Spanish were the primary lessons. In Providence, Rhode Island, I belatedly wondered if creating safe space was a teaching I'd not yet appreciated. I recalled other protected places where truths had been bared. A sunroom full of Orisha. The Taíno in caverns. Nuchi in the bathroom, my hands in her hair. The bathroom at Yale where mom prayed over the coconuts. Flor upstairs on the couch for an hour. Could I build a safe space on the page, in the theater? A place where ritual could flow, where I could connect honestly with myself, with my own story and the stories that inhabited me? A place where I could control the narrative, center myself and my loved ones? Sure, all art was destined for outside (mis)interpretation. But basic theater decorum and etiquette entreated all present to listen respectfully, to watch attentively where the light was thrown.

Once, life had happened to me. Now, my desk became a nexus of agency. Writing is plodding work, its progress measured in lines and paragraphs. The sun arcs across the sky and little changes. Eight hours elapse and you've not budged from your chair. But within slow hours, rapture can unfold. Draft by draft, I unveiled the Perezes, fitted us in protagonists' clothes, recorded the hum of our music. My Perezes were gorgeous, monstrous creatures whose flaws proved their humanity rather than obscured it. We would hide no more. To megaphone our genius when the nation denied us, to force a bearing of witness, that became my North Star.

I thought now of all the times mom dragged me to fabric stores. Her searches for the perfect button or trimming bordered on ecstatic. If it meant driving from Delaware to New Jersey in a night, she was uncompromising—she would build the best throne Oshun had ever seen. I had not realized in those textile hunts and woozy car rides that my apprenticeship was in full swing, that I would become altar-builder, too, that I would place photos of ancestors and goblets of water at my windowsill. But my daily candle-lighting and batá prayers were warm-ups. My main practice was the plays. I was building the throne.

Paula told us most artists begin with a naïve phase. More voice than skill, naïve works are saturated in point of view. They are bold and startling, if imbalanced and inelegant. I lacked the craft and dexterity to match my narrative intoxication. But the son montunos and Mozart of my adolescence offered themselves anew, this time as dramaturgical structures. Fugues and batá songs had sturdy architectures. Bach gave me motivic momentum. Batá gave me slow-build suspense. One scene ended tempestuously, raucously. What next, after all that explosion, how to start anew? Schubert offered clues. There lay the answer in his A-major sonata, the one I'd recorded at Yale. After fortissimo, a note or two to test the water. After cacophony, a single solitary melodic line.

34

SILENCE=DEATH
(DÉJÀ VU ALL OVER AGAIN)

Because I fled us, even to go write us, my grip on the present-tense Perez reality loosened. I was farther from home and more removed from my family than ever. Each monologue drew me closer to my cousins. Scene by scene, I loved my sister in new ways. Line by line, I unearthed Titi Ginny's layered womanhood. But these were acts of memory and reflection.

Reality travels fast. The present tense has a phone book and I got a call. No matter how far I traveled, how old I grew, or how loudly I voiced us, our old silences chased me down, reaffirmed their hook.

"Did you hear about Nuchi?"

"No."

"She's not well."

"How so?"

Mom sighed instead of answering.

"What does she have?"

"She's skinny, Quiara. Sabes que she was always thin pero esto . . . Los ojos no tienen vida. Her cheeks are gone, Quiara. Nuchi used to have cheeks, verdad?"

"Yes, Nuchi had cheeks."

"She dropped by the other day. She said, 'Titi, can I show you something?' Ay, her voice, Quiara, como una niña asustada. She unbuttoned her shorts." Mom sighed and sighed and sighed. "There was a sore on her belly."

"What kind of sore?"

"You know . . ."

"No, I don't."

"A purple sore."

"A lesion?"

Mom sighed and sighed and sighed. Just name the fucking disease already, I thought.

"Who knows when she was first infected, or if she was re-infected over the years? Apparently—quien sabe, I'm telling you what she told me—she was undetectable for a long time."

"So Nuchi's HIV positive?"

Mom sighed and sighed and sighed. "According to her, the tests say one thing one day, another thing the next. All I can tell you is your cousin's sick, Quiara."

Mom's silence was not about prudishness. It was a strategic non-naming, a wound that cut too close to the bone. If you stare directly into the sun, you go blind. And it had another benefit. It gave my fury an easy target, it let me blame her silence rather than my cousin or the virus or, for that matter, the world. Much time had passed since my first brushes with AIDS. Back then I had only Keith Haring and Mapplethorpe. Now I had Tony Kush-

ner's *Angels in America,* Larry Kramer's *The Normal Heart,* Tom
Hanks in *Philadelphia.* But none of those were us. The virus was
superficial, the only thing we shared. Even Angel in *Rent* died
amidst a rapturous love story and Mimi looked like an MTV superstar.

We were nowhere.

I next saw Nuchi at mom's birthday. Mom's summer parties always kept the back door open so people could come in and out
with beers, burgers, and pernil. There she was, my first cousin,
chillin' on the porch swing.

"How's your health?" I asked, joining her. She didn't mention
AIDS. Instead she pulled off a shoe, revealing a whopper of a
bunion. Unleashed unto the sun like a dinosaur bone from a dig.

"Ain't that nasty, Qui Qui? I wear two sizes bigger on the left
foot now!" Ever the prankster. Two more of her teeth were gone,
and for what implants cost, she told me, she could buy a car.
Maybe not a new one, but more than a lemon. "Not that I could
get a title." She pinched my knee to emphasize the scandal. "I got
a warrant on my ass for twelve years of unpaid tickets. I owe the
city something like two thousand bucks. Mm-hmm." Nuchi always pinched my leg when gossiping, especially about herself.
She had a stand-up comic's instinct for self-deprecation. Given a
stage mic and Friday night crowd, she'd slay.

"Qui Qui. Even if I paid every one a them tickets and all them
bullshit fines, cuz you know they be charging interest and fees on
top a the initial price tag, even if I paid all that I still couldn't get
a car." She was reeling me in. Waiting for the ask.

"Why not?"

"Because I ain't never had a license not a day in my life. They'd lock me up for unlawful driving. That's why I can't pay my parking tickets!"

Yeah, Nuchi wasn't getting dental implants or a car. And she'd need a miracle to get rid of that bunion. She had mastered a new closed-mouth smile, pursed lips that hid the dental issues. Her figure had whittled away, a wisp of her previous form. A decade prior, at that Fourth of July party, her ass and thighs were majestic. Redwoods. Now her jeans were held up by a rope. Even with so much less of her, Nuchi's hostile beauty cast a spell. The eroded landscape of her cheekbones, her eyes sunken like water holes. There's a reason the Badlands capture our awe—in their decay, a life cycle sings.

By certain measures, Nuchi had weathered the storm. One daughter who'd walked the stage to get a bachelor's. Another on the path to a nursing degree. Plus, one rap-sheet-free son training to be a prizefighter. Sure, some of her sons were doing the lockup dance, and her lawyer, Thom, was on speed dial. But Nuchi had a parcel of grandkids she'd been entrusted to babysit as their parents pursued day-job adulthoods. Success. The next gen, one step ahead of the last. Really, though, such metrics were red herrings and I knew it. I'd stuck to the "made good" script long enough, fronting like Yale's rigor (and prestige) meant that spiritually I had done my work. All those up-and-up notions aside, it was Nuchi's ability to land a great punchline that remained her most impressive humanity. Maybe that's what mom had meant when whisper-urging me: *It's in your blood. The resilience. The deep memory and experience of survival.* Humor like Nuchi's.

An intention formed as I sat beside my ill cousin. Faintest voice, this desire. No sooner had I heard it than I hushed it. Naming a goal, after all, invites the possibility of failure. One day, I hoped, I would claim and really know a resilience of my own.

"Hey, Qui Qui, which potato salad you like more?" Nuchi asked, pursing her lips. Studying my paper plate, I pointed to one of two mayonnaise-y blobs. I chose right. "Don't tell Flor. You know my secret? Eggs and pickles. Hey, Qui Qui, which arroz con gandules you like more?" Again I chose correctly. "Don't tell Titi Ginny. She puts in too much oil. She be oiling the caldero like she 'bout to fry alcapurrias!"

Sitting out back at mom's, listening to the birdsong, squished together on the garden swing so our legs touched, asking about AIDS struck me as inappropriate and unkind. Still, for one second, Nuchi shot me sad eyes, like, "Do you know, little cuz?"

35

THE BOOK OF OUR GENIUS

Though the Perez women wore clothes when necessary, they were butt naked, half-naked, and somewhat-exposed a lot, too. Any given day at Abuela's, half the jeans would be unbuttoned cuz, *ay comadre ya tu sabes:* PMS, heatstroke, menopause, and Abuela's exagerada servings kept us trapped in perma-bloat. After an El ride north through the desolate landscape, my matriarchs' bodies were natural wonders. Nuchi's eroded cheekbones were my Grand Canyon. Mom's thigh jiggles my Niagara Falls. The tattoo on Ginny's breast my Aurora Borealis. North Philly's vast, vacant stretches of blight were increasingly visible from each house Abuela migrated to. The female Perez form stood out against the gray rubble, fulsome and bold. Facial moles like cacti in the sierra, front-tooth gaps like keyhole nebulae. The cellulite rippling over their asses shone with a brook's babbling glimmer. The sag of each tit—big ones and small—like stalactites of varied epochal formation. Stalactitties! Upper arms of all shapes, sizes, and textures, like varied river stones. And oh (swoon) the guts! Abundant flabdomens, some inhabited by earthworm-shaped stretchmarks. Brown bellies like Philly's own Half Dome and Black Hills.

The nipples you see in skin flicks, dirty rags, and R movies? Bullshit. Ours were a motley combo platter of puffy, inverted, asymmetrical, enormous, dainty, bumpy, smooth, and protrusive that resembled nothing ever glimpsed in commercial media. Some of us had smaller nipples growing out of our main ones— nipples stacked up like Russian nesting dolls. By *Playboy* standards we were some kinda freak show, and yet the way my elders swung their milk pendulums with easy posture was twice as confident as any pinup girl.

People use "fat" as some catch-all descriptor, but the variety of our curves revealed the slur's downright laziness. The Perez matriarchs ballooned in my adolescence, but even in my hopscotch days, prekindergarten, I remember Ginny's runner legs: thick firm tree trunks. In sepia eight-by-tens, mom's teenage thighs rocket down from miniskirts, sturdy willful things. Some fatness was green-mango firm, other fatness pooled and jiggled. Gravity, that universal law, played out differently from one body to the next. Blubber might protrude horizontally and turn your belly into a shelf where you could prop your cafecito, or ripple and drape down like Victorian curtains. Skinniness was something I didn't learn about till bloodsickness rolled into town. Skinny meant the doctor had bad news for you, the steep grade of a downhill ride.

There was so much pubic hair. You could upholster a fucking mansion. By the time I was grown and saw the hairless pussies that had taken over porn? Poor things looked like E.T. in the plastic lab—overexposed, malnourished creatures. Save E.T.! Grow some hair!

One of my Brooklyn cousins had a C-section scar thick as a thumb, bisecting her abdomen from pubes up to navel. Little dots ran alongside it from the stitchwork, giving the appearance of caterpillar feet. Cellulite spilled out on either side of the taut, shiny scar. She would show off her bifurcated belly, jiggle it, tuck it in her jeans like a shirt. There was no small dose of bragging in her demonstrations. "I can't get liposuction," she said, smiling, "because the fat will eventually pool around the scar again." The scar thickened with each new child and reopening. To the Jersey Shore and Rockaway beaches, she wore one-piece swimsuits. But at Abuela's, her jeans were reliably unbuttoned and zipper-ventilated. "Have you seen how the doctors ruined me?" she'd ask, and even if you said yes, she'd unzip. *Witness me, behold.*

The thick shiny scar up mom's thigh resembled a strip of tape holding her together. She had stepped through a rotted floorboard in our West Philly twin while pregnant with me. So when I ran my finger along the scar's glassy pathway, life in the womb felt close at hand.

Abuela's batas were so threadbare they'd turn a PG movie NC-17. Her daughters came through and exclaimed. "Mami, where are the new housedresses I bought you from Penney's?" But Abuela had a proclivity toward the broken in. She rarely wore a slip before noon. If she stood before the east-facing window early morning, stirring stovetop café, the flower print magically faded in the sunlight. You could see everything. It was a shadow puppet show of titties and butt dimples. Abuela often sat upstairs, naked in the AC, slow-rolling stockings over her varicose veins. In this seated, hunched position her pendulous flat breasts cascaded over her tiered belly, two slinkies heading downstairs. At some point in her life, I assumed, Abuela's nipples had been darker, but now they were the same color as her pale skin so you couldn't tell where breast ended and nipple began. They seemed the very essence of regality. Vintage rarities whose value accrued with age. A front-facing superhero cape. I wanted a pair like that one day.

Some of my older cousins had a subtle dark stripe up their abdomens. A shade darker than their particular color brown, adorned with peach fuzz. I admired those velveteen lines. They seemed feminine, a girly mustache. I used to think their belly button was thirsty and the stripe was the straw. I would study my belly's reflection, anticipating my stripe. When puberty did not bring it, I thought maybe pregnancy. Something to look forward to. Now at forty, having closed up shop after two kids, I sometimes catch my unstriped belly in the mirror and think wistfully, maybe menopause.

My girlish body hadn't accrued much character. There were no hard knocks or tall tales writ on my flesh, no scars or distinguishing marks beyond freckles. All us young'uns were blank canvases, awaiting life's paintbrush. I had Cuca's flat butt and mom's water-jug belly, but no real narrative you could read on my curves. That's what made me a girl. One day I would be a woman whose body told tales, and I would show them to other women with equally epic, if distinctly shaped, bodies as a younger generation beheld with awe. This would be my defiant adulthood. The messy book of womanhood's flesh was something to aspire to.

In middle school I learned despising one's boobs, body hair, and ass was American as apple pie. White girls stood before the locker room mirror coaching each other on suck-in-the-pouch tactics. I played my part, drawing in the stomach and standing taller. Made a girdle of my breath until the next girl's turn. As instructed, I named aloud all my body's flaws: inverted nipples that pointed down rather than giving the perky salute of a young cadet. I was supposed to behold fleshiness and corpulence with repulsion, and take corrective action where necessary. That "supposed to" let the joy of Abuela's ring more fully. I was coming of age in a *Vogue* nation. Heroin-chic was selling Calvin Klein underwear. *Don't hate me because I'm beautiful* was a national refrain. But not at Abuela's. There, the Perez DNA wrote different rules. The notion of a single beauty mold, be it size or skin color, was dismantled by our fleshy testimony. To glance at us was to know plurality, to behold beauty's parade.

Mom had told me once, as she prepared to receive Changó, that initiates' clothes are torn away so they arrive on their great spiritual path as newborns. It shone light on the fleshy world of mom's home and Abuela's. I understood with retrospective clarity why Titi Ginny, when teaching me how to shampoo my hair, did not coach little me from the side of the shower. No, she undressed and stepped into the water, too. She hoisted me to her naked hip and water poured over our connected bodies. Perez nudity was rebirth of a daily order, a resetting of the spirit to its naïve state, both a freedom and a strong protection.

In my adolescence, a relative from dad's side sat me down for a talk. "I've been wanting to bring this up, but I know how sensitive you are. I say it with love, because the Puerto Rican culture has many beautiful things about it, things that have made you who you are. But when you grow up, don't become fat like your mom and aunts." That word. *Fat.* How to make a human disappear in three moves. F-A-T, checkmate. I had marched on Earth

Day. I knew overconsumption was rupturing the ozone. But hey, fatness was the problem, right? I silently swore to excise "fat" from my vocabulary. I had already put "bitch," "witch," and "whore" on a shelf. "Fat" would be in auspicious boycotted company.

That was the same year my little sis, Gabi, ran into her bedroom naked. Beheld her reflection and declared her curves miraculous as mother nature: "My belly is round as the earth!" She had been four then. That Gabi was, by eight, one of the toughest kids in third grade came as no accident. You tryin'a step with some dumb-ass recycled fat joke? Best be prepared to have your buck teeth, onion armpits, or mummy breath flung right back at your donkey face. She threw insults like party snaps, quick blacktop detonations. Tuesday afternoons when I picked her up, I'd sometimes hang back at the monkey bars, unnoticed, and watch as she brought her bullies to tears. She could flip a mob with a single insult. The kids would circle round, amped up that some alpha was about to take her down. Within seconds that same mob was rolling laughing at the bully's defeat. Ding-ding-ding! We have a winner! Most fat jokes, Gabi had learned, are generic low-brain-cell taunts. They hurt, yeah, but not from artfulness. Gabi would spit some bespoke shit your way. Now all of third grade knows you snack on your boogers during science plus you're an idiot who can't clap back. Double victory. Yeah, sure, Gabi would be quiet the whole subway ride home. Yeah, sure, she'd disappear into her room without saying hi to Pop. Better to weep into her pillow than talk about it. Cuz if Pop got wind? "Well, then, lose some weight! You're too fat!" I would sneak into Gabi's room and praise her body, mind, and spirit, and confirm, *Yup, the world sucks* and then, *You make no mistake, little sis, your success is preordained.* (Later I'd pray myself to sleep: *Dear god, let her thrive.*) You don't want kids to develop grit that coarse. Medium grit sure would be nicer.

The Perez bodies became a play. After a decade-long boycott, "fat" made an energized return. Now I could own the slur, twist its intention, transform it into an honorific. "Queer," "bitch," "dyke," "witch," and "whore" joined my reclaimed lexicon. In my play they became high praise, a code for belonging.

I wrote the one-act play in my Providence corner apartment. A huge Victorian estate had been chopped into student housing and mine had the godsend of two exposures. Weeks after our wedding in the old Quaker meetinghouse, the boy and I had driven to Providence, stepped foot in the idiosyncratic crib, and sniffed a future amongst its dusty built-in bookshelves. Now my Lukumí library filled those shelves.

As writing nooks go, none could be more romantic. My first-floor desk looked out onto the sidewalk. The brick herringbone pattern, clatter of heels, scratch of skateboard wheels—a sensory world that cushioned my solitude. Between classes students ambled back and forth in cloud drifts. Snippets of conversation bled in. The blue-collar construction workers next door said "fuck" with gusto from sunup till three P.M. My desk window was nearly five feet tall and from my salvaged-trash chair I was eye level with the pedestrians. In warm weather, window propped up with a dictionary, there wasn't even a pane of glass separating inside from out. When I first moved in, the window was painted shut. It took a butter knife and an afternoon to get the thing opening and closing. Now, on its sill, the boy would leave me a fresh cafecito, for inspiration, and scuttle away.

Every morning I lit a candle, played batá music, and warmed up with a poem for Oshun, Orisha of female sensuality who undoubtedly held sway over this developing piece. At times, thoughts flowed quicker than I could write them. All those naked bodies lived in me again, as did the ways I'd been told to despise them. It was painful, yes, but rebellious and right.

I brought the pages in. The feedback was positive. *More,* my colleagues urged. *How could it end there? Give us act two!* Paula said. *Make it full-length and I'll produce it as your thesis.*

How to continue? Act two eluded me. The desk began to mock. I had run out of ideas and inspiration. The passersby became distractions, bad juju. The construction workers were now assholes imposing on my peace. The morning hours, which I loved most, became taunting as the day stretched before me with no voices to follow. The play gained a strong resistance to my efforts.

I needed a Plan B. I began leaving for the graduate cluster after dinner. White particleboard desks stretched beneath fluorescent lights. No dividers, no delineated workstations. Just row after row of communal tables and overworked computers. Stacks of library hardbacks created semiprivate nooks. Snacks—forbidden—remained squirreled in knapsacks, so there was the constant motion of hands plunging into bags, a pickpocket's dance. Magnetic key cards and the baroque sign-in sheet made entry an event—once inside, you stayed. Self-imposed lockdown. The cluster was open till some ungodly hour, and I was not a night person. The air of communal misery offered a strange brew of courage. Blank screens, unite.

One such night, around ten, I was plodding along on act two. The cluster was packed. Midterm deadlines loomed. The play was styled as a flesh-and-blood comic book. There were fight scenes, chase sequences, and cape-wearing alter egos. Fatness, slut shaming, and sexual violence were the themes, all told through a bi-curious Latina's coming of age. It was raunchy, X-rated, and naïve all at once. I felt a particular affection for the lead character, a fictional chubby Latina who captured my little sis's essence. I enjoyed putting Oshun into a comic book, having the Orisha of sweet rivers usher in a girl's first wet dream. But where to next, what did act one demand? What sort of ending was I building to? Comic books ended in apocalypse or redemption. Either option, on its own, felt incomplete for my chubby hero.

The cluster didn't allow for my usual indulgences. The lit candles. The blasting batá CD. The pacing back and forth as I improvised a warm-up poem aloud. Daily steps inviting imagination's looseness. In the cluster, without my gradual strategies for entering a creative state, I just sat and wrote. A blunt entrance.

I don't remember that blackout like I do the others. In previous possessions, the on-ramp, that first surge and tremble, remain vivid. The initial denial, my desperation to still the tremors, to not be mounted—I remember, quite palpably, losing the fight each time. For this—my fourth surrender, and the final of my life that I recall—I have no memory of its arrival.

I remember only the off-ramp. Sitting there, disoriented and unwell, as though an alarm clock had startled my eyes open. Headphone-wearing students typed on adjacent computers. Their banal slouches indicated life as usual. My asphyxiated gulps and strained heartbeat, indicators that the storm had hit. Time had elapsed: four hours. The page count read 87. Last I remembered, there were half as many. On the screen, the words "End of play" preceded a blinking cursor. It was one in the morning.

I scrolled back to page 40 and began to read. At first the play's mischievous, irreverent tone continued apace. Then scene by scene, it began lurching toward darkness. Threat and violence

overtook playfulness and sensuality. The antagonists were closing in and they intended real harm. The comic book vibe
morphed into horror. It was not what I had in mind when con-
ceiving the project. I wanted warmth, rebellion, corporeality, defiant silliness. Reading on, I grew upset. The play's mounting
fury seemed imported from a stranger, but I was that stranger.
Judging by the words, my subconscious had been incubating a
beast. How could I be so unfamiliar to myself? I began to hate
the play, not because it was good or bad, but because it unmasked
me without permission.

In the final scene, the antagonists caught up with my young
hero. They'd been populating the subplots since page one, clown-
ish satirical ciphers, comic relief. They were buffoons who called
my heroes whores, and I reveled in making them ridiculous. But
now they infiltrated the main plot. They gave chase, weapons
drawn. My lead character was trapped. In the play's climactic tableau, as the bad guys moved in close, poised to kill her, my superhero made one final declaration. I AM A WHORE.

Blackout. End of play.

Whaaaa?

Record scratch!

I almost fell out my seat. What the fuck was that? I AM A
WHORE?

That wasn't the play I wanted to write! I could see that the
way my character said it, she wasn't yielding to the slur or dimin-
ishing herself. She was reclaiming monstrosity as her earned,
rightful power. She got the last laugh, owned her whole self on
her dying breath. And yet I loathed the line, rejected it completely. I highlighted the text, finger on the delete key. Teeth digging into my bottom lip, my eyes unblinking lest the tears drop
down. But the words were stronger than my will to undo them.

I stood, agitated, brushing against knapsacks and chair backs in a space too cramped for pacing. Then I sat, opened a browser window, and emailed Paula. "I'm scared. I wrote something that disgusts me. I do not want to feel this way. I do not like who these lines reveal me to be." I was too horrified to walk home, certain my antagonists were lurking in Providence alleyways, ready to annihilate me as they had my lead character. So I sat and sat, awaiting a response, strange to myself, as neighboring students typed away.

Was this what I signed up for? Was speaking the Perez wounds reopening them? Though I couldn't remember the possession itself, I knew it was a purging of inherited trauma. But also a tasting. The fire gave me truth even as it burned me. Having left myself in those unremembered hours, did I know myself at last?

The goat, turtle, and chicken whispered old warnings, doomed animals whose pain I wanted no complicity in. Once upon a girlhood their blood made me wail, told me too soon about the mortality I was made of. But seated in the computer lab, I remembered an asterisk beside each death. Previously, the sacrifices had loomed so big they'd erased what came next. Now I saw each animal's forgotten epilogue: how after ritual sacrifices mom labored into the night. The next morning meant waking up to a transfixing aroma, and there it would be on the stovetop over low flame: chicken soup or goat stew, the fruit of her overnight labor. I had tasted each of these special meals, though doing so broke my strict adolescent vegetarianism. Out of respect for each animal, I had eaten. Though I would only eat alone, so I could weep, unwatched, while lifting spoon to lips. The soup's flavor humbled me. Delicious. Every bowl was a braid of suffering and renewal and now, in a computer cluster, I could not say if those sacrificed animals broke me or built me.

What did I know?

I AM A WHORE. . . .

Old crank calls rang, a jangling disturbance. Cut it out, stop calling! *Simpsons* volume low as vulgarities lanceted mom. Hoe. A tool for turning up earth, rejuvenating soil, making way for new growth. Ho. All the shame a woman carried. How mom branded the word unto her heart. AZADA AZADA AZADA! But what use was a garden tool, I railed, when the Perez women had divorced mother nature? Abuela's gandules harvest, over. Mom's circle of sage, dead. My horse farm woods, gone. Ripped and rent from all soil, we who had once been earth-women and were now North Philly—treeless rubble, tire-strewn and derelict. But wait. Hadn't one plot of land persisted? Migrated with us all this way? One human-size patch of earth? Our bodies.

I am tired soil, break me, wound me.

I AM A WHORE. . . .

Around three in the morning my inbox dinged. Paula was up late. "I have been scared, too," she said. "Trembling as I wrote about old violations. Certain I would be chased down once again. I locked every door in my writing cabin and hid in a closet. A lunatic was in the house, I convinced myself, so I sprinted to the car and locked myself inside, key in the ignition, hand on the key, as the owls screeched till sunrise. The actual threat, of course, was internal: the fact of myself laid bare, removing the armor and seeing the wounds still bled."

I closed the browser window and lingered in my chair, wrecked by gratitude. Why was I the bewildered repository for grand matriarchal bequests? Paula's email still jolts me today: walk toward the internal fear. Skin zapping, arm fuzz half-raised from the lightning bolt, I printed the play and collected warm pages. Empty now, the graduate cluster seemed ready for my leave-taking. The final line, which I was unable to delete, had become part of the material world, slumping in my backpack above pens and snack wrappers.

In a matter of months houselights would dim, ink on paper would become actor's voice on audience ears, and I would tremble, hermana, as you saw the anarchical yarn I had spun from the Perez body. As you witnessed, at fourteen, a roomful of strangers witnessing you. Seated at your side in that dark theater, fear would convince me my words were a knife in your back, my play was a sisterhood-annihilating machine. Seconds after houselights rose, I would admit these fears, needing to know: are we through, did I break us? And you would say through tears, as folks filed to the lobby, "I feel seen. I feel, like, I don't know, like, fuckin' powerful. Yeah, it hurt but, like, I'm a lead character of a whole play, yo! Thass a honor! Thass right, people, y'all better hear my story!" You would tell me, hermana mia, that your grip on shame had loosened a bit.

For now, I exited into the dark Providence night. Past unlit alleyways, looking over my shoulder, finding not danger but serenity. The breeze's cool fingertips snapped me conscious. I was real. I quickstepped home and climbed into bed. The slightest awareness, not a worded koan but a pulse's nod, swam through me that excited, sleepless night. *This is what a beginning feels like. The apprenticeship is over.*

It was, indeed, the last time. Four possessions, my life's allowance. Quaker meeting, Dr. Phillips's essay test, Holly Hughes's identity list, and *I am a whore.* Even at forty, over a decade later, the final one lingers. The hush vines up my arm, a thrill robes my skin, and I am reminded viscerally of my inheritance. You, my Perez women, understand because you are the throne and the dance. You shook your asses as the world's walls tried to crush you.

Mami, primas, hermana, no one else qualifies for the job. We must be our own librarians because we alone are literate in our bodies. By naming our pain and voicing our imperfections, we declare our tremendous survival. Our offspring deserve to inherit these strategies. We have worked hard to be here. We owe them ourselves. We owe each other.

And since our archive is in us and of us, let it grow not in word alone but also flesh. The hum of our bodies together is nothing less than the book of our genius. That is why, on opening nights, you sit beside me and I touch you. Your elbow perches on the armrest, my hand finds the flat smoosh of your knuckles, and we watch our old silences become loud songs. We are here.

ACKNOWLEDGMENTS

For Ray Beauchamp, my husband, whose emotional and logistic support made this years-long work not only possible but enjoyable, I am grateful beyond words. He brought me meals as I wrote. Grasped my hand as I stumbled through rough patches. Said, "You better get to it," and also, "Maybe put it down for a bit." In taking care of Cecilia and Julian, our children, he modeled for them how to nourish and cheerlead a writing woman.

For Chris Jackson, my editor and publisher, whose literary gift and communicative finesse urged me ever inward. His precision of thought and stewardship leave me humbled and improved.

For Virginia Sanchez, my mom, whose insightful, splendid, and astute notes on various drafts led me to a breakthrough in this book. Her immense knowledge is not taken lightly.

To loved ones mentioned briefly or not at all in these pages, please know that word count does not represent my depth of feeling for the safe havens, companionship, and joy you've given me. Aunt Linda the punk rocker and Uncle Rik the wild trumpeter who included me in their artists' universe. Fay and Gary, whose levity and togetherness are a balm. Ariel and Forrest, whom I treasure. Edie, a big cuz and heart-healer. Nick, Rachel, Rafi, and Ellie, an adventurous foursome. Cap Rush, who directed *Sweat of the River* at Yale. Awilda Peña, who ran Casa Comadre alongside mom, and the dedicated network of Casa supporters. And many more relatives, friends, and collaborators who participated in the events described here. And John Buzzetti, who entered my life after the events of this book, and then made the telling my bread and butter.

Ian Kleinert, my agent, asked me: "If you could do anything, what would you do?" When I told him, *It's time to write my book,* he shepherded this endeavor into being.

Gratitude, aché, and peace, y'all.

ABOUT THE AUTHOR

QUIARA ALEGRÍA HUDES is a playwright, wife, mother of two, barrio feminist, and native of West Philly, U.S.A. Hailed for their exuberance, intellectual rigor, and rich imagination, her plays and musicals have been performed around the world. They include *In the Heights,* a Broadway musical soon to be released as a motion picture, and *Water by the Spoonful,* a drama about an online recovery community. She recently founded a crowd-sourced testimonial project, Emancipated Stories, that seeks to put a personal face on mass incarceration by having people behind bars share one page of their life story with the world.

Twitter: @quiarahudes
Instagram: @emancipated_stories_project